IYENGAR
His Life and Work

Front cover photograph: Derek French

Library of Congress Cataloging-in
Publication Data

Iyengar, his life and work.
Compiled by B.K.S. Iyengar 60th Birthday
Celebration Committee.
Rev. and enl. ed. of: Body the shrine,
yoga thy light. 1978.
1. Iyengar, B. K. S., 1918-   . 2. Hindus—India—
Biography. 3. Yogis—India—Biography. I.
B.K.S. Iyengar 60th Birthday Celebration
Committee.   II. Body the shrine, yoga thy light.
BL1175.I9I95 1987   294.5'092'4 [B]   87-7058
ISBN 0-931454-14-X (pbk.)

First edition published by B.I.
Taraporewala, 1978

This edition published by Timeless Books, 1987

Published by

Box 160
Porthill, ID 83853
Printed in U.S.A.

IYENGAR
His Life and Work

Timeless Books

1987

ACKNOWLEDGMENTS

To COLLECT A VOLUME of this kind, covering the life's work of a man with this much energy, and spanning this many years, takes an effort of many people. When the call went out to the Yoga community for help in documenting the life of B.K.S. Iyengar, many responded. Several old pupils and friends offered up new articles and photographs never before available to the public. To all those who contributed articles, quotations and photographs, we are most grateful. Special thanks must be given to:-

Carol Cavanaugh, Diana Clifton, Trudy Davis, Colly Dastur, Mary Dunn, Mardi Erdman, Derek French, Marian Garfinkel, Bill Graham, Beverly Graves, Elizabeth Kent, Sri Kulhalli, Geeta S. Iyengar, Liz McLeod, Sri Mahadevan, Mira Mehta, Silva Mehta, Donald Moyer, Kalyan Namjoshi, Lyn Oliver, Mary Palmer, Ramanand Patel, Melinda Perlee, Chris Saudek, Karin Stephan, Joyce Stuart, Joyce Zouves Van Rensburg.

These names must be added to the acknowledgements listed in the original autobiography *Body the Shrine— Yoga Thy Light*. Thanks also to the Yoga Journal, East-West Journal, San Francisco Iyengar Institute Review and Victoria Yoga Centre newsletter for permission to reprint articles and interviews from these publications.

I would like to make special mention of Shirley Daventry French and Trish Graham of the Victoria Yoga Centre: Shirley for crafting the new book and editing the manuscript, and Trish for her design of this new edition. Thanks also to Celia Ward for her illustrations, and all those Yoga students in Victoria, B.C., who helped with proof reading.

Lastly, very special thanks to Terence Buie of Timeless Books, whose idea sparked the enthusiasm for this project and who oversaw the publication of this book.

It should also be noted that Shri B.K.S. Iyengar gave me access to his personal set of family albums to help with the visual portion of this work. His encouragement for my personal work without care as to his own personal gain continues to amaze me.

Manouso Manos
San Francisco 1986

TABLE OF CONTENTS

GOOD WISHES
  from B.K.S. Iyengar   xiii
BEYOND THE THRESHOLD: *Introduction*
  by Ramanand Patel   xvii
ON THE THRESHOLD: *Introduction to the First Edition*
  by B.I. Taraporewala   xxi
MANGALASISH (BLESSINGS)
  from Shri T. Krishnamachar   xxvi

The Body is My Temple by B.K.S. Iyengar
  Childhood and Education   3
  How Pune became my Home   19
  Marriage and Family   35
  Call of the West   59
  Rama—The Light of my Life   73

Articles and Extracts by B.K.S. Iyengar
  Why the West is Interested in Yoga   83
  Yoga Discipline in Athletes   89
  Yoga and Meditation   93
  The Art of Relaxation   99
  Yoga and Mental Peace   107
  Yoga—An Answer to Problems of Today   113
  Yoga—A Path to Self-Realization   117

Yoga and Dance — 121
Yoga and Brahmacharya — 125
Prana and Pranayama — 131
Similarity in Treatment of Yoga and Ayurveda — 139
Pilgrimage to the Vatican — 159
Is Yoga for One and All? — 167
On Food — 168
On the Effects of Pranayama — 168
On Samadhi — 169
Yoga and Dharma — 169
Importance of Sarira-Dharma — 171
The Need for Yoga Education in Schools
and Colleges — 172
The Importance of Asanas — 174

Interviews and Comments *with B.K.S. Iyengar*
Personality Through Yoga
All-India Radio — 181
An Hour with Shri B.K.S. Iyengar
—Arvind Mulla — 189
A Visit with B.K.S.Iyengar
—Carol Cavanaugh — 197
B.K.S. Iyengar Talks on Yoga
—Karin Stephan — 209
A Commonwealth Interview
—Victoria Yoga Centre newsletter — 219
Quotes and Comments in Southern California — 233

The Flowers
Our Brother
by B.K. Doreswami and B.K. Vendantachar — 241
Iyengar and the Queen of Belgium
by S.B. Taraporewala — 245

With No Instrument
by Yehudi Menuhin 249
Contributions to Knowledge by Mr. B.K.S. Iyengar
by Dr. Bruce M. Carruthers 253
Iyengar—An Enigma
by Col. D.I.M. Robbins 259
B.K.S. Iyengar—A Tribute
by Joyce Stuart 263
The Man of Action and Perfection
by Madhu Tijoriwala 269
Iyengar—The Guiding Light
by Freny S. Motivala 277
Our Guruji
by Kalyani Namjoshi 283
The Evolution of an Acharya
by B.I. Taraporewala 291

Pot-pourri
B.K.S. Iyengar comes to the United States
by Mary Palmer 303
The Lion and the Lamb
by Elizabeth Kent 307
The Self is in Every Cell
by Mardi Erdman 317
Iyengar—a Retrospective 321
A Gathering in San Francisco
by Manouso Manos 331
B.K.S. Iyengar . . . HIMSELF
by Bill Graham 335
Portrait of B.K.S. Iyengar
by Karin Stephan 343

The Fruits: Curative Aspects of Yoga
Who is a Truly Healthy Man
by Sam Motivala   357
Yoga Therapeutics
by Geeta Iyengar   359
My Cure
by Freny Motivala   367
My Fight Against Arthritis
by Pushpa Gurumani   369
Yoga and I
by Dr. A.S. Batliwala   371
Double Cure
by Mary Sethna   373
Bamboo Spine
by Pervez Irani   375
Cures Galore
by Dhan Palkhivala   379
The Lure of Yoga
by Mary Palmer   383
Robert's Story
by Marian Garfinkel   389
Yoga for Women
by Geeta Iyengar   395
Yoga and Ayurveda
by Geeta Iyengar   401

The Essence
A Musical Light on *Light on Yoga*
by Peter Leek   423
How *Light on Yoga* was written
by B.I. Taraporewala   427
Light on Pranayama—a review
by Swami Venkatesananda   433

Iyengar—The Artist
  by B.I. Taraporewala   437
The Yoga Institute
  by Madhu Tijoriwala   445
Iyengar—The Teacher
  by B.I. Taraporewala   455
Issue of Certificates—Swaziland 1975
  by B.K.S. Iyengar   471
Essential Qualities of a Yoga Teacher
  by B.K.S. Iyengar   481

Wisdom of the Master: Maxims *by B.K.S. Iyengar*
  compiled by B.I. Taraporewala
  and Shirley Daventry French
Yoga   487
Health   490
Asanas   495
Sadhana (Practice)   512
Learning and Teaching   523
Pain   531
Wealth   532
Pranayama—Dhyana—Meditation   533

GOOD WISHES

from Shri B.K.S. Iyengar

I AM EXTREMELY PLEASED to hear that Timeless Books Publishers are planning to bring out a North American edition of *Body the Shrine, Yoga Thy Light,* which was compiled by the B.K.S. Iyengar 60th Birthday Celebration Committee of 1978 and published by "The Light on Yoga Research Trust," Bombay.

Body the Shrine, Yoga Thy Light is a misnomer. This book covers the life and works of a man whose hopes of survival at one time were literally at the nadir. No-one, including myself, ever thought that he would hit the headlines all over the globe or touch the zenith in the unchosen field of Yoga.

I was a creature of contempt from my people due to constant ill health from birth. It is my brother-in-law (sister's husband) who chose this path for me and became my Guru. This path was untreaded by any of my family members before. Due to fear of my Guru, I kept going in Yoga. It was a very painful process when I began. Circumstances came in chains creating restlessness, discomforts, disappointments and despair. I moved with circumstances and lived with them. The spirit inside me helped me to accept the situations without surrendering to them.

Hence, the title of the book may be very appropriate if it is changed into *Iyengar—His Life and Work*.

The first chapter begins with the chosen title, "The Body is my Temple," for one simple reason: that for each one, the body becomes the temple of the soul or the seer who resides in it. In the same way, the house of the seer or the Individual Soul becomes the shrine for the Universal Spirit or God.

It is as clear as daylight that no one likes to stay in a dilapidated house or remain without a bath. Each and every one loves to keep his house clean, tidy and airy so that the surroundings elate his heart, mind and intelligence. Similarly, one wants to take a bath as often as possible to keep the body free from smell. Hence, body being the coat of the self or the core of Being, it demands attention for health and cleanliness for its owner to live in bliss, freedom and beatitude. If the body is neglected or abused, the indweller too feels unhappy, dejected and lonely. In order to keep the owner and the owned (self and body) judiciously healthy and clean, the sages and yogis of India invented yogic practices so that the individual self enters the sanctum sanctorum or the holy of holy place within. Thus, the chapter begins: "The Body is my Temple."

Whether one is theist or atheist, religious or irreligious or an agnostic or infidel, yet he or she is sure of the existence of his or her body. They are also certain that disease might affect them if they neglect their bodies. Even for them, body becomes the shrine to do day to day work with ease without interruptions in health. Attention to health and care of the body is a must to one and all.

In my early life, I was deprived of essentials of life, like food, health and shelter. When I gained a glimpse of health, the candle of zeal increased the urge to practice Yoga and slowly Yoga became my guide, friend and philosopher.

It lifted me from the position of ill-health and frustrated mind to the level of contentment and spiritual fulfilment. Through the practice of Yoga, my parasitic and useless life became worth living and fruitful to experience glimpses of that absolute indivisible state of existence. It also made me go out of my way to help afflicted people by passing on what I had derived from Yoga.

I am indebted to that hidden spirit in me which created such difficult situations to test my sincerity and determination and kept the switch of my will power on, to maintain, sustain and uphold the best of what I learned on my own through Yoga and led me to what I am now.

I wish that this autobiography and biography ignites fire in the readers who are better blessed than me to peep into this noblest human art of living and carry its effects of peace, poise, bliss and freedom wherever they can take it.

I once again thank the Timeless Books for their effort to present this book to a greater audience.

B.K.S. Iyengar

BEYOND THE
THRESHOLD

Mangala Moorti Marutinandana,
(Embodiment of Auspiciousness,
O Son of Maruti [Hanuman],)
Sakala Amangala Mool Nikaandana.
(Dispel the very Root of
Everything Non-auspicious)

Today by coincidence, it is exactly eight years since
Mr. B.I. Taraporewala wrote the preface to the first edition of this book. In writing that preface on the occasion
of the 60th birthday celebration of Yogacharya Shri Bellur
Krishnamachar Sundararaja Iyengar, Mr. Taraporewala
delineated the contents of the book in a very eloquent and
precise manner. He talked of the titanic stuggle and
eventual triumph of our beloved "Guruji" as we have
come to know him.

For many years he declined this title because of its
negative connotation indicating a cult. To his pupils it
was always obvious that his message and teachings were
not in the nature of a cult. In the years that have followed
since that first publication, this fact has become so
obvious even to the outsiders that the title "Guruji" so

spontaneously bestowed upon him by his pupils as well as the coined phrase of "Iyengar Yoga" have become standard phrases of the Yoga world's vocabulary. From its humble beginning this seed has sprouted to become a mighty tree with branches all over the world.

If the first edition marked the triumph of this spiritual giant, this next edition seeks to enlarge the frontiers of that triumph. While his many devoted pupils have done a magnificent job, the very nature of his rising glory is such that perhaps no book, however elaborate, will ever succeed in doing anything more than a cursory justice to his noble work. It is in this ongoing quest to let the world know of his life and his work, that the film *Guruji* has now been released in 16mm, and even as this book goes to print the film is being made available in video cassette. Video cassettes of his early as well as more recent practices are also being made available. While all these add to the understanding of his work, for those of us close to him such records serve to indicate how powerless we are to capture or evaluate his astonishing prowess in every aspect of Yoga through such mechanical means.

It has been observed elsewhere that what pertains to his autobiography may have more human interest but does nothing to add to or subtract from his untarnished record of achievements. I beg to differ with this view. Such biographical records indeed do nothing to "subtract" but they do indeed "add" to the glory of his achievements, marked every step of the way by human trials, human tribulations and human triumphs, showing Yoga to be much more than a subject of dry scientific achievements.

Generous and magnanimous, often in the face of overwhelming odds, I have seen him happily and quietly give away hard earned money to some "worthy" cause, swallow untold suffering to protect his family, friends and pupils, and take it all in his stride in such an unassuming manner that the scene might completely escape one's notice unless one was carefully attentive. It has always been refreshing to see him in activities outside the "Yoga scene;" he gets as enthusiastically involved as if they were all some gigantic and perpetual Trikonasana. Transcending all barriers of culture and time, I have seen him reverentially take in the beauty of all cultures that crossed his path. I have seen him at play with children as though he was himself still a child, very quickly making other adults join in the fun without ever threatening the domain of the children. I have also seen him at meetings of the most serious nature, there quietly letting everybody have their say and respecting their views, but then without the slightest fear stating his honest and most direct opinion.

Many of his pupils remember his most loving manner and his large, dark, motherly and very kind eyes, his charming, melodic and favorite phrases such as "Is it not?" and "Follow now!" On the other hand, should an occasion warrant it those same eyes glow with such fire, his loud roar challenging the fake yogis abusing his generosity, that I have witnessed even the proudest of them run for cover. I have seen him lost in the most divine laughter that captivates his audience, only a moment later to be withdrawn like some shy child. In complete contrast I have seen him stand proud and take in the standing ovation of hundreds of spectators with the dignity that befits an emperor.

I join his pupils, friends, family and well wishers in the prayer that this emperor reign long and victorious.

It is my proud privilege to present a revised and enlarged North American edition of this book. It is an honor for which I am very grateful.

Ramanand D. Patel

San Jose, California
December 9th, 1986

ON THE THRESHOLD

Grow old along with me!
The best is yet to be,
The last of life, for which the first was made,
Our time is in His hand
Who saith "A whole I planned,
Youth shows but half; trust God;
see all nor be afraid!"
—Robert Browning's *Rabbi Ben Ezra*

This book entitled *Body the Shrine, Yoga Thy Light* is published on the occasion of the completion of the sixtieth year of life of Yogacharya Bellur Krishnamachar Sundararaja Iyengar, which according to old Indian tradition marks a turning point in life.

The book starts with the Mangalasish, the invocation of blessings specially composed in Sanskrit for the occasion by Yogacharya T. Krishnamachar, brother-in-law of Yogacharya Iyengar who initiated him into Yoga.

The spark of Yoga brought to him by his Guru ignited his spirit. He learned by experience that the body indeed is the instrument for achieving spiritual aspirations and realising the latent divinity within oneself.

With courage, determination and unrelenting practice for years on end, he kept the light of Yoga burning in his heart. He strengthened and purified his body. He transformed it into a shrine worthy to house the light of Yoga. This light guided him slowly, steadily and surely along the paths to glory, prosperity and victory.

The first part of the book is autobiographical in its nature, dealing with the titanic struggle of Yogacharya Iyengar for survival and his gradual acquisition of knowledge and mastery over Yoga. It speaks of the hidden years before he became famous. His life during these years is known to very few. It tells how from a poor, uneducated and under-nourished body dogged with ill-health, he rose to become one of the best Yoga teachers, who inspired many and gave health to them.

God was his anvil, the circumstances gave the hammer blows, his own body was the metal, his *tapas* and devotion provided the fire, and the indifference of the world and grinding poverty were the waters. These tempered and honed his intellect and spirit to become like a true-edged, trusty sword and forged his character into the mould of a Yogacharya.

The autobiography is followed by Yogacharya Iyengar's tribute to his late wife Rama. Her cherished memory inspired the foundation of the Ramamani Iyengar Memorial Yoga Institute, which has become a centre of attraction for the pupils of the Yogacharya from all the continents.

The spirit and temper of Yogacharya Iyengar are shown in the interviews given by him and in the articles written by him on various aspects of Yoga. There is also an account of his pilgrimage to the Vatican, and a short account of his meetings with Elisabeth, the late Dowager Queen Mother of Belgium.

The second part of the book consists mainly of essays on Yogacharya Iyengar contributed by several of his friends and pupils from various walks of life. These include Yehudi Menuhin, Dr. Bruce Carruthers, Colonel Robbins, Secretary of the British Wheel of Yoga and many others. The chapter on the curative aspects of Yogacharya Iyengar's teachings describes the benefits experienced by his pupils who followed his methods under his supervision. Yogacharya Iyengar's eldest daughter, Geeta, a Yoga teacher in her own right, has contributed articles on Yoga Therapeutics and on Yoga for Women.

The third part of the book deals with work of Yogacharya Iyengar. There are essays on how *Light on Yoga* was written and how the Ramamani Iyengar Memorial Yoga Institute was established. There are also essays on two important aspects of the Yogacharya's unique career as an artist and as a teacher. The essay on the artistic aspect of the Yogacharya's career in India and abroad attempts to describe his control of body and mind backed by a wealth of wisdom and humanity. The essay on his career as a teacher deals with his ever-growing influence. He has taught leading political figures like Jayaprakash Narayan, philosophers and savants like J. Krishnamurti, internationally famous musicians like Yehudi Menuhin and Clifford Curzon, generals of the Indian army, and pupils of his pupils number several thousands. Yogacharya Iyengar never went through any University training. Yet what he acquired through his single-minded devotion to Yoga for over forty years now provides courses for several universities abroad.

The book ends with the sayings and teachings of Yogacharya Iyengar gathered over the years by his pupils in India and abroad during the course of his teaching sessions.

Yogacharya Iyengar is still thirsty for knowledge. He is ever eager to refine himself. He is busy writing his book on Pranayama, the discipline of breath. Originally, it had been proposed that the publication of his *Light on Pranayama* should coincide with his sixtieth birthday, but it was not possible to complete this work in time. A wealth of material and photographs, however, were available for preparing a book on his life and work. By the concerted efforts of many of his friends and pupils spread all over the world, the material and the photographs were gathered. Articles were prepared, selected, arranged and edited in a few months.

The Tata Press came to our rescue and acceded to our request to bring out the present publication economically and well within time to coincide with the auspicious occasion of Yogacharya Iyengar's sixtieth birthday.

It is not possible to mention individually the numerous friends and pupils of Yogacharya Iyengar who gave their time and efforts most generously to bring out the present work, and we thank them for helping us. Our special thanks are due to:

Shri Shantilal Tolat for his valuable suggestions in editing the book, Shri J.A. Dave for the English translation of the Mangalasish, Smt. Freny S. Motivala and Smt. Sheru B. Taraporewala for selecting the material and photographs from numerous and voluminous sources, Kum. Villoo Pithawalla for her suggestions on the art work, Mrs. Eileen Piercey (Mrs. E.B. Moon) for granting permission to reproduce her line drawings of yogasanas embellishing the book, Kum. Srimathi Rao for preparing countless typescripts for the book, and the Shri Xerxes S. Desai, Shri M.S. Petkar and the Tata Press for the care and promptness with which they brought out the present publication.

B.I. Taraporewala, Chairman,

B.K.S. Iyengar 60th Birthday
Celebration Committee

Bombay, December 9, 1978

॥ श्री टी. कृष्णमाचार विरचित॥
॥ मङ्गलाशिषः॥

॥ श्री हयग्रीवाय नमः॥

इष्ट देवता प्रार्थना

श्री लक्ष्मीहयवदनो लक्ष्मीरमणश्च दंपती दिव्ये

(दवते दिव्ये) ।

अन्यास्तामनवरतं सुंदरराजं सपुत्रपुत्रीकम् ॥

आशिषः

प्रतिवादि भीतकारी बहुविध योगासनेषु संचारी

(योगाब्धि संचारी) ।

सुंदरराजः सुकृती जीवतु सुचिरं जनस्य सुखकारी ॥

षष्ट्यब्दपूर्त्युत्साशीर्वचनानि

षष्ट्यब्दपूर्ति संज्ञिक शुभोत्सवाभिषिक्त सर्वांगम् ।

सुंदरराजं यमिनं रक्षतु लक्ष्मीपतिर्देवः ॥

पर्यायेण च

विनतातनुजारूढः प्रणताभीष्ट प्रदान धृतदीक्षः ।

अवतात् सुंदरराजं प्रशांत सुतसहित मनवरतम् ॥

अस्य वंशः

श्रीवत्सगोत्रजातः सुंदरराजः स्वयोग विभवेन ।

श्रीवत्सप्रतिरूपः सक्तो भक्तो वृषादे रमणेऽस्तु ॥

अस्य स्वरूपम्

योगी भोगी रागी त्यागी चायं तथापि समयोगी ।

देशे स्वस्य विदेशे सुंदरराजः समानदृग् हा हा ॥

BLESSINGS
from Shri T.Krishnamachar

Salutation to Lord Hayagriva

Prayer to the Family Deity
May the Divine couples, Sri Laksmi-Hayagriva and Laksmi-Narayana, constantly protect Sundararaja along with his son and daughters.

Blessings
One who has defeated his opponents, one who is adept in manifold yogic asanas (who has dived deep in the ocean of Yoga)—this Sundararaja of pious acts who works for the good of the people—may he live long.

Blessings on the Occasion of His Completion of Sixty Years
May Lord Laksmipati Narayana protect Sundararaja who has practised self-control when his whole body is getting sprinkled with holy waters at the time of the auspicious celebration of his completion of sixty years.

In the Alternative
May Lord Visnu who rides Garuda the son of Vinata, and who has vowed to fulfil desires, protect Sundararaja constantly along with his son Prasanta.

अस्य कार्यक्रमाणि

क्वचिच्छिक्षयन् अत्यन् शिष्टशैलीम्
क्वचिद् बोधयन् योगभेदान् वचोभिः ।
क्वचिच्चाचरन् नित्यमात्मानुभूत्यै
अयंगार अयं वर्तते पुण्यपुर्याम् ॥

अस्य सप्रदायः

लब्धब्रह्मोपदेशश्च स्वगुरोर्नियमैः सह
प्राप्ताद्यभिक्षश्च ततः गुरूपल्या व्रती भवन् ।
स संप्रदायं योगांगान्यभ्यस्य बुबुधे लघु
तथैव गुरुणा साकं प्रचाराय चचार च ॥

विवाह गार्हस्थम्

ततोऽभिजातां कन्यां नु रमामणिशुभाभिधाम्
उपयेमे सुविधिना ब्राह्मं पाणिग्रहं चरन् ॥

संतानवृंढ

तस्यां हि जनयामास पंचकन्यां सुशोभनाः ।
एकं पुत्रं शांतचित्तं प्रशांत इति नामनः ॥
पंचस्वपि च कन्यासु ज्येष्ठा गीतेति विश्रुता ।
अद्य गीताप्रशांतौ च योगे तु परिनिष्ठितौ ॥
स्वपित्रा शिक्षितौ सम्यग् विख्यातौ योगतेजसा ।
शिक्षयन्तौ पुण्यपुर्यां अन्यत्र बहून् जनान् ।
आसाते सह पित्रा तौ योगाभ्यासप्रचारकौ ॥

मातृवियोगः

ततो दुर्योगतो माता तयोः कालवशां गता ।
रमामणिरथौ तस्या पतिः सुंदरराट् कृती

Lineage

Born in the Gotra (clan) called Srivatsa, Sundararaja has become a replica of Srivatsa (symbol of auspiciousness) on account of his yogic effulgence. May he remain attached to the Lord of the Seven Hills (that is Lord of Tirupati).

Personality

Sundararaja is a yogi, sports in that art, is attached to it, has made sacrifices for it and has attained the Yoga of harmony. He looks upon all in India as well as abroad with equanimity.

His Work

Sometimes he is engaged in teaching Yoga without giving up the authentic classical way. Sometimes he gives lectures about the different varieties of Yoga. He himself is also engaged in practising Yoga constantly for his own spiritual experience and he is established in the city of Pune.

His Yoga School and Student Career

He was given sacred thread and Vedic instructions by his teacher according to Sastric rules. He received his first alms from his teacher's wife and he began his life of austerities. He quickly grasped and studied the traditional Yoga and its details and travelled to various places along with his teacher for its propagation.

Marriage and Life as House-holder

Thereafter he married a girl of noble family called Ramamani according to the Brahma form of marriage.

Children

He begot through her five accomplished daughters and one son called Prasanta of unruffled mind. Of his five daughters, the eldest is known by the name of Geeta. Geeta and Prasanta have dived deep in the study of Yoga. They have been taught well by

तन्नाम्ना स्थापयामास सुंदरं योगमंदिरम् ।
तत्राधुना योगविद्याप्रचारश्चलतीति ह ॥
अयंगारप्रणीता च प्रसिद्धा योगदीपिका
इति गाम्ना प्रकटित कोऽपि सा गंथ उत्तमः ॥
नानाभाषासुभातीति को न वेदति पृच्छति ॥
रमामण्यभिधं योगमंदिरं लीकसुंदरम्
अंतेवासिभिरापूर्णं वर्धतामभिवर्धताम् ॥
आशास्ते शस्तात्मा कोऽपि श्रीकृष्णनामकी योगी ।
इत्थं भदागारे मद्र५२ास्पुर्या शठारिवंशीयः ॥

their father and they have become well-known on account of their mastery of Yoga. They, too, have taught many people in Pune and elsewhere and have disseminated the knowledge of Yoga along with their father.

Their Mother's Demise

As willed by fate, their mother Ramamani expired. Her husband Sundararaja of firm actions established in her name an excellent Yoga institute in her memory. In that institute yogic instructions are being given.

Iyengar wrote and published a standard treatise of Yoga called *Yoga-Dipika*. It has been rendered into many languages of different countries. Who does not know about that excellent treatise?

This beautiful Institute in memory of Ramamani is always full with large number of pupils. May it prosper more and more.

Thus are conveyed the blessings of Yogacharya Sri Krsna, a descendant of Sathari, of disciplined mind and residing in a pure dwelling in the city of Madras.

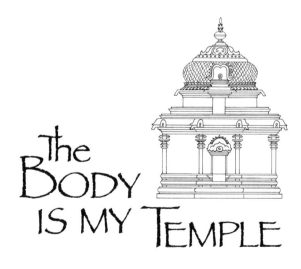

The
BODY
IS MY TEMPLE

CHILDHOOD AND EDUCATION

MY FATHER, BELLUR KRISHNAMACHAR, came from a poor family in a village called Bellur, in Kolar District, now a part of the Karnataka State. He was the headmaster of the only primary school in Narsapur, a small town. He retired in 1924 after serving as a teacher for thirty-three years.

I was born on the night of Saturday, December 14th, 1918. My mother, Sheshamma, had an attack of influenza. It was a country-wide epidemic and thousands of people died. By the grace of God my mother and I survived. I was very dark, my head used to hang down and I had to lift it with an effort. My head was bigger in size to that of my body and my brothers and sisters often teased me. When I was a boy of five my father left the village and settled at Bangalore. He got a clerical job in a big provision store owned by a Muslim named Abdulla. My father was very sincere and hardworking and the proprietor was interested in my father. He treated my father as his brother and helped our family financially. We were thirteen children and I was the eleventh child of my parents and only ten survived. My father celebrated marriages of three daughters and three sons before he died.

Professor T. Krishnamachar during his younger days went to Nepal, where he met a Yogi named Ram Mohan Brahmachari and learned Yoga from him. He was educated in the subjects of Sanskrit, Philosophy, Logic, Sankhya and Mimamsa in the Universities of Benares, Allahabad and Calcutta. He came to Bangalore and was giving religious discources. He taught asanas also. One day in 1927, he came to our house with some of his relatives. My maternal uncle was also with him. My maternal uncle asked my father for an alliance with Shri Krishnamachar, as my third elder sister Namagiriamma was of marriageable age then. My uncle was keen on this alliance and so my father consented and the marriage was celebrated. He thereafter returned to Mysore and started popularising Yoga. The late Majaraja of Mysore, His Highness Sir Sri Krishnaraja Wadiyar, heard about the accomplishments of Shri T. Krishnamachar. The Maharaja was a keen student of philosophy and took great interest in Shri T. Krishnamachar and later he became a student of Yoga.

After practising under the guidance of Shri T. Krishnamachar and realising the value of Yoga, the Maharaja started a Yogashala in the Jaganmohan Palace in 1931 for the benefit of the royal family. Gradually outsiders were permitted to attend the classes with a written permission.

Shri T. Krishnamachar is a versatile man and a great scholar, who stood first in first class in all the public examinations in Mimamsa, Vedanta, Sankhya and Yoga. He had been awarded many titles from different universities like *Mimamsa-Ratna, Mimamsa-Tirtha, Sankhya-Yoga-Shikhamani, Vedanta-Vagisha, Veda-Kesari, Nyaya-charya* and Professor of Yoga. In addition to Yoga he knows Astrology, Ayurveda and classical Karnatic Music. He also plays on the Veena. He is an excellent cook and it is difficult to say which of his preparations is the best. However, he has his own pecularity. For instance, while walking he does not see hither and thither; so people who see him on the road often have mistaken notions about his pride. I know that he does not stand before a mirror and see his own body. He insists that everyone should look after his body, but he does not care for himself. Yet he possesses an ideal body with proportionate limbs.

After my father settled at Bangalore for a few years all went on well. My father had suffered from appendicitis in youth and had taken no treatment. The malady flared up again and he died in 1928 at the age of sixty. He was very kind to us all and never ill-treated us. If anyone questioned him about his fortune, he answered that his children were his fortune. From his sick bed he used to call me and tell me that he would die when I would be nine. It seems that he had lost his own father when he was nine so he felt that he would die when I also would be nine. He also told me: "I have struggled very hard in my youth and you also will have to struggle very hard, but eventually, you will lead a happy life." I dare say his prophecy came to pass.

My mother passed away in 1958 at the age of eighty. She was innocent, kind-hearted, religious and highly orthodox in her habits. She had implicit faith in God. Ever since I began to earn I shared the responsibility of providing for her needs. I continued to do so till her death. Her orthodox habits kept her at Bangalore. She used to drink water only from wells and would refuse to drink water from taps. Though I had asked her to come and live with me at Pune after I settled there, she had refused to do so because of difficulty in getting well water. It was not in my destiny to serve her as I would have liked to do.

When my father was alive I was studying in the primary fourth standard. After his death the burden of bringing up the younger children fell upon our three elder brothers, who were the earning members of our family. The eldest, Doreswami, was an accountant. The second, Rajaiyangar, was a school master. Doreswami and Rajaiyangar were settled in Bangalore. Our third brother, Vedantachar, was then a relieving junior clerk in the Madras and Southern Maratha Railway and later a station master at Malur, about twenty miles from Bangalore. Our brothers had to fulfil their responsibility to their own respective families, and we became burden to them.

My fourth elder brother, Ramaswami, could not get through in the lower secondary examination, stopped further studying and thereafter took tailoring as a professional career. My younger brother, Cheluvarajan, stayed with my second elder sister, Rukkamma. My youngest sister, Jayamma, remained with my third elder sister Namagiriamma.

I had a weak constitution. In the year 1931, I suffered from malaria and later on again I was laid down with fever. The doctor suspected that I had typhoid and advised my brother to have me admitted as an in-patient in the Victoria Hospital, Bangalore. I remained as an in-patient for nearly one month before I was discharged. Even after the fever had subsided and one year had passed I did not show any progress in my health. I was as weak as before, and my schooling was affected and in 1932 I failed in English. In 1933, with the blessings of the elders, I got through in the lower secondary school examination. However, on the last day of the public examination, I fell down from the cycle I was riding and became unconscious. I reached the examination hall late. I recollect that the paper was on hygiene. For the first half hour my mind was blank. Slowly I gained confidence, scribbled something and came out. I got through the examination. Without passing this public examination it was not possible to join the High School.

I stayed with my eldest brother to join the High School. I remember when I was in Mysore in the year 1934-35 a doctor examined me in school. My height then was four feet ten inches. I weighed seventy pounds. My chest measurement was twenty two inches and chest expansion was only half an inch. Today my height is five feet six inches, weight is one hundred and forty-five pounds and my chest expands by five inches.

In those days education was free up to Lower Secondary School. In the High School we had to pay fees for eight months only during the year. My brothers expressed their inability to finance my studies. Fate was kind to me. My brother Rajaiyangar, the school-master, took me to some merchants in Bangalore who were known to my father. They were kind and contributed and in all I collected about 8 rupees towards my education. This encouraged me to apply for a seat in the High School. The admission fee was 1 rupee, the monthly fee 3 rupees, sports and library fees 1 rupee 12 annas, and the medical fee was 8 annas. The total fees amounted to 6 rupees and 4 annas. So my brother asked me what I would do for the monthly fees. I knew I could get nothing from those merchants. I had no answer for my brother and kept quiet.

With great effort I managed to get a letter of recommendation for freeship from Shri K.T. Bhasyam, an influential lawyer who had defended cases of my father's employer. Bhasyam later became the Law and Labour Minister in the Government of Mysore. I was lucky enough to be declared as a half-free student. I passed the annual examination.

I was very weak physically and the doctor suspected that I had consumption. During April-May 1934 my brother-in-law, Shri Krishnamachar, was asked by the Maharaja to go to Bombay to meet Swami Sri Kuvalaya-nanda and to see for himself the Yogashrams conducted by Swamiji at Lonavla and Bombay. Shri Krishnamachar came to Bangalore on his way to Bombay. He asked me to stay with my sister till his return from Bombay. As there were summer holidays I agreed to go to Mysore. He paid my railway fare and I proceeded to Mysore. I was very keen to see the palace of the Maharaja. When Shri Krish-namachar returned from the tour I requested him to send me back to Bangalore. He asked me to continue my studies in Mysore. So I stayed on in Mysore. I joined the Maharaja High School at Mysore. My half-freeship was continued here also.

In the beginning I enjoyed the school. My brother-in-law, though a very kind-hearted man, was hot-tempered. Gradually fear cropped up in me and I grew nervous even to stand or sit in his presence. None of my school fellows was allowed to visit me. Though I stayed in Mysore for two years I could not make friendship with any of my classmates. I was asked by Shri Krishnamachar to practise Yoga asanas, but for several months no asanas were taught to me. However, when I tried to do some asanas on my own I found that my body was stiff as a poker. It was impossible for me to do any bending. Shri Krishnamachar did not teach me or permit me to go to the Yogashala. For

8

several months I did not even know where the Yogashala was located.

Yoga Initiation

Shri Krishnamachar had brought up an orphan boy named Keshavamurthy. He had even celebrated the boy's thread ceremony and taught him Yoga. The boy was no doubt an expert. He and I shared the same room and he was my only friend and I felt sure that one day he would shine in life. But Providence willed otherwise. One morning in June or July 1935 he left all of a sudden and never returned. I was left alone. When Keshavamurthy was with us, Shri Krishnamachar used to wake us up at four in the morning and ask us to water the garden. We were so sleepy that we used to close the door and sleep outside the house for a few minutes and then start watering the garden. This task took us about an hour and a half.

After Keshavamurthy left, his share of the work also fell on me and I was ever hungry. I had no guts to ask even my sister for something to eat. We were to eat when called for, and to eat only what was served. I used to steal some money. Pangs of hunger drove me to steal some money to appease it. A hungry man will commit any sin.

I remember that in May 1935 I went to Bangalore for my father's death anniversary. One day I took a cycle of a lawyer who was a tenant in the house where my brother Rajaiyangar resided. By ill-luck I met with an accident. I sustained no injury, but the cycle was badly damaged. The lawyer demanded four rupees eight annas for repairing the cycle, which I did not have. My sister Seetamma paid a part of this and I earned the rest by doing domestic service and defrayed the balance.

Prof. T. Krishnamacharya and his Disciples, Pune.
SREE YOGA SHALA,
JAGANMOHAN PALACE, MYSORE.

Chair: G.R. Sakhalkar, Prince of Mysore;
M.G. Madan Gopal Raj Urs; Yoga-prof.T. Krishnamacharya;
V.N. Mudliar; B.K. Sundar Raja Iyangar, Yoga Instructor
2nd Row: S.K. Mudliar, M. Putta Raj Urs.

When I returned to Mysore in June 1935 my brother-in-law needed someone to perform the asanas at the Yagashala in place of Keshavamurthy who had left. This was the turning point in my life

Till that time Shri Krishnamachar did not think of teaching me Yoga asanas. Whenever I asked him to teach me some asanas he used to answer that it all depended upon one's *Karmas* in previous birth. It was my good fortune that due to Keshavamurthy's absence my brother-in-law taught me for a few days and he thus became my Guruji. Soon he performed my thread ceremony and became the Acharya initiating me with the Gayatri Mantra.

My legs pained terribly, backache was unbearable. Out of fear, I could not express my difficulties to anyone. For years I practised the Yoga asanas mechanically and I had no interest in learning asanas in the beginning. In spite of my difficulties, within a month of my learning a few asanas I gave my first public performance along with others in the Mysore Town Hall. It was in the month of September 1935. This was done in the presence of the late Maharaja of Mysore, who in appreciation of our performance awarded each of us 50 rupees. Guruji asked me to deposit that amount in the Postal Savings Bank. I kept the money in the Bank but gradually withdrew small sums for my food. Fortunately, Guruji never asked me about the deposit amount.

Soon after this performance I was asked to attend the Yogashala to train students both in the morning and in the evenings. My daily routine was to get up at 4 in the morning, water the garden and study up to 7 am. At 7:30 am some students also used to come to the residence to learn the difficult Yoga asanas for about half an hour. At

My brother-in-law needed someone to perform
the asanas at the Yogashala.
This was the turning point in my life.
Iyengar at 16, 1934.

8:30 am I took my bath, went to the Yogashala and returned home by 10 am. I took my food at 10:15 am and then walked three miles to school. Though the school closed at 4:30 in the afternoon, I was not allowed to go to the Yogashala direct though it was only a ten minute walk. I had to go back home just to leave my books there and then return to the Yogashala. I practised and taught at the Yogashala up to 7 pm and returned home for evening prayers and at 8 pm we had our food. Due to this hard life I felt very drowsy both at school and at the Yogashala. I could not concentrate on my studies and became a back-bencher. With great difficulty I collected the fees for the Secondary School Leaving Certificate Examination. Though I had little confidence in getting through, I appeared for this public examination. After the summer vacation the results were announced. I passed in all subjects except English.

As I had not managed to secure three more marks in English I was not eligible to join any college. According to the rules then prevailing, I would have to reappear for all the subjects and pass in each of them to be eligible to join college. It was beyond my means to rejoin the school without freeship and reappear for the examination.

Here ended my formal educational career.

The Yogashala also conducted its annual examinations and awarded certificates to the candidates who were successful in the elementary, intermediate and advanced diploma courses in Yoga. I appeared for the examination in October 1935 and I was awarded certificates. I stood first, securing ninety-eight marks out of a hundred in each course.

Even though I could perform the asanas I was not satisfied with my presentation. Also I had no stamina to retain the pose. After long practice and persistence, today I can stay in any pose conveniently for much longer duration. My hard work in mastering them has helped me now to teach the simplest of poses to the maximum stretch.

In December 1935, the World Y.M.C.A. Conference was held at Mysore. The Maharaja of Mysore gave an "at home" party to the delegates. At that time there was a Yoga demonstration. I took part in it and did the asanas. I got an award of 50 rupees from the Maharaja. I kept the amount in the Post Office. At this time, when I was attending the Yogashala to conduct classes on behalf of Guruji, a Sanyasi named Sri Swami Yogananda had come from America to Mysore as a palace guest. He visited our institution and saw all the work carried on there. He liked it immensely and praised Guruji for the work. His eyes fell on me and he asked me whether I would accompany him to America. But as I was very young Guruji did not agree to my going to America and told him that he might take me with him on his next visit.

Ventures in the Unknown

In 1936 the Maharaja of Mysore requested Guruji to go on a tour of North Karnataka. As it was summer, Guruji asked me to follow him along with his pupils. One of them was Shri C.M. Bhat, now settled in Bombay as a Yoga instructor. We gave two performances at Chitradurga. From there we went to Harihar and gave a demonstration. From there we proceeeded to Dharwar and remained there for three weeks. We gave a number of demonstrations, both public as well as private, at Dharwar and Hubli. The staff of the Karnataka College took keen interest. We were housed at the College quarters.

14

Many professors and doctors along with their families began to learn the asanas.

The ladies and girls demanded a separate class. Being the youngest of the group, I was put in charge.

This was the beginning of my independent teaching career.

In July, Guruji and his party had to return. But before returning to Mysore he fixed up a programme of two performances in Belgaum, one at the Sardar High School and the other at the Lingaraja College. At the Lingaraja college there was a big crowd. Dr. V.B. Gokhale, then Civil Surgeon of Belgaum, was also present. He took keen interest in Yoga. After his retirement he corresponded with the Mysore Yogashala to send a man to train the students in Pune colleges.

Dr. Gokhale had seen all the asanas performed by us. He has also checked pulsations and heart beats of my Guruji and was astonished when Guruji stopped them. There was another instance of Guruji stopping his heart and pulse. This was during the visit of two eminent doctors—Dr. Marcault and Dr. Brooce, heart specialists from France, who visited the Yogashala in 1935. They were great admirers of Yoga. First they observed all the asanas. I also showed them a number of poses. Guruji showed them the different varieties of pranayama and the reactions of breathing on the heart. They remained twenty days in Mysore experimenting the reactions of pranayama on the nervous system by the cardiogram machine. On the last day, the doctors were recording Guruji's heart beat and pulsations on the machine when it stopped and the lights also went off. For some time as there were no activities recorded the doctors announced that Guruji was dead. Soon thereafter the machine started

The body is the temple of the Spirit.
Let the temple be clean through Yoga.

re-recording and the doctors in amazement told us that Guruji was alive. The doctors confessed that Guruji had shown the stopping of the electrical beat of the heart which was considered impossible. Such was Guruji's control over the involuntary organs of the body.

Seeds of Teaching—Will of the Divine
After our performances were over, we were planning to return. The professors of the Karnataka College at Dharwar desired that one of us should remain and teach Yoga. Guruji wanted to leave a boy named Panduranga Bhatt. But the professors insisted that I should remain there. Guruji was first reluctant as I was only seventeen years old. Then he consented to my stay in Dharwar. I continued to work very well to the satisfaction of all for a month and a half and trained a good number of people. When the classes came to an end, they all presented me with clothes, silver tumblers and paid my fare to Mysore. They also gave me a shawl for Guruji.

Ethical discipline of the asana is when you extend
correctly, evenly, and to the maximum.

HOW PUNE
BECAME MY HOME

In THE MONTH OF FEBRUARY 1937, I went on a tour of several districts of Mysore State and gave a number of lecture-demonstrations. In this tour I got experience but not encouragement. On the contrary, I had to spend my own money. After this I returned to Mysore.

At that time one Shri Narasingarao from Koratagere came to Mysore and requested my Guruji to send me along with him to Koratagere. I accompanied Shri Narasingarao to Koratagere. I commenced treating him for hydrocele. After a few days I gave performances there. Shri Narasingarao did not pay me any fees for the tuition. Guruji wrote asking me to return to Mysore. When I returned he told me to proceed to Pune to train students there for a period of six months from September. My monthly salary was to be 60 rupees. As I was the only person at the Yogashala who knew a little English I got the chance to go to Pune.

At that time Guruji had been asked by the Maharaja to go on a tour of Bezwada and other places. I had 30 rupees in the savings bank. I withdrew 28 rupees for my trip to Pune. Guruji asked one of my colleagues to accompany him to Bezwada on condition that he should bear his own railway fare. My colleague asked me for a loan of 15 rupees. I loaned him the amount. With 13 rupees in hand I left for Hubli on July 2nd, 1937. Hubli is half way to Pune. I had to reach Pune by the end of August. I had not sufficient funds to maintain myself for two months till September. I broke my journey at Hubli in the hope of earning more money there. I had worked at Dhawar, which is fifteen miles from Hubli, the previous year. This time I took my chance to work in Hubli. I had taught one Shri Ramaswamy, who worked in the Bharat Mills at Hubli, when he was at Mysore. I wrote to him that I would stay at Hubli for a month. Shri Ramaswamy was very kind and found a place for me at a friend's house where I could board and lodge. I started teaching five or six students along with my hosts. It was arranged that all of them should contribute towards my expenses and pay my railway fare up to Pune. I also planned to go to Dharwar to take my chance there.

My schedule was very hard. Every morning at 6 am I left my place and walked a distance of about three miles to catch a train to Dharwar. The fare from Hubli to Dharwar was two annas (twelve paise) only. The response at Dharwar was disappointing. Whereas in the previous year I had taught about thirty pupils, this time I could get only one pupil on the understanding that he would only provide for my lunch. After the lesson, followed by lunch at 10:30 am, I walked back between Hubli and Dharwar—in all eighteen miles daily. During this time I gave two lecture-demonstrations, one at Hubli and the other at Dharwar. As I had to be in Pune by August 30th, I was given a ticket to Pune and 5 rupees for my expenses in Pune. I left Hubli on the 29th. Shri Ramaswamy and my other pupils came and saw me off at the station. When I reached Pune on the morning of August 30th, 1937, I had only a sum of four and a half rupees with me.

Little did I realise then that Pune would be my home for the rest of my life.

I did not know Marathi then. I engaged a coolie for four annas to guide me to the Deccan Gymkhana. I made enquiries about a cheap hotel where I could board and lodge. I found one called "Cafe Unique" where the daily rate for a room with meals was one rupee twelve annas. I paid the amount for two days. I had only twelve annas left with me. On August 31st, I met Dr. V.B. Gokhala who took me to the Gymkhana Club and introduced me to my prospective students who would work with me. When the introductions were over I requested Dr. Gokhale to inform the proprietor of the Cafe Unique that I was employed and that I would pay my bill at the end of the month. The charges were 40 rupees per month. Dr. Gokhale kindly informed the hotel proprietor and I was able to remain in the hotel. I could not get any money in advance. I had to manage with only twelve annas for the whole month. All my worldly goods were a pair of shirts and *dhoties* and bedding. I used one dhoti as a towel. I had no soap. I had no money even for a shave. I bought a razor-blade for one paisa and with that naked blade shaved twice without soap during the month.

Though my class had started, students were very few. It was arranged among the Fergusson College, the Wadia College, the S.P. College, the Nutan Marathi Vidyalaya, the Deccan Gymkhana, the Maharashtra Mandal and the Maharashtra Education Society School that each institution should contribute 10 rupees per month with a right to depute ten students for the daily classes. This worked out to be the princely sum of three naya paise per lesson per pupil per day. At first only three students from the Fergusson College, two from the Wadia College, five from the Nutan Marathi Vidyalaya, six from the Maharashtra Mandal and one from the S.P. College turned up. No students came from the M.E.S. School or from the Deccan Gymkhana Club. Outsiders were charged one rupee per month. I had in all ten students. The classes went on for six months. The pupils wanted to continue but three of the institutions withdrew their contribution. Some outsiders took the responsibility that they would bear the loss and that the classes should continue. So the classes got another lease on life for six more months.

I could not afford to stay at the Unique Cafe, so during the second month I shifted to a cheaper place.

During the Ganpati Festival days, Dr. Gokhala arranged lecture-demonstrations by me along with the gymnastics staff of the Deccan Gymkhana Club. The staff was non-cooperative and only at the close of the functions did I have my chance to show my art for about ten minutes. Even these short demonstrations were appreciated by the audience.

Dreams of Prophecy
One night towards the end of 1937, I had a strange dream. I wanted to drive a nail into the wall. As I was hammering the nail, two heads of a thousand-headed cobra fell down. I got frightened and turned towards the other wall where I had fixed a picture of Narayana. When I turned I saw a huge eagle—Narayana's Garuda—intently gazing at me. Feeling panicky I prayed to the Lord to save me as on one side there was the cobra and on the other side there was the eagle.

All of a sudden I saw a brilliant light, ten times brighter than the Sun. In that light I saw the Lord in the form of Adi-Shesha (the Divine Serpent, on whose Head the Earth rests), Narayana, Shri Devi and Bhu Devi. I fell at their feet and did *Satsanga Namaskar*. The Lord asked me to have his *darshan* fully. When my eyes fell on Adi-Shesha I saw two heads in the centre missing. I asked why the two heads were missing and the Lord answered that I had cut off the two heads. I woke up with a start feeling greatly disturbed. I do not know how to interpret the dream. Perhaps it may be that I have yet to take more births to realise God.

One night in 1938, in my dream I visited Trivandrum with Guruji to have Darshan of Ananta Padmanabha Swami. Both of us went to the temple where there was a huge idol of the Lord in the centre. The temple had three doors. The first door was opposite the head. The middle door was near the trunk and the third near the feet. I went to the head-side door and then to the centre door. From the third door I took the last chance to see the entire idol as I had to leave the place.

As I prayed a fire emerged from the face of the idol and came towards me. I prayed to the Lord to forgive me if I had committed any sin. The more I prayed the more the flames came towards me. I felt that I would have to give up my body immediately. I turned to Guruji and asked him to pardon me and bless me. As soon as I turned to Guruji the flames slowly lessened and vanished. This dream strengthened my faith in Guruji.

In August 1938, Dr. Gokhale again arranged lecture-demonstrations for schools and colleges. This was liked by all and the improvements made by my students of various institutions enabled the institutions to continue my services for another year. Guruji came down to Pune and saw for himself how my class was functioning. As my pupils made good progress an examination was held and certificates were issued to them by the Mysore Yogashala. Taking advantage of Guruji's presence, I arranged lectures and demonstrations which were presided over by Shri G.V. Mavlankar, the then Speaker of the Legislative Assembly of Bombay, and by Smt. Sarojini Naidu, who later became the Governor of Uttar Pradesh. The demonstrations generated enthusiasm amongst my students. The S.P. College again agreed to enrol students and contribute funds, provided I gave my classes at the College premises. About sixty to seventy students attended at the S.P. College. The authorities of the M.E.S. School for girls expressed their desire to restart the class for their pupils. A class for ladies and girls only was started at the Deccan Gymkhana Club.

My students wanted to organise a function and some college students approached the then Chairman of the Municipality, Shri P.K. Atre, noted Marathi writer and dramatist, to preside over the function. Seeing their youthful enthusiasm he consented. He appreciated our efforts and asked the authorities of the Gandhi Training School, which was under the control of the Municipality, to train their students in Yoga. Many individuals asked me to teach them at their homes.

I was very young then and the interest shown by the public inspired me to greater efforts. However, the physical strain was unbearable. I suggested to Dr. Gokhale that he should request the individuals who wanted training at home to go over to the Gymkhana Club. He did not agree. For the Gymkhana it became almost a business proposition. I was treated by the Gymkhana authorities as if I were a domestic servant. They did not care for me or for my health.

Some of the Rulers of the Deccan States, including the late Shrimant Bhavanrao Pant, Raja Saheb of Aundh, founder of the Surya Namaskar System, visited our class. My students and I gave a good show. In appreciation, the Rulers presented me with a purse. The presents were taken away and I was told that so long as I served the Gymkhana I was not at liberty to accept presents from anyone. What was gifted by generous hands was grabbed away by greedy hands.

All who visited my Yoga class were impressed. The number of students had swelled to two hundred. The class got a fresh lease on life for a year. The gymnasium staff of the Gymkhana Club envied my success. One night, in their intolerance, they broke open the lock of the pavilion of the Gymkhana, where items used for the Yoga classes like mats, carpets and ropes were kept, and burnt them. The culprits could not be traced. My classes, however, did not close as there was a surplus amount accumulated as a result of my hard work. New mats and carpets were bought and the classes proceeded as usual.

The Deccan Gymkhana Club was the first to introduce the Indian style of physical exercise and, therefore, got a good grant from the Government of Bombay. I recall that in 1944 or 1945, the Chairman of the Physical Board of Education of the Bombay Province, Swami Kuvalaya-nandji, had visited the Gymkhana. I had been asked to give a lecture-demonstration, though at that time I was not connected with Gymkhana. Later I learned that due to this demonstration the Gymkhana got a grant from the Government for that year also.

Some of my students and I attended the All Maharashtra Physical Conference held at Bombay, Satara and Miraj and gave good performances. We were taken to Hubli by Dr. Gokhale for a demonstration before the Bombay Medical Conference which was held there. Then we proceeded to Jog Falls and Bangalore. Dr. Gokhale bore the expenses of those tours.

I recollect that in 1938, some of my students had taken me to a temple near Shivaji Nagar to meet Phadke Maharaj. He looked at me and said that though I had practised Yoga for some time I was lacking in spiritual practice. He also said that if I was given the right training I would turn towards spirituality. Later, Phadke Majaraj accompanied me to my room where I showed him a photoraph of Guruji. Phadke Maharaj stared intently at the photograph for a long time. At that time I did not know Marathi well. Phadke Maharaj asked for a paper and pen and he wrote about Guruji. He said that Guruji was a great soul and that I should never forget him or neglect him. If I were to do so I would be doomed. Padke Maharaj said that I would get everything from Guruji alone as he had a great liking for me.

In January 1939, Guruji asked me to attend the Ayurvedic Conference at Gudiwada in Andhra Pradesh. At Gudiwada we met Shri V.V. Giri, who later became the fourth President of India, and Dr. Lakshmipati, then Health Minister of Madras. They were impressed by the demonstration. After visiting Bangalore I returned to Pune.

In February 1940, the Pune students had their gathering once again when Shri S.M. Joshi, (Socialist leader) presided and certificates were awarded.

26

During September 1939, Dr. Gokhale had taken permission of the Maharaja of Mysore to make a movie of about 2000 ft. of my Yoga asana poses. With the help of one Shri Sardar Ponde, Dr. Gokhale started filming my poses near the Bhandarkar Institute at Pune. When Guruji was in Pune in July 1940, I had arranged a performance before His Excellency Sir Roger Lumley, the then Governor of Bombay. The governor had invited many people for the occasion and they were impressed by the demonstrations. Taking advantage of Guruji's presence, I requested him to appear in the film of Dr. Gokhale, who was to take a few shots of my students also. The movie was to be in black and white. Due to some misunderstanding which arose between us, the film remained unfinished.

In July 1940, Guruji visited Pune, and asked me to accompany him to Bombay for a few days. I accompanied him and took part in a demonstration arranged at the Convocation Hall of the Bombay University where Sir Rustom Masani, the then Vice Chancellor of the University, presided. There was another performance at Sir Cawasji Jehangir Hall where Smt. Sarojini Naidu presided. As the Maharaja of Mysore died at that time, Guruji cancelled his remaining programme and returned to Mysore.

Darkness before Dawn

My services with the Deccan Gymkhana Club were to terminate by the end of August 1940. I had taken a loan of 100 rupees from the Gymkhana in April 1940 for the marriage of my younger sister Jayamma. By July 1940, I had cleared half the amount. When my services came to an end the Gymkhana deducted the balance of the loan amount along with interest and all I had at the end of August 1940 was a sum of 4 rupees. My lodging bill was still unpaid.

At this stage of my life I did not know where my next meal could come from. I had no roof over my head since the room which I was occupying had to be vacated. My only reason for staying on in Pune was that it was better to continue in a place where I had established some contacts for three years rather than start afresh in an unknown place.

In September 1940, however, there was an Industrial Exhibition held at Sambhaji Park, Pune. My performance was arranged there and it was presided over by Shri L.B. Bhopatkar, President of the All India Hindu Mahasabha. In that gathering there was a Gujarati gentleman by the name of Shri L.M. Motee, official race card publisher describing the forms of horses for the Pune and Bombay horse races. Shri Motee liked my performance and asked me to teach his children and he agreed to pay me 40 rupees a month. This started the second phase of my life in Pune.

Before closing with the first phase it is my duty to thank Dr. Gokhale for the great pains and personal interest he took in me to ensure running of the Yoga class even against opposition. But for his efforts my career as a Yoga teacher would have ended. With the help of Dr. Gokhale I trained more than six hundred students, many of whom still practise Yoga asanas sincerely.

I started teaching Shri Motee and his family as soon as I was called. I had found a big hall located in the Main Street in Pune Cantonment to conduct my classes there. The rent was only 10 rupees a month, but when I shifted to Main Street my students avoided me fearing that the place was haunted. Some students from the Cantonment area came for a month or two and left. My old students did not come to Main Street because of the distance. Shri Motee had supplied mats and carpets for the class. He was also kind enough to send to me a bottle of milk every day. But my ill luck persisted. I had to close my class in September 1941, because I could not afford to pay the monthly rent of 10 rupees. This was perhaps the darkest period of my life. It lasted for three to four years.

In September 1941, when I closed my class in Main Street my pupils were only Shri Motee and his family and one Shri Dinshaw who owned a restaurant. Shri Dinshaw was almost paralysed when he came in contact with me in September 1940. He suffered from nausea after meals and so he chewed beetle leaves and smoked. After starting Yoga asanas he gradually gave up these habits. He turned a vegetarian and a teetotaller. He began to lead a regular life and became pure in body and mind.

Search for the "Known"
In March or April 1941, when I was cycling I had a jerk as a result of which my testicles were jammed under the seat, causing severe pain and swelling. I suffered for about three years. I consulted a doctor pupil of mine and he was of the opinion that my complaint was due to hernia and advised me to take rest. I very cautiously practised some asanas to relieve myself of the pain and swelling. Slowly my trouble disappeared.

In September 1941, I read a news item about Uday-shankar, the world-famous dancer. It stated that he was visiting Bombay and persons keen on learning dancing could correspond with him at his address in Bombay. I met him personally and had discussions with him. I told him of my interest in dance and offered to teach him and his troupe Yoga asanas, if he in turn could teach me dancing and maintain me during the period of study as I could not afford to maintain myself. He turned down my offer and my interest in dancing faded.

I carried on correspondence with various publications like *Health Magazine, The Illustrated Weekly of India, Life* magazine published in America and United Publications of Delhi. I also corresponded with the Information Films of India and requested them to present Yoga in its proper perspective. But all the journals and the Information Films of India replied that they were not interested.

The Body is a Temple and Asanas are Prayers

My daily routine had not changed. I got up at four in the morning, practised pranayama for half an hour, relaxed and went to work. If the work was less I did asanas first and then practised pranayama.

I was completely down and out. The physical effort of perfecting my asanas poses exhausted me. I was mentally depressed due to failure in my Yogic practices. There was always difficulty in earning my livelihood. In those days food was relatively cheap and one could have a plate of rice for two annas (twelve paise). But even this was beyond my reach. There were occasions when I had a plate of rice once in two or three days. The rest of the time I had to fill my belly with tea or with tap water. It was a real testing time of tears and failures and anxieties. My heart, nerve and senses were giving way. However, an inner voice urged me to persist and carry on. Sometimes I cried that even God had forgotten me. Now, by hindsight, it seems that this was the darkest hour before the dawn of prosperity. My will alone held on. I persisted in my practices. Slowly the grace of God started descending upon me and my mind turned inwards.

I regarded the body as my temple and the asanas as my prayers. My practice in Yoga increased more and more.

I made up my mind that I would continue in my practice, but I would not give any publicity nor beg anyone for tuitions or recommendations. My conviction grew stronger that I should continue in my yogic practices and live the same life as long as God willed it.

I had come in contact with one Shri Prahlad (a film actor) of Mysore who was then working with Prabhat Film Co. He introduced me to various people in the film industry. He had a charming personality and I lost a good friend when he died in 1943.

One of my acquaintances through Prahlad in the film industry was Shri Bhal G. Pendharkar, who was a producer and director of films. He saw my poses of all asanas and asked me to teach him. He also asked me to give up all tuitions except those of Shri Motee and Shri Dinshaw. He wanted me to become more worldly and offered to be my manager and make arrangements about fees from people desiring to take lessons from me. Unfortunately, my association with him was short-lived. His own film concern at Pune was running at a loss. He closed it in October 1941, went to Kolhapur and settled there.

Charity Show
In August 1941, members of the National Guard of Bombay had organised a Charity Show for relief for victims of floods in Malabar and Gujarat. Some of the organisers were friends of Pendharkar. One of them, Dr. Nair, requested me to give a demonstration of Yoga asanas.

31

When I practise, I'm a philosopher. When I teach, I'm a
scientist. When I demonstrate, I'm an artist.

Pendharkar photographed some of my asanas in his studio and sent the results to Bombay. The photographs were not published but my name did appear in the newspapers. I went to Bombay two days before the performance. The organisers wanted to curtail my programme, thinking that it would not interest the audience. I asked them to give me a chance and they agreed to give me ten minutes towards the end of the programme. The function was to be inaugurated by Smt. Sarojini Naidu. Amongst the performers were well-known film stars of those days, Snehprabha Pradhan and Vasanti. The famous dancer Gaurishankar was also there. They were introduced to Smt. Sarojini Naidu, but other participants, including me, were not introduced. Fortunately, as I was going on to the stage to make my arrangements, Smt. Naidu, who was to inaugurate the function and then leave for another engagement, met me. She remembered me from my previous demonstration, and suggested to the organisers that they arrange my item first as there were some foreign delegates with her who would like to see my demonstration. The organisers, therefore, had my item first. It was greatly appreciated by the audience. At the end of the performance Shri Dhirubhai Desai, President of the National Guard, who later became the Indian Ambassador to Switzerland, told the organisers to thank me as mine was the best performance in the show. Later I became friendly with Shri Dhirubhai.

MARRIAGE AND FAMILY

IN 1943, I VISITED BANGALORE for my father's death anniversary. When I reached Bangalore I received a letter from Guruji asking me to accompany him to Rajahmundry to attend the Ayurvedic Conference which was to be held at a place where the Godavari river flows into the sea and we had to go by launch. When we reached the place, Guruji asked Dr. Lakshmipati to arrange our lecture-demonstration first. He spoke in Telugu whilst I performed the asanas. I was fagged out by my travels yet I was not discouraged and our performance was a success. Dr. Lakshmipati requested Guruji to render his speech in Sanskrit and Guruji spoke in Sanskrit as if it were his mother tongue. This was the first time that I had heard him deliver a speech in Sanskrit.

After the conference was over we returned to Madras and then proceeded to Malur where my brother Vedantachar was an assistant station master. He had gone to Bangalore to attend the marriage of my cousin. We stopped for a few days at Malur. Guruji told my brother Vedantachar that it was time that I got married. My brother took a personal interest in me. But due to my hard life at Pune and lack of financial stability, I was unwilling to marry. My relatives suspected my resistance as being due to some flaw in my character. Guruji, however, felt that it was time that I established myself as a married man. My brother had carried on correspondence with various relatives for a prospective bride for me and had asked my relatives to bring the girls to Bangalore for formal talks. My uncle's son, Shamachar, had brought a sixteen-year-old girl named Ramamani. She was the daughter of Anekal Ramachandrachar and Shingaramma. Shingaramma was the sister of Shamachar's son-in-law. Ramamani had dark complexion but was tall and of good appearance. They had come to Bangalore during the afternoon and had been waiting there since about two o'clock. At that time I was at Malur and knew nothing about their visit to Bangalore. My brother Vedantachar had been transferred from Malur to Bangalore and he had packed up his belongings and all of us proceeded to Bangalore which we reached at about 10 o'clock at night.

At the Bangalore railway station my younger brother informed Vedantachar that a prospective bridal party had come to see me. I understood the situation and felt perturbed. When we reached home I was asked to see the girl Shamachar had brought with him and give my views. I told my brother that I was not against marriage but I wanted a little time to think. My brother did not like this. The party had been waiting for hours. My brothers, sisters, uncles and aunts all insisted that I should give my consent. My mother, who was also related to the girl's mother, liked the proposed alliance, but could not interfere. Ultimately I consented to the marriage. The bride's party wanted to celebrate the marriage early, while I wanted the marriage to be postponed until December.

At the insistence of the bride's party, the wedding was fixed for July 9th, 1943.

I had very little money with me. It was less than 100 rupees. The marriage had been fixed in haste. The marriage was to be performed at Tumkur. I did not ask for any dowry. The bride's party paid me 150 rupees for clothes and for the railway fare to Tumkur. I wrote to my friends in Pune for help. Shri Motee and Shri Dinshaw sent 100 rupees each. I wrote to other students who owed me tuition fees and in all I managed to collect about 500 rupees. I had the invitation cards printed and sent them to friends in Pune. All my brothers and sisters attended my marriage. I paid their railway fares to Tumkur and back. Half of all the wealth I had was spent for railway fares. I did not even possess a new *dhoti* for my wedding. But I took everything with calmness. The marriage functions were over and on July 11th, 1943, we all left for Bangalore with Rama.

After my marriage I prolonged my stay at Bangalore as my people wanted to invite all the relatives for lunch. An auspicious day was selected and the lunch was held. The expenses of the lunch were borne by me.

At the end of July 1943, I left Bangalore with my wife and niece. My wife got down at Tumkur and proceeded to her parents' place. She requested me to alight at Tumkur, but I could not do so as I had to return to Pune. My niece got down at Arsikere and I proceeded to Pune.

I met my students at Pune. Shri Motee had been like a father to me since September 1940, but when I returned in August 1943, he told me that he would discontinue the tuitions. This was a severe loss of income for me, but I kept silent. Shri Motee very kindly told me that he wanted to send 200 rupees as a wedding present but he had sent only 100 rupees as he wanted to pay the further sum of 100 rupees personally. Shri Motee also refused to take back the loan which I had taken from him and said that amount was also a wedding gift.

It seemed that when Shri Motee started my tuitions he had three daughters but no son. Shri Motee and his wife both had a great desire to have a son. I had told Shri Motee and his wife that they would get a son by God's grace if both of them did asanas. They did the asanas and after about three years were blessed with a son. Their desire for a son was fulfilled and thereafter Shri Motee discontinued my tuition.

Shri Dinshaw, however, continued as my pupil and also gave me another present. I had no other tuitions for about another three months and I was very worried about my wife. Alone, if my financial position did not improve, I could bear the physical and mental strain, but I did not like the idea of my wife sharing my sufferings. I never lost hope though I had no money.

Luckily in October 1943, the Superintendent of the M.E.S. School asked me to train some girls from the school and I willingly accepted. One Dr. R.V. Gokhale also asked me to teach him. My financial position improved and I asked my wife to come over to Pune. This was in November 1943. She was brought to Pune by her brother. We started our new life with very few things. Every household article was borrowed or gathered from friends as neither of us had been provided with household articles by our parents. We had a single pot for cooking. Those were the days of the Second World War. Prices were soaring. But I was happy because God had blessed me with a good wife and contentment.

Guardian Angel
Ever since I started teaching Yoga at the age of seventeen

I taught many girls and women. When I taught in Dharwar, the ladies ignored my presence and had frank discussions of their intimate problems amongst themselves. This enabled me to learn the psychology of women which helped me greatly later in life. On several occasions temptations arose in me, which was but natural at that age. The grace of God kept me clean. Gradually my thoughts turned towards study of philosophy, though I was not completely free from temptations. When I married Ramamani I loved her passionately. She was very kindhearted, serene and patience incarnate with understanding. She became my excellent adviser. She was my helpmate, always encouraging me in my times of difficulty and stress. She never interfered in my practices and teaching and sacrificed her comforts on my account. On several occasions I sat at night, while she was asleep, gazing at her serene face. I thanked God for giving me such a faithful wife who was also my guardian angel. Ours was a blessed union as we were united physically, mentally and spiritually. Our union was blessed with seven children, of whom we lost one.

In December 1943, Shri F.P. Pocha, a famous seed merchant of Pune asked me to train him and his daughter at his residence. He was a victim of sciatica and got relief only through Yoga. He induced many of his friends to take to Yoga.

In 1944, I wanted an album of photographs of my asana poses. One of my friends Shri S. Ram, working at the Royal Western India Turf club, had a camera and I asked him to take photographs of my poses. He agreed to do so but films were extremely scarce at that time and I had to pay an exorbitant price for getting films in the market. Ram photographed me doing about a hundred and fifty poses within two days. This exertion affected my health adversely and I had high fever. My wife was then in the seventh month of her first pregnancy. I, therefore, asked Ram to come and help me. He did so but he himself fell ill and the task of nursing us both fell upon her. A friend of Ram had us admitted to the Sassoon Hospital and one of my brothers came from Bangalore to our aid. I was discharged after four days, but Ram had to remain in hospital as he had an acute attack of malaria. After my discharge from the hospital I moved all over Pune to tell my students that I was proceeding to Bangalore for rest, as I was weak. This brought about a relapse and when I reached Bangalore the doctor diagnosed my fever as malaria. I was confined to bed for about twenty days. I had to borrow money from Pocha and Motee.

After recovery, my wife and I went to Mysore to seek Guruji's blessings as he had not been able to attend our marriage. This was during the last week of October 1944, which was the time of the annual gathering of the Yoga-shala. The pupils at the Yogashala had some grievances against Guruji and they had decided to refrain from participating in the annual function unless they had their own way. I felt that this was not the proper occasion for the pupils to air their grievances and that the function should proceed smoothly. However, as the pupils did not participate, I alone gave a demonstration of asanas although I had not fully recovered. My performance was appreciated and the function ended successfully. We returned to Bangalore. From there I proceeded to Pune after leaving my wife at Tumkur for her delivery.

On December 7th, 1944, my wife gave birth to our first daughter, Geeta. She returned with the baby to Pune in April 1945.

Pocha's recommendations greatly helped in furthering my career. I was introduced to some patients of Dr. Dinshaw Mehta. Dr. Mehta had a Nature Cure Clinic where Mahatma Gandhi had taken treatments. The patients at his clinic, who had benefitted by taking Yoga lessons from me and Pocha, tried to persuade Dr. Mehta to utilise my services at his clinic. Dr. Mehta made an offer, but it was unremunerative, as he insisted that I should not take up any outside work. He further said that he would choose the appropriate asanas out of a number of them selected by me. I could not accept his suggestion.

When Pocha visited the United States in July 1946 to participate in the International Rotary Conference in his capacity as Governor of the Rotary Club, he did not discontinue my services. He requested me to teach Dr. (Mrs.) Vasundhara Gharpure, wife of Dr. K.C. Gharpure, a noted surgeon of Pune. I started teaching her. After a month Dr. Gharpure also started learning the asanas. At one of my demonstrations at the Pune Medical School in 1947, arranged by Dr. Gokhale, Dr. Gharpure admired my performance. However, he felt that it was too rigorous for an average person. When Dr. Gharpure himself consented to learn from me I was very happy to teach him. On his return from the United States, Pocha arranged my performance at the Rotary Club of Pune. Dr. Gharpure was then the president of the Rotary Club, and he explained to the audience how asanas did not strain the heart and that the yogic system of physical exercise could be practised by all persons, even those having a weak constitution. Dr. Gharpure was also kind enough to refer patients to me for treatment by yogic asanas.

I was perhaps the first person to take this art to the masses and also to introduce the training of Yoga asanas for ladies.

Vision of Divinity

One night in October 1946, both my wife and I had strange dreams. In my dream I saw Lord Venkateshwara of Tirupati blessing me with one hand. In the other, the Lord held out a grain of rice and said that from that day onwards my struggles would be over and that I should devote all my time to teaching and practising Yoga. In my wife's dream a gracious lady in a yellow *saree* appeared. She had long hair and broad *kumkum* mark on her forehead. The lady gave my wife a coin and told her that she and her husband owed us a debt which she wanted to repay. We narrated our dreams to each other in the morning. I believe that the lady who appeared in my wife's dream was Lakshmi, the goddess of wealth. From that day onwards we never felt the want of money.

These dreams became turning points in our lives.

Experiments and Successes

I came in contact with many more people and I started treating persons suffering from various complaints through Yoga.

Perhaps I was the pioneer in India in the field of introducing Yoga teaching to groups of students, both male, female, and mixed groups.

In March 1947, Dr. Gharpure introduced me to Shrimati Fatima Ismail, now nominated as a member of the Rajya Sabha. Her daughter Usha was afflicted by polio. She had taken Usha all over India for treatment. She had shown Usha to Dr. Kini, a famous orthopaedic surgeon of Madras, who after examination said that though Usha's leg might improve, the spine would not. Smt. Ismail had tried to bring about improvement in Usha by getting her to undergo treatments with many masseurs and physiotherapists. Dr. Kini's treatment brought about improvement in Usha generally. There was, however, no change in the condition of Usha's spine. On the advice of Dr. Gharpure, Smt. Ismail decided that I should teach Usha. I was happy to do so and she showed improvement in her spine in about a month. This created confidence in Smt. Ismail about my work. She took Usha to Dr. Kini for a check-up and the doctor advised her to let Usha continue with the Yoga treatment. Smt. Ismail often wanted to test my sincerity. She would tell her servants that she was away when I came to teach Usha. Actually she would be at home. The mother's presence or absence made no difference to my line of treatment, so far as Usha was concerned. After seeing the improvement in her child, she was extremely pleased and continued my further training.

Smt. Ismail founded a rehabilitation centre in Bombay for disabled children at this time. She very kindly offered me a job at the centre. I visited the centre at her request and worked there for a week. The children co-operated with me joyfully. Their parents also took keen interest in my way of handling the children but the work involved was more than could be handled by one person. Smt. Ismail was not willing to give me any assistants as she did not have faith in others. I could not continue the work at the rehabilitation centre. Later, in 1952, Smt. Ismail raised her offer, but I could not accept it as it was not possible to handle disabled children single-handed. Each such child required individual attention and the work involved demanded total absorption.

At the time of Smt. Ismail's first offer, Shri Bankim-chandra Mukherji, a political leader of Bengal, who was then the President of the Indian National trade Union

Congress, came all the way from Calcutta to Pune to see me. He had been advised at the Institute of Tropical Medicine to take a course of Yoga asanas with me. He had intestinal complaints since childhood and I was happy that Mukherji got considerable relief as a result of the treatment.

Smt. Ismail introduced me to one Shri Pakseema, proprietor of Muratore's restaurant in Pune. His daughter was also a victim of polio. He had taken her to eminent doctors in Bombay and after trying out various treatments had given up hope of improvement. Within a few months of my teaching her, she recovered strength in her leg and her limping almost disappeared. Pakseema later migrated to Pakistan and his daughter continued to maintain her practices there and improved gradually. She is now happily married and has children.

During my association with Pakseema I had an opportunity to know something about the Holy Koran. We often had discussions on philosophy and he gave me a number of quotations from the Holy Koran which were very similar in thought content to the Vedic and Upanishadic texts. Pakseema explained to me that the "Namaz" was an Islamic form of worship. He also explained that though men belonged to various faiths the soul is one—undifferentiated and it was the immutable Self—*Atma*. I belong to one of the orthodox sects of the Hindu community. Formerly I was even reluctant to share food with men of other communities. Gradually my outlook changed and the feeling of differentiation lessened and ultimately disappeared. I look upon my friends of all communities as my kith and kin. I feel that the inner purity of a person alone counts and that human thoughts and feelings are the same all the world over.

When Pakseema left for Pakistan, my income was reduced but this setback did not diminish my faith in the mercy of God. On many occasions I felt that I was bargaining for God's mercy and this thought made me feel miserable at my lack of faith. Later I learned to pray only without thought of any return or favours from the Lord.

What is the Truth?

Towards the end of December 1947 or the beginning of January 1948, Swami Ramanandji visited Bombay. He was a Yogi from the Himalayas. He gave a public performance in which he stayed buried underground for twenty-four hours. This news was flashed all over the world and I was curious to meet him. It was not possible for me to go to Bombay. Fortunately after about a week in Bombay he visited Pune and another similar performance was arranged at the Deccan Gymkhana Club. I saw this performance, and was introduced to Swamiji. He spoke in Hindi for a few minutes. He talked about his desire to start an Ashram at Almora in Uttar Pradesh, for which he was collecting funds. Swamiji was buried. The following day I went two hours before he was scheduled to be disinterred. It seemed that his pupil had got a call from him to bring him up and the pupil had done so, and I watched Swamiji perspiring profusely. He said that he had been in Samadhi and was feeling extremely tired and could hardly speak. His words sounded strange because according to the yogic texts a person who has experienced Samadhi does not feel hot or cold. During the experience of Samadhi there is no sense of smell, taste or touch and there is neither a sense of happiness nor sorrow. Once during my practice I experienced Samadhi for a few brief moments but my experience was completely different from that of Swami Ramamandji. My body was at rest. My soul was calm. I had no sense of awareness of things around me. All my thoughts, actions, body and ego were completely forgotten. I was only conscious of that moment of rapture. A movement of the head brought me back to normalcy.

There were diverse comments in the newspapers about Swamiji's performance. It appeared that the cell where Swamiji had been buried was found to have a hole in it about the size of a rupee coin and a flower had been placed upon the hole so as to cover it. A sentry posted near the cell had complained that he had heard sounds made by a chisel, apparently when the hole was being bored by a disciple of Swamiji, and the sentry had seen the hole. The disciple of Swamiji had an argument with the sentry. This news created doubts as regards the genuineness of the performance. Through friends I learnt that Swamiji was staying with his host in my residential locality and I wanted to meet him personally. His disciples made people who wanted to visit him stand in long queues. I did not get my chance on two occasions to see Swamiji. On the third occasion I was told that Swamiji allotted only an hour and a half for interviews with members of the public and during the rest of the time was in Samadhi. When I ultimately met Swamiji and told him about our introduction at the time of his public performance at the Deccan Gymkhana Club, he could not recollect our meeting. I broached the topic of my desire of showing my asana poses to him and obtaining his guidance. Swamiji willingly gave me time in the morning. Taking this opportunity, I requested Swamiji to permit my wife and others to see me perform the asanas. My wife's presence gave me great encouragement and I gave a demonstration for an hour and a half. Swamiji was all praises for my demonstration and stated that even in the Himalayas he had not come across anyone who could perform asanas like this. Swamiji's praise made me happy. After this performance Swamiji gave me permission to meet him every day during his stay in Pune at any time I liked. I wondered how I could do so when he was said to be in Samadhi except during the time allotted to meet visitors. I met him almost daily during his stay in Pune and I found him to be free and not in Samadhi at all. I had asked him once to give one more performance of Samadhi so as to remove the doubts created in the public by the newspaper reports. He did not give any performance thereafter. After a lapse of two years I learnt that Swamiji had come back to Bombay. One of his pupils had met me and had told me that Swamiji proposed to visit the United States and had desired me to accompany him. Much as I liked the idea of visiting the United States I declined his offer as I was not sure about Swamiji's practices in Yoga.

Approaching Dawn

In June 1948, one of my elderly lady pupils, Smt. Khurshid Kapadia, introduced me to Smt. Mehra Jal Vakil (now Smt. Mehra Dinshaw Malegaumwala). Mehra's husband, Dr. Jal Rustom Vakil, was a leading cardiologist. Mehra talked with me regarding yogic exercises and their efficacy, and she planned to stay in Pune for a month to learn about the yogic method of healing. Her husband and mother-in-law wondered whether she was practising asceticism, but when they met and talked with me their doubts disappeared. Dr. Vakil's mother learned from me some exercises for toning her body and a few breathing exercises for her heart trouble. Prior to her learning these exercises and breathing, even a few steps left her fatigued and gave her palpitations. After practising breathing exercises for a few weeks she could climb stairs without difficulty and walking tired her no longer. Mehra's mother, Lady Karanjia, also learned some exercises from me and all the people in her family became Yoga enthusiasts. When Mehra and Dr. Vakil went to England in 1950, she carried with her an album of my Yoga asana poses. She showed the album to many doctors in England and also to her other friends and did propaganda about the efficacy of yogic asanas.

In the middle of 1948, Shri J. Krishnamurti, well-known philosopher, came to Pune to give discourses over a period of three months. I attended most of his lectures. I was introduced to him by Pocha and I showed him my asana poses. He appreciated my performance and told me that it was the skill of a professional. I requested him not to brand me like that as I had not taken to this art as a professional man. It had come to me of its own accord and I would stop teaching my art when God willed it. After finishing my performance, when I was talking to some friends who were present, Krishnaji asked me to see his own asana poses and he started performing them. I was glad to see him do many asanas. His poses, however, were not accurate and he was getting out of breath. I told Krishnaji that he could perform the asanas to perfection if he wanted to and I casually mentioned that one never got out of breath while doing asanas. He said that he had already performed his asanas in the morning and, therefore, he felt exhausted doing them again. I then told him that I could make him do all the poses over again without his getting out of breath. He performed the poses again while I supported him and corrected the postures. Krishnaji was pleased that I was not critical of his performance. He requested me to teach him every morning at five during his stay in Pune and accordingly I changed my schedule with Pocha and worked with Krishnaji till his departure from Pune. Krishnaji was a man of great will power. He was true to his practice and he readily responded to my instructions as regards asanas and pranayama. I taught him Yoga for twenty years.

My acquaintance with Krishnaji brought me in contact with Rao Saheb Patwardhan and his brother, Achyut, heroes of the Quit India Movement in 1942. Achyut Patwardhan took training under me and realising the value of yogic exercises advised young men and women he met to learn the art of asanas from me.

Proposal to introduce Yoga in Schools.

In August 1949, I read in newspapers that the Central Government and the Bombay Government had given grants to Kaivalyadhama, an institution devoted to Yoga practices, organised by Swami Kuvalayananda. This news item induced me to make a representation to the State and Central Governments. I also requested Guruji to forward his representations. We carried on correspondence with the Education Minister for about two years with no effect. I represented to Shri B.G. Kher, the Chief Minister of Bombay, that an All-India Conference should be called to chalk out a common programme and then to give grants to institutions which were considered the best. Shri Kher personally replied that the matter would be considered. After a month I got an envelope from the Dead Letter Office of Bombay. Opening it I found that it was my own letter which had been sent by me to Shri Kher, who had forwarded it to Swami Kuvalayananda for consideration.

Swami Kuvalayananda was then the Director of the Board of Physical Education, Bombay. I sent the same letter back to Shri Kher and this was acknowledged by his personal secretary.

When the government moved from Bombay to Pune, I took the opportunity and wrote to Shri Kher to grant me a personal interview. In the meantime Shri Kher had come to dinner at Pocha's house. One of Shri Kher's sons had suffered from an attack of polio. Pocha spoke to Shri Kher about my treating Smt. Ismail's daughter. Smt. Ismail was known to Shri Kher. Pocha's introduction had a good effect and I was granted an interview on October 17th, 1949. I asked Shri Kher if he remembered our meeting when I had given a performance in Deccan Gymkhana Club in 1938. I told him that I was the pioneer to introduce Yoga exercises for girls and boys in schools and colleges. He asked me what I wanted. I told him that I was placing the importance of Yoga before him not because he was the Chief Minister but because he was the Education Minister, also. He could do something to introduce Yoga exercises in schools and colleges. It was within his power to call a conference before granting aids to institutions. Shri Kher mistook my visit as being one for personal gain. I told him that I was not begging for any help for myself. I gave him my album of asana poses so that he could see them at his convenience. He saw some photographs and asked me to give a demonstration of poses at his residence on the morning of October 21st, 1949, which was Diwali day. Accordingly, I went to his residence at the time appointed. My punctuality surprised him. Shri Kher had invited some friends, two of whom turned out to be my students. After my performance Shri Kher thanked me and said that a day would come when I would get recognition from the government. Someone present remarked that the government of the day had removed former Maharajas who at least patronised the arts, but the present government did not care to give any help to artists. Shri Kher laughed and said that the government had no funds. I also laughingly remarked that the recognition would come to me posthumously. Then one of Shri Kher's sons took me to a private room and offered me a cup of milk. While we were talking I learned that Swami Kuvalayananda was Shri Kher's maternal uncle. I could then see why various donee institutions got government grants.

In December 1949, Dr. Gokhale met me in connection with the Maharashtra and All-India Physical Culture Conference. He wanted me to give a performance in January 1950, for the conference when the Commander-in-Chief of India, General Cariappa would preside. Dr. Gokhale had written an article on "Integral Fitness" and had distributed its copies freely. In that article he had written how Yoga helped an individual physically, mentally, morally and spiritually. I gave the performance at the conference which was appreciated by General Cariappa. Dr. Gokhale also arranged another performance of mine at the Army School of Physical Training.

In September 1950, a Body Beautiful Competition had been arranged. When the organisers of the competition requested me to act as one of the judges, I was hesitant to be a judge as I knew little about Western methods of exercises and body development. The organisers insisted and ultimately I did act as a judge. The competitors were divided into three groups and the presentation was judged on the basis of measurement, quality—that is muscle formation, skin and hair—and lastly for posing.

The competitors were satisfied with my criticism and judgment.

Swami Vibhutijyoti Nityananda

In October 1959, I learned from Pocha and Shri P.T. Anklesaria (another student of mine) that Swami Vibhutijyoti Nityananda, Swami of Kotagiri Hills, Nilgiri, was to deliver a lecture at the Rotary Club. I got the opportunity to meet Swami Nityananda at the residence of Anklesaria when he came for lunch. Swamiji told me that he had been guided in the Himalayas by a Yogi who was nearly three hundred and sixty years of age. This did not surprise me much as my Guruji's Guru had lived for about two hundred and thirty years. I attended Swami Nityananda's lecture at the Rotary Club. The lecture was on Astrology and he predicted world events. Swamiji was pleased to hear me speak in Tamil. He asked me to arrange a lecture in the South Indian Society in Pune. I did so and he spoke on Bhakti Yoga—the Yoga of Devotion. At my request Swamiji saw me perform asanas and pranayama at the residence of Shri Walchand Hirachand, with whom Swamiji was residing. At the end of the performance he told me that he had not come across any performer like me. He said that the flow of my performance was uninterrupted like a perrennial river. He called me a *"Siddha Purusha"* (a man of attainment). Swamiji advised me not to be discouraged by my poverty. He said, "Poverty was the garland for knowledge." He advised me to be always cheerful and happy. At a public gathering he spoke of my *tapas* (arduous discipline) for fourteen years and the achievement thereof.

Family

During these years my family had grown. My daughter, Vanita, was born on August 29th, 1947. Prior to Vanita's birth we had lost a daughter. On July 2nd, 1949 my son, Prashant, was born. Two years later on July 3rd, 1951, my daughter, Sunita, was born. My last two daughters, Suchita and Savita, were born on July 21st, 1953 and May 5th, 1955 respectively.

In 1950, Dr. Gokhale had arranged my lecture-demonstration for members of the police force. There he spoke on physical fitness with the intention that the system of Yoga should be introduced in the physical training course of the police. The District Superintendent of Police, Shri Kolhatkar, had presided. Though my performance was appreciated, nothing came out as regards introduction of Yoga asanas in the physical training course of the police.

Dr. Gokhale had also arranged for another lecture-demonstration with the authorities of the Army Training School. After the demonstration the military doctors wanted to test my vital capacity. They brought an instrument called the spirometer and tested my blowing capacity. I was ignorant of the technique of blowing into the instrument. Seeing my demonstration they put me Class A-1 category. However, on test, my capacity was found to 0.1 less than the A-1 class. The difference was negligible but the military doctors made a fuss about it. It had to be remembered that preceding the test I had just given a lecture-demonstration after having conducted my classes for the day. The lecture-demonstration, however, was greatly appreciated. Col. Khandhuri, who was in charge of the Armed Forces Physical Training, took a number of photographs of my asana poses. He said that he was

Iyengar, Ramamani and their children

prepared to introduce the Yoga asana system in the army provided the system was modernised. The doctors wanted anatomical and physiological movements x-rayed and pathological values of each pose explained as was done in Western countries. It was not possible for me to undertake such a research. Dr. Gokhale suggested that as the army had all the facilities they were the proper authorities to undertake such work. He told the army doctors that I was available to the army for research in the matter. No such research project was taken up. The armed forces did include some of the asanas in their physical training course.

Swami Shivanandji

Towards the end of 1950, Swami Shivanandji visited Pune. He had written many books on Yoga and I was keen on meeting him and showing him my asana poses. I approached the organiser Shri Vishwanathan, then Director, Public Health, Bombay. I was not given a personal interview, but was asked to meet Swamiji at Rishikesh. Before leaving I thanked Shri Vishwanathan and introducing myself told him that I was a Yoga instructor in Pune. He recollected that he had heard a lot about me and then told me that I could find out from Swamiji himself where I could meet him. However, I gave up the idea of meeting Swamiji personally though I attended all his lectures. After his Pune visit, Swamiji went to Bombay. There my friend Mehra Vakil saw him and showed him the album of my poses. He showed such keen interest that he wanted to keep the album for himself. Mehra presented another album of my poses to Swamiji. Swamiji remarked that it was as he was seeing Matsyendranath, the founder of Yoga asanas, reborn.

In March 1951, my pupil Anklesaria requested me to give a lecture-demonstration at the Rotary Club. At his request, I gave a brief introductory talk and then started my demonstration with my pupil Dinshaw who was then seventy years old. It was one of the best lecture-demonstrations I had given and it lasted for about an hour and a half. I highlighted the benefits of various asanas while performing them. The doctors in the audience were surprised to see the range of bodily movements. Col. Basu of the medical corps, who was in the audience, said that there must be something extraordinary about my spine as otherwise such movements were not possible. I replied that there was nothing unusual and that it was possible for all the persons who diligently practised asanas with perseverance to achieve similar movements and that I had trained many of my pupils in such movements.

During the same period several eminent European doctors, journalists and writers visited India with their wives to study Indian culture. They visited various places of tourist interest. When they came to Pune, Col. Basu arranged for my lecture-demonstration at the Napier Hotel. The visitors watched the demonstration with great interest and enthusiasm and said that certain movements were beyond their belief as no textbook had given such a range of bodily movements. They were also of the view that the demonstration was perhaps the best thing that they had seen in India.

Closure of the Mysore Yogashala

When my family and I had gone to Bangalore during April-May 1951, I received a letter from Guruji asking me to attend the Yogashala gathering. I could not go to Mysore for the gathering as I had some religious ceremony to perform. The function was presided over by Shri

K.C. Reddy, former Chief Minister of Mysore. Within a week of the Yogashala gathering I received another letter from Guruji stating that the Yogashala had been ordered to be closed down within a month. At first I could not believe the news. The reason for the closure was not known. Guruji corresponded with various authorities to revive the institute. I wrote articles in two Bangalore newspapers requesting the revival of the Yogashala. Guruji and I wrote several letters to various Government Departments and the authorities concerned including Ministers but the end result was that the Government of Mysore did not revive the famous Yogashala.

"Yogi Raja"

Mehra Vakil had sent an album of my photographs to Swami Shivanandji as a New Year gift in the year 1952. Sometime later I was very agreeably surprised to receive a letter from Swamiji conferring upon me the title of "Yogi Raja" in recognition of my work. Though Swamiji had very kindly bestowed that title upon me I felt that the proper person to receive this distinction was Guruji.

During this time I started treating Dr. M.S.H. Mody, a leading physician of Pune, for his backache. Dr. Mody was Pocha's family physician. Initially, he had no faith in any system of healing other than allopathy. He had consulted many doctors abroad for his trouble. When he noticed the progress in Pocha, he, too, wanted to try Yoga for his back trouble. He improved so much that he resumed horse riding and induced his wife and children to learn under my guidance. One of his sons, Dr. S.M. Mody, is now a leading physician and heart specialist practising in Pune. The senior Dr. Mody still maintains his asana practices and recommends yogic practices to his patients.

Iyengar Teaching Menuhin.

CALL OF THE WEST

IN 1952, AT THE REQUEST OF Pandit Jawaharlal Nehru, Prime Minister of India, Yehudi Menuhin, world famous violinist, visited India and gave several concerts to collect funds for the Prime Minister's Famine Relief Fund. Menuhin and his wife were guests of the government of India during their visit. Prior to the visit I had read in the newspapers about his interest in Yoga. I had, however, felt that it was not possible for me to come in contact with him personally. A movie called "The Magic Bow" was screened in Pune prior to Menuhin's arrival and it showed Menuhin playing the violin. I saw it to learn more about him and I felt that Menuhin was a born artist.

Dr. Meherhomji, a dentist of Pune, sent word that I should see him. When I saw the doctor, he told me that one of the members of the reception committee to greet Menuhin, Shri Mehli Mehta (father of Zubin Mehta, internationally known music conductor), had met the doctor. Mehta had told the doctor that since Menuhin was interested in Yoga he wanted to meet an expert on Yoga and had asked the doctor if he knew one. As the doctor knew that I had taught Krishnamurti he suggested my name. The doctor had sent for me to enquire whether I would be willing to go to Bombay to show my Yoga asanas to Menuhin. I told the doctor that I would be happy to do so provided the members of the reception committee paid my travel and lodging expenses. The doctor told me that he would let me know. A day or two later the doctor told me that the committee had arranged with some other Yoga exponents in Bombay to meet Menuhin and that I might also get a chance later if the committee felt it necessary. I wrote to Mehra Vakil about my talk with Dr. Meherhomji. Mehra phoned Pocha on March 2nd, 1952, that she had arranged for an interview with Menuhin for me on March 4th, in the morning, and intimated that she would bear the expense of my trip. I went to Bombay and met Mehra. She told me though she was a member of the reception committee she did not like the idea of taking the initiative of introducing me to Menuhin. She had met Menuhin at a tea party and had shown my album to him. Menuhin was impressed and requested her to ask me to come to Bombay. The Governor of Bombay, Shri Maharaj Singh, had earlier arranged meetings between Menuhin and Swami Kuvalayanandji and my former colleague Shri C.M. Bhatt.

Contact with Menuhin

Mehra took me to the Government House on March 4th, 1952 and introduced me to Menuhin. He said that though he was greatly impressed by the album he was very tired and he could spare me only five minutes. I told him: "You are tired. Will it be possible for you to watch my demonstration?" He said, "Though I am tired I am very much interested in Yoga and I would like to see you perform." In fact, I immediately put Menuhin in Savasana—pose of relaxation. Menuhin slept for an hour. When he woke, I asked him whether his fatigue was gone. He said that he felt as though he had got up after a long, deep, refreshing sleep. He was very enthusiastic to see my demonstration. He showed keen interest in each and every pose and was impressed by what he saw. My allotted time of five minutes lasted for three hours. Smt. Menuhin was not present when I demonstrated my asanas to him. She came very late. He introduced me to her. He sat pensively and then he suddenly asked me whether I could see him the following day. He had several programmes, but he requested the organisers to cancel them. I agreed to see Menuhin the next day.

The next day I proceeded to the Government House with Mehra. She told me that at the previous night's dinner party, Menuhin had spoken to other guests about me and my asanas and had expressed a desire to take me to America to train him and his family. Amongst the guests were Smt. Vijayalakshmi Pandit and Smt. Eleanor Roosevelt, widow of the late President Franklin Roosevelt of the United States of America.

When we reached Government House I taught Menuhin. His wife and his accompanist Marcel Gazelle were present. Menuhin grasped his lesson better than on the first day and remembered the points I showed him. He then asked me to show some poses. Smt. Menuhin, who had been a ballerina, watched the asanas with great interest and stated that she had not seen such movements. The second day I was with Menuhin for about three hours and a half. Later, when I was dressing, Menuhin suddenly came to me and asked me if I was prepared to visit his home for a year. I could not answer him immediately. He wanted me to come for four months at least. I could not agree to stay so long as I had my own family to look after. He was happy to learn that I could go to him for a few months. He came out and announced to the party waiting

Contact with Menuhin was a great inspiration to me and we regard our meeting as one of the great events in our lives.   *Iyengar*

outside that we had made a pact. Then he asked me if I would like to attend his concerts. He got me the tickets and I heard his recital that night at the Regal Theatre. After the recital I received a letter from Menuhin confirming his previous offer. He wanted me to meet him the same night back stage. When I went there he received me with both hands and asked me for my answer regarding the proposed visit. I requested him to give me a fortnight's time. He said that I could take the time. The news about his offer had spread and a number of people asked me when I was proceeding to the United States.

Menuhin was a violinist of rare distinction but he was very simple, modest, noble and humane. With all his fame and greatness he was humble. It was a pleasure and privilege to come across such a personality and to teach him. Unfortunately, owing to difficulties which cropped up, my visit to the United States could not materialise that year. My contact with Menuhin was prestigious to us both. Members of the public started to appreciate my work. I reiterate that the happy turn of events was entirely due to the grace of God.

Yoga—Bridge between the East and the West

Menuhin visited India again in February 1954. He wanted me to teach him. I started giving him lessons earnestly at the Government House, Bombay. This time he got a better impression of my teaching. During the ten days that he was in Bombay he benefitted so much that he invited me to Delhi to give him further lessons there. It was through him that I had the privilege of meeting the noblest son of India and idol of millions, Pandit Jawaharlal Nehru, then Prime Minister of India. Menuhin introduced me to Pandit Nehru, Shri Krishna Menon, Phiroze and Indira Gandhi. In remembrance of our meeting I presented Pandit Nehru with an album of my Yoga poses. My lessons helped Menuhin to acquire better control over his violin. He invited me to Switzerland for a period of six weeks for further training. I had to stay for more than six weeks. Not only did he himself practise asanas but his children did so. In appreciation of what Yoga had done for him, he presented me with an Omega wrist watch. At the back of it was the inscription, "To my best violin teacher B.K.S. Iyengar. Yehudi Menuhin, Gstaad, Sept. 1954." His later recitals showed the benefits he derived from Yoga.

Contact with Menuhin was a great inspiration to me and we regard our meeting as one of the great events in our lives.

Through Menuhin I came in contact with the then top Pianist, W. Malcunzinsky. The India Ambassador in Switzerland, Shri Y.D. Gandevia, arranged a lecture-demonstration of mine at the time of the Swiss National Exhibition, where the government of India was also represented. The organization for the demonstration was done by Shri S. Sen, Consul General of India for Europe. Menuhin presided over the function. The performance was appreciated by all and I met many musicians of repute. After this I went to London with Malcunzinsky and then joined Menuhin again in Paris in the middle of October 1954. I gave another lecture-demonstration there presided over by Menuhin. The Indian Ambassador to France, Sardar Malik, was also present at this demonstration.

Jayaprakash Narayan
After my first meeting with Menuhin in August 1952, I came in contact with Shri Jayaprakash Narayan. Shri

Narayan had undertaken a fast of twenty-one days at Dr. Dinshaw Mehta's Clinic at Pune. Shri Achyut Patwardhan had spoken to him about me and had requested him to perform some Yoga asanas and breathing exercises under my guidance. On August 19th, 1952, when I had gone to Vithalwadi to teach Achyut, Shri Narayan came there and I was introduced to him. Shri Narayan had already heard about me and he liked to perform asanas with me for his sciatica and abdominal trouble. Shri Narayan was sincere in his practice and put his heart and soul into it. What he achieved within a short time was amazing. I was very happy to serve such a great patriot and a man of God as Shri Narayan. Countless millions look to him for guidance. I think he is a true karma yogi.

I feel that it was as a reward for my past good karma and blessings of Guruji that I came into contact with eminent people like J. Krishnamurti, Yehudi Menuhin, Shri Jayaprakash Narayan and Pandit Nehru.

In December 1952, Mehra wrote asking me to visit Sadhu T.L. Vaswani, a mystic and philosopher. Sadhu Vaswani worked for the upliftment of the poor and had attended many religious conferences. I met him on December 11th, 1952, at St. Mira School. I had a talk with him and later taught his nephew, Shri J.P. Vaswani. At the request of Sadhu Vaswani, I showed him a few asanas and explained to him the significance of Yoga. He was pleased and requested me to give a demonstration before the students of the St. Mira School as he wanted them to learn about the noble art of Yoga. Accordingly, I gave a performance which was appreciated.

On New Year's day in 1953, I had the honour to give a demonstration before eminent scientists of the world who had assembled at the Taj Mahal Hotel, Bombay, for the International Cancer Commission. At the last minute, as I was going on the stage for my demonstration, I was advised by the president of the commission, Dr. Khanolkar, not to give any talk during my demonstration. This dampened my enthusiasm. Yet without losing heart I went ahead with the performance, which was appreciated by the audience. At the end of the demonstration, Dr. Khanolkar stated that the United Nations Organization and the World Health Organization should invite me for performance. He also said that I had pupils aged over seventy and that every one should take to the practice of Yoga.

In 1953, I had the privilege of teaching Shri Krishnamurti again. During our talks he gave me a piece of advice: "Fulfilment leads to frustration and frustration leads to fulfilment." He asked me to stay unaffected both in frustration as well as in fulfilment.

In October 1953, I had the good fortune to teach one of the most respected Jain Gurus, Shri Bhadrankarji Maharaj. The Maharaj was a very pious soul with profound knowledge. He derived such benefit from asanas and pranayama exercises that he wrote to his followers that he got more benefit from pranayama practice than from his study of Jnana Yoga. I was teaching Guru Maharaj on weekends at Bombay. Learning about my visits to Bombay during weekends, Mehra suggested that I should start a class in Bombay. Accordingly I started a class at Bombay from January 1954 with six students. Gradually more and more students came to the Bombay class, and the class is still functioning.

Yoga and the Defence Forces
During 1954-55, Major-General E. Habibullah, then

commandant of the National Defence Academy at Khadakvasla, started taking training in Yoga with me. His body was very stiff and he was affected by dysentry while serving in Burma. Within a few months of practice his condition improved and he regained his lost vitality. He became a complete convert to Yoga. He desired to make Yoga popular at the academy and in June 1955, directed the instructors there to undergo training in Yoga. I trained the instructors for a month and made them realise the efficacy of Yoga asanas on the human system. The instructors were initially of the view that only their set of exercises were the best for army training. They were surprised that my methods of training were tougher than theirs. The commandant then thought of the weakest boys of the academy. After consultation with the deputy commandant, fifty weak cadets were selected for experiment, for a term of four months. Twenty-five cadets were given the regular army exercises daily. I instructed the remaining twenty-five cadets twice a week. At the end of the term the Yoga group, who could not improve earlier by regular military training, showed improvement as regards their health, agility, lightness of the body and mental development. Their performance was superior to that of the other group.

I learned that the records of the cadets maintained by the academy showed the steady progress made by the Yoga group who had passed their tests. This encouraged the commandant to extend the Yoga training to all cadets and my services at the academy were extended for another year. At the request of the academy officers, the commandant consented to have a special class for them.

It was kind of Commandant Habibullah to have given me the opportunity to demonstrate the benefits of

Iyengar leaves for his second trip to Europe.

Yoga for army personnel. The Yoga training at the academy was stopped in 1958. I am happy to relate that in 1976, Commandant Awati reintroduced Yoga training at the academy and classes are now being conducted by my eldest daughter, Geeta, and my son, Prashant.

My contacts with the National Defence Academy enabled me to present my art before our first President of India, the late Dr. Rajendra Prasad, and before the visiting foreign dignitaries. One of them was Dr. Mohammad Hatta, then Vice President of Indonesia, who had come on a goodwill mission. He visited the academy on November 10th, 1955, when a group of cadets performed asanas before him and I gave a demonstration for twenty minutes. Again in the same month I gave a demonstration at the academy before Marshal Bulganin, Premier of Russia, and Nikita Krushchev, First Secretary of the Communist Party. Russian cameramen filmed the entire demonstration throughout for screening in Russia. After the demonstration I was introduced to the distinguished visitors, and when they were told that I was training the backward boys of the academy, they replied that they had heard about my teaching the Army Chief of Staff, General Shri Nagesh. Krushchev thanked me for the impressive show and said that Yoga was not meant for weak people only but for all. Lt. General Thimayya, General Officer Commanding, Southern Command, also congratulated me for the fine exhibition of India's culture. I also performed before the Chinese military delegation who visited the academy. They were thrilled to see the agility and skill and remarked that such training was needed in guerrilla warfare.

In November 1955, I gave another lecture-demonstration in Bombay under the auspices of the Theatre

Why should you practice Yoga?
To kindle the divine fire within yourself.
Everyone has a dormant spark of divinity in him
which has to be fanned into flame.

Unit. I impressed upon the audience that the internal contentment and peace derived by the method of Yoga training is a weapon to establish world peace as it creates healthy understanding between people of different nations and generates feelings of tolerance.

The Tree Blossoms

I am concluding the reminiscences of my days of struggle. Though I experienced difficulties from 1955 to 1960, life for me and my family was not as hard as before. From 1960 onwards things began to change. My work was better appreciated and I had several occasions to go abroad and take workshops there. These activities of mine are now known the world over and, therefore, I do not think it necessary to describe them. I have dealt with my earlier life because the incidents during that period were known only to a very few persons closely connected with me. I feel that the present occasion of my completion of sixty years of life is an apt one when I should narrate the events of my earlier days.

The tree of Yoga has blossomed.

Ramamani
Rama was the personification of patience and magnanimity.
She was simple, generous and unostentatious. She was
kind to one and all.

RAMA—THE LIGHT
OF MY LIFE

MY LIFE STORY IS INCOMPLETE without reference to my wife, Ramamani.

Rama was born on November 2nd, 1927, at Anekal near Bangalore. She was the ninth child of her parents. Her father was a teacher of the primary school, like my father. Although brilliant in her younger days, she could not study beyond the fourth standard.

Our marriage took place on July 9th, 1943, when Rama was sixteen. We started our life in Pune in November 1943. When she came, she brought only her *mangalsutra* as she had nothing else to call her own. I had nothing in my possession to make her comfortable. We borrowed an aluminium vessel and two plates from Motee. The first fire at our home was lit from a stove also borrowed from him.

Rama and I struggled hard to maintain ourselves. She was content with what little we could get each day and remained unperturbed though our economic problems remained unsolved.

Every day I got up very early in the morning for my Yoga practices. Rama also got up at the same time to prepare coffee for both of us. She used to observe my

73

practices, but never interfered. For her even the word "Yoga" was unknown. She did not know then what it stood for, and she never ventured to ask what Yoga teaching meant or what I learned. However, in the course of time, she evinced keen interest in learning the art. I started teaching her daily and she became my pupil. As she made progress, I taught her how to assist me towards improving my methods. My instructions to help me during practice made her a good teacher. This enabled her to teach one or two lady students from my group independently. As our family responsibilities increased and her attention towards the welfare of the children took much of her time, she could not take to teaching. Whenever she found time, she practised Yoga for herself. She was ever ready to help whenever I wanted a support to get a better position in my practices.

As already mentioned, we both had dreams the same night in 1946. The dreams came true which indicated our bright days ahead. People started enquiring for lessons. Our suffering decreased and with the blessings of God our wants were fulfilled. Fortune favoured us and our domestic life became secure. We had not imagined that our life at home or in the field of Yoga would make such good progress. Slowly we understood each other, and lived happily, spiritually and were devoted to each other. Her interest in life was to take care of our children and me so that my practices and teachings were not hindered. I was everything to her. We shared the nectar of divinity through each other. Rama was the personification of patience and magnanimity. She was simple, generous and unostentatious. She was kind to one and all. She had great forbearance even towards people who did not wish her well. She was quiet, serene, peaceful and remained unruffled in adverse circumstances. She took everything in her stride coolly. She looked after those who came to her for help or advice with love, joy and devotion. She served us extending both her hands. I remember how the late Dr. N.B. Parulekar, proprietor and editor of *Sakal*, Pune, compared her to Sharadadevi, wife of Shri Ramkrishna Paramahamsa. How true his words were, I realise more and more as days pass by.

Hospitality, kindness and self-sacrifice were very much in her blood. She treated her maid servants and sweepers of the street as if they were members of her family. During festival days, she used to reserve their share of food, lest they should be overlooked. Her feelings and thoughts were noble and she never wished ill of anyone. Such was her disposition. Her love was unique, she had a heart full of compassion and people called her "Amma" which means "mother". Her physique was big, her mind great and her soul noble.

She was philosophical in her thoughts and philanthrophic in her dealings and never brooded over her past discomfitures. She betrayed no sorrow at her distress nor felt jubilant at her affluence.

Rama was an accomplished vocalist and was singing quite a large number of *krtis* of Purandaradasa and Thyagaraja while cooking or combing the children's hair. Along with Karnataka classical music, she had great liking for Hindustani music also. This created a love of music and dance in her children. She was an excellent cook. She was able to prepare a number of dainty dishes even for large parties at home on special occasions like festivals and gatherings. These skills created a unique combination in a housewife.

I do not recollect any occasion of misunderstanding between us. My impatient nature—speed, quick decisions and impulsiveness—were counterbalanced by her soft

We lived without conflicts as if our two souls were one.

voice and the quiet expression in her eyes. We lived without conflicts as if our two souls were one. She was never harsh to the children; yet she commanded high respect and moulded them with discipline.

She suddenly became weak after performing the Bhumi Puja on land purchased by us for our proposed new house on January 25th, 1973.

On January 26th, 1973, I got her admitted to a nursing home so that she might rest and recover from fatigue. I was with her for a few hours. She was feeling better than at home.

What a noble lady my wife was! She knew her death was approaching. That night my two daughters, Sunita and Suchita, had a sitar recital. She did not want to disturb them nor did she stop me from going to Bombay. Noticing the time when the concert would be over, she asked the doctors at the nursing home to phone Dr. Pabhalkar, our neighbour, who had a telephone. It was three o'clock in the morning when my son, Prashant, and daughter, Geeta, went to see her. She asked them to go home immediately and to light up the lamps to our deity and to come back soon with the other children. All the children could not go as no transport was available at that hour. She just asked them why they did not bring the other children. She said to Prashant and Geeta that her duties and responsibilities were coming to an end and she would be departing in a few moments. She did not want to die on the bed of the nursing home. She wanted to be closer to mother earth and lie on a carpet on the floor but the doctors did not permit it. So she sat reclining. Placing the childrens' palms in hers, she blessed them and told them to bear the future responsibilities on their own. She breathed her last like a great *tappaswini* who knew of her death beforehand. Her soul merged with the Universal Divine Soul.

I had left for Bombay to conduct Yoga classes, as it was a Saturday. On Sunday, January 28th, 1973 at four o'clock in the morning, my pupils, Madhu Tijoriwala and Barzo Taraporewala came to the hotel where I was staying. I had been restless the whole night and I was already up when they knocked at the door. They asked me to proceed to Pune, saying that they had a message from my son, that my wife was serious. As I had seen her the previous day, I did not assess the gravity of the situation and told them that I would finish the Sunday class and then proceed to Pune. My pupils insisted upon my returning forthwith, accompanied by them. I understood the situation although I could not express my fears about the survival of my wife. They hesitated to put the fact to me, with a view to giving me the shocking news as late as possible. On the way, Smt. Freny Motivala, a third pupil, joined us to go to Pune. However, I was thoughtful and was prepared for any eventuality.

When we were about to reach Pune, my pupils asked me whether we should go home or proceed to the nursing home. I said that if she is alive, she will be in the nursing home or otherwise at our residence. Then they broke the news that she was no more. Then I said that my children must have brought her body home and so I advised them to drive straight to the house, which we reached at 6:30 am. As I entered, I saw many of my pupils and people and knew that everything was over. With coolness, I comforted my weeping children, telling them not to weep for their mother, who was a pious soul. From then on I was both their mother and father.

When she embraced mother earth on January 28th, 1973, people from all walks of life, known and unknown, thronged the house, as if it were a temple, to pay their homage to the departed soul. Pupils who had come from South Africa for lessons witnessed her body being laid to rest. Messages poured in from all parts of the world, expressing their grief and sorrow. She embraced death with the same graceful serenity with which she had lived—with patience and forbearance.

The foundation which Rama laid later became the famous Ramamani Iyengar Memorial Yoga Institute. It was built in her memory by raising donations from friends, pupils and admirers as a token of their love and affection.

As long as she was alive, I lived a carefree life as she managed the house, the children and myself. She left me completely free to devote my time to the practice and teaching of Yoga. After her passing away I have become a householder and now my children are substantially bearing the burden of the house. While she was alive I was married to Rama and Yoga and now Yoga only had remained in my life. I am never separated from her for she is always in my heart.

ARTICLES
&
EXTRACTS

WHY THE WEST IS INTERESTED IN YOGA

FOR 25 YEARS I have been visiting the West regularly for periods of three months or so. On these visits I have met many eminent personalities, as well as common people, and the question is often asked, "Why is interest in Yoga increasing day by day in the West?"

India is a land enriched by its ancient but ever-fresh and flourishing culture. Although we were ruled for a long time by foreigners and in the clutches of poverty, we did not lose our ground; our culture and our strong faith in its philosophical thoughts, along with our strong faith in the inner Self, have always protected us from all sorts of disasters. Facing the calamities of life, we have understood the meaning and the depth of life. Even the Hindu religion has not remained within limited boundaries. It has often proven that it is not meant only for Indians, but is a universal religion.

Yoga was evolved centuries ago. It is an ancient and perfect science which takes one toward the innermost truth. Yoga means union. It means evennesss of attitude in our day to day life. It is also a skill which arises by itself in our action or meditation. To achieve union and evenness one has to still the mind. One has to cross the frontier which separates the stillness in one's mind from one's thoughts and emotions. Actions that are colored by thoughts and emotions are not pure. Pure emotion is that by which skill comes into being, which brings serenity, morality, and creativity. That is true Yoga. Thus Yoga brings purity in action, clarity in thought, and stability in mind. The West has realized that there is a fundamental need to introduce Yoga into its way of life.

When I was first introduced to the West in 1954 by Yehudi Menuhin, I began to sow the seeds of Yoga and today I am proud to say those seeds have grown into a forest. I see enthusiasm growing. Hundreds of Westerners have worked hard and have learned well. They are now conducting classes in different centers in Europe, North America, Africa, Australia, New Zealand, Mauritius, etc., often on a purely humanitarian basis. Thus more and more people are being introduced to Yoga.

Western people have always been interested in Indian philosophy. Not only are they keen to know about the Indian way of life, but they are also keen to adopt it. However, impeded by all their book knowledge of Yoga, they could never quite grasp what Yoga is actually about. In 1954 when I arrived at London airport, I was looked upon as a miracle man. I was asked whether I, being a practitioner of Yoga, could chew glass, drink acid, or walk on fire. When I denied all such demonstrations, the audience was very surprised and enquired what kind of yogi I was. I immediately realized that some gross misconceptions of Yoga existed in the West, and I felt that there was a lot of work for me to do to make people there understand what Yoga is. It was then a kind of challenge for me to dispel so many misconceived notions.

The West has progressed very rapidly in technical and scientific knowledge. But the simultaneous growth of materialism has created a great spiritual void. Discipline has become a mechanical format in a barren existence. Bored with materialism, the people in the West are searching for something which will give them peace of mind. The lack of any spiritual touch in human life and relationship has led many frustrated people to turn to the East for solace and inspiration. They realize that happiness and peace elude them. The art of living has been drained from their lives. A hectic life has eclipsed their peace of mind; the soft and sophisticated material comforts have robbed them of life's simple happiness; an externally imposed discipline has kidnapped their inner freedom.

Now Westerners are realizing that Yoga can keep their minds out of bondage. Though physically able to sustain the pace of modern life, they are often not able to bear its mental pressures. The artificiality has hurt the core of their consciousness. A lopsided and pampered existence has not protected them from enormous mental tensions generated by so many hectic claims on their lives. Though Western society recognizes and permits divorce, remarriage, free sex, independent living even for adolescents, still the people have not been able to bring peace to their inner selves. On the contrary, this so-called liberty has produced innumerable mental and psychological worries and problems. Westerners are intellectually developed but emotionally starved, as they are cut off from the fountain of inner life. They talk a lot from the brain, but their hearts are empty and sterile. This has separated them from spirituality, and because of all this they are drawn to Yoga, to regain some inner balance.

While explaining why the West has taken to Yoga, I cannot refrain from saying that we Indians have neglected Yoga, this rich legacy which has come to us from our ancient sages. While the West wants to adopt the

Indian way of life, which is known for its simplicity and straight forwardness, we Indians are trying to imitate their way of life. Not only have we neglected our own art, Yoga, but we are forgetting it. We talk a great deal about our philosophy, but we do not convert it into action. We are merely glorifying the past. We do not live according to what is morally important; we live on ideals. We are humble and simple; belief has a very strong hold on us. But we are very slow and even slovenly in action.

The Western mind is intellectually well-trained. In India we believe that one cannot improve society unless one is evolved spiritually. As the Westerners are people of action, they go all out to improve society. Both types of approaches are partially correct and productive. No doubt we Indians are proud of our civilization and culture, and of our great yogis and rishis. But that feeling is not going to lift us from lethargy. We must work steadfastly and purposefully, as did our great masters in the past. We have to act in our chosen paths earnestly and not casually and merely intellectually. Only action with understanding and a desire to learn with humility will bring us once again to that past glory. We are patient, tolerant, simple and humble, but we lack keenness and interest and the drive to get results.

Being of just the opposite frame of mind, Westerners, once they set their minds to something, will persevere with it. Once they take to yogic practice, they do not treat it casually but try to project it. Yoga has gone to every nook and corner in the West, whereas we in India think that it is in our blood and neglect the real art.

The West is eager to know about our philosophical approach to life. The Western mind is in search of peace, but peace canot come from outside; it has to come from within. Unless people learn to distinguish essentials and nonessentials, peace will ever elude them. The West thought that the soul could be realized through intelligence. Now India must teach that the head can take us only so far and no further; we must instead hitch the wagon to our hearts. There should be coordination of head and heart. The proper mental approach and a firm moral background are essential factors; without them, a spiritual approach is an impossibility. The West seems to have realized that Yoga is the only path which is universal in its nature and which can bring about a fundamental change in its way of life.

When I came in contact with Westerners, the first thing they told me was that they are tired of lectures on Indian philosophy and weary of so much endless theoretical knowledge; they wanted something practical and tangible of which they were ignorant. We do not distinguish between body and mind. There must be an integrated approach. I then had to teach the yogasanas and pranayama with this wholesome approach. At every step I had to insist and make them understand how the body and the mind work in coordination, how each asana and each breath is treated with a kindred spirit. Their bodies being very supple and elastic, could perform movement, but I had to make them aware that the mind has also to be kept alert, living all the time in the present, and how the current of spiritual awareness has to flow in each movement, each action.

The family structure in the West, Western habits, conventions, and social living are all opposite in nature to the yogic way. Smoking and drinking have never been regarded as unacceptable behaviour. Their idea of morality is such that they never considered it necessary for spiritual life. Yet after beginning the regular practice of Yoga, many of them stopped smoking and drinking, and even attending social parties so often.

Yoga is an excellent solution for mental and psychological problems, and therefore it is becoming very popular. It is of course true that popularity can sometimes damage the real and original nature of a subject, and it is here that I have found the second stage of my work. In the fifties and sixties I worked hard to popularize Yoga; now I must work to correct the distortions that have appeared since that popularization. On television and especially in physical fitness classes, Yoga is being presented, not in its true form, but in a Westernized version that is more like any other form of physical exercise. Whenever I appeared on Western television, it became my duty to point out the discrepancies between these adapted versions and the true original Yoga, and to emphasize that Yoga is not done merely to "keep fit." If one practices well, health will be an inevitable by-product.

Westerners are enthusiastic, courageous, sincere, and hard working. They are always awaiting with humility guidance from the East. I think that their scientific and technical knowledge, coupled with our spiritual understanding and maturity, could perhaps work hand in hand to bring human beings once again to the religion meant for universal peace which was founded by our ancient masters.

Perhaps one day it will be Westerners who bring Yoga back to India. But the East was the original source of Yoga, and I pray that it will always be the main source— that it will continue to be the preserver of this great art.

(Reprinted with permission from *Yoga Journal,* July/August 1977 Copyright © 1977 *Yoga Journal*)

YOGA DISCIPLINE
IN ATHLETES

Y OGA HAS BECOME A WORD much bandied about. It has been linked with several esoteric groups and popularised by such pop groups as the Beatles. In the frantic search for spiritual and transcendental experience through Yoga akin to psychedelic and hallucinatory experience induced by drugs, the strong physical foundation of Yoga has been ignored. For this reason too the immense advantages of yogic asanas or postures for athletes and sportsmen have been very largely forgotten.

Athletics and all sports demand vigorous physical discipline to develop speed, strength, endurance, precision and agility. But while the muscular portion of the body is developed, very often the inner organs remain weak or stifled and the mind may actually be dulled. Athletes and sportsmen are unable to maintain supremacy in their fields for very long, and while the consumption of energy is at a maximum the recuperative powers are hardly developed.

It is here that the art of Yoga can assist athletes and sportsmen. The yogi's understanding and mastery of the body is far more intricate than that of the sportsman. He recognises five layers of human consciousness: the anatomical or physical body, consisting of bones and muscles, the physiological body, made up of the respiratory, nervous, circulatory and alimentary systems, the psychological or emotional layer, the mental or intellectual inner layer, and finally the innermost layer or blissful state of being. No other human system has mapped out with such precision the development of these various layers of consciousness.

The usual repertoire of exercises for the athlete and sportsman includes exercises for contracting and expanding the muscles. Weight-lifting, running, swimming and playing games develop the anatomical structure of the body, but very little attention is paid to its physiological development. We often have a huge bulk hung on to small, poorly developed internal organs. Yoga, however, is not simply content with the external development of the muscles. It believes in the proper communion of the internal organs and the anatomical structure of the body. Freedom and strength are to be given to the spleen, pancreas, liver, heart, kidneys, and other organs by the same process of contraction and expansion that is normally used for the development of the muscles. Elasticity is given to the joints, and the lungs' capacity is enhanced by the breathing techniques known as pranayama.

The basic pranayamic technique employs breath inhalation, breath retention and breath exhalation. With the inhalation there is an intake of energy. Retention distributes this energy throughout the body, while exhalation expends this energy. (Athletes and sportsmen usually expend more energy than they take in). This creates a great deal of acid in the body and results in fatigue and stiffness. The body also becomes heavy and is no longer agile. Yogic techniques, both the asanas and pranayama,

90

teach conservation of energy. They also help quick recovery from fatigue.

To return to pranayama, deep breathing is not forceful inhalation with simple pulling of the intercostal muscles. It is more than that. Every small fractional part of the lungs must have time to absorb the energy slowly and rhythmically drawn in from the pelvic diaphragm to the top of the lungs, so that the topmost ribs feel the full extension of the lungs. The forward ribs should move up, while the ribs on the side should move with horizontal-vertical stretch.

As a heavy shower runs off the ground, but a gentle drizzle soaks into it and is of more benefit to the crops, so a sharp, forceful inhalation will not be as beneficial as a quiet steady intake of breath. Retention of breath increases the circulation of blood and keeps the body warm and clean. Whereas the sportsman and the athlete use the upper portion of the lungs while active and the intercostal muscles while resting, the yogi—with one rhythmic movement—employs the full lungs. Even the exhalation is slow, to retain energy as much as possible.

The learning of yogic techniques of breathing will not only be beneficial to athletes and sportsmen, but will also help them to withstand strain at any altitude. The asanas together with pranayama tone the nerves so that the acclimatisation is achieved soon. The warming-up process in cold countries is helped by the inverted poses such as headstand and shoulderstand. Yoga also gives emotional stability and many of the ugly scenes at sport and track meets can be avoided if sportsmen learn through Yoga to keep their tempers under control.

Emotional stability leads automatically to clarity of mind and greater energy output.

Today man needs first and foremost physical firmness,
emotional poise and intellectual clarity.

YOGA AND MEDITATION

$\mathbf{M}$AN MUST TOUCH THE SPIRITUAL at some point. Yet if a journey to outer space demands rigorous discipline covering a period of years, it should be clear that a trip to the transcendent is not that easy. The demands of meditation properly performed are more exacting than the discipline needed by the cosmonaut. A space trip can fail due to a fault in a tiny wire and so does meditation if the body is neglected.

Meditation must begin with the body. It is the vehicle of the Self, which, if not controlled in its desires, prevents true meditation. The ancients in their wisdom knew this, but modern make-believe would ignore the body. Ignoring the body springs from ignorance of the body and for that matter of the soul. For the body cannot be ignored. A mosquito bite, a stomach ache, a running nose divert attention to themselves, and the sublime is caught up in the ridiculous. A dull body begets a dull mind; a distracted body, a distraught mind. Has one ever tried to still one's own body, nerves and emotions? The *Yoga Sutras* of Patanjali, classic meditative wisdom, begin not with the esoteric but with common sense.

"Choose a place," says the *Hatha-Yoga Pradipika,* "free of insects, noise and evil smells, and spreading a rug, sit on it." The choice of time is also important—before sunrise or after sunset, for at early dawn and late evening the Spirit of God pervades over the earth like a healing benediction.

Body posture is important. The awareness from within of every pore of the body in the various asanas is itself meditation. It is like the turning on of millions of spiritual eyes. The mind impregnates the body and yet remains an observer; the body becomes mind and yet remains supremely alert as body. And so mind and matter are fused in the dynamism of sheer energy, which is active without being spent, creative without bringing on exhaustion. The asanas are not simply important because they strengthen the nerves, lungs and other parts of body but also for their role in meditation. They are themselves vehicles of meditative action.

The classic meditative pose is the cross-legged *Padmasana* pose with the spine held straight and rigid. When the ancients counselled, "Sit in any comfortable position with the spine straight," they certainly did not mean that slouching would do. To sit in a loose, collapsed sort of way induces sleep. Drowsiness is not to be mistaken for meditation. Meditation does not make the mind dull. Rather, in meditation the mind is still but razor-sharp, silent but vibrant with energy. This state cannot be achieved without a firm stable sitting posture, where the spine ascends and the mind descends and dissolves in the consciousness of the heart, where the true Self reveals itself. The whole body, far from being ignored, is taken up in this spiritual alertness, till the whole man becomes pure flame. An alert, erect spine creates a spiritual intensity of concentration that burns out distracting thoughts and the brooding over past and future and leaves one in the virginal, fresh present.

In *Dhyana* or pure meditation, the eyes are shut, the head held erect and the gaze directed downward and backward as though the parallel gaze of the eyes is searching the infinity of darkness that lies beyond the back of the head for Him who is the true light that enlightens every man. The facial skin is relaxed and descends. The brain is released from the pull of the senses. The eyes, ears and root of the tongue become passive and consciousness passes from the active, aggressive front part of the brain to the quiet, observant back part of the brain. The hands are pressed together, palm against palm, in front of the breastbone. This classic pose of all prayer is not only symbolic but also practical. Symbolically the palms salute the Lord, who is within. The mind is drawn to surrender to the Holy One. This surrender, by breaking the chain of distracting thoughts, increases the intensity of one's concentration. The hands are locked together by the magnetism of the human body. The increase or decrease of the pressure on the palms is the sensitive gauge of one's alertness and one's freedom from distracting thoughts. The exact balance of the electric currents of the body can also be tested by the palms pressed against each other. If both palms press equally against each other, both mind and body are in balance and harmony. If one palm exerts more pressure than the other, that side of the body is more alert also. By increasing the pressure on the weaker palm a delicate adjustment should be made to bring the body-mind unit back to balance. For Yoga is nothing if it is not perfect harmony.

It has been maintained that yogic meditation is without content, a mere emptying of the mind. For those who have had the experience of its richness and satisfying fullness, such an assertion can only sound ridiculous. The intellect of the mind may cease its roving but the intellect of the heart goes out to the Lord. And it is the heart that matters. Is there really need of the petty content of our own thoughts, when the heart is drawn to the Infinite One, who is always near and ever receding, imminent and transcendent at the same time?

The yogic pranayamic or breathing techniques are meditative in their origin and in their effect. The rhythmic movements of inhalation, retention and exhalation of breath still the mind by withdrawing the senses and help one uncover the depths of the Self. Unlike *Dhyana,* in pranayama the head is sunk on the chest with a firm chin-lock. Physically the chin-lock releases the breath from the egotistical domination of the brain and makes it more gentle and impersonal. The chin-lock takes one to the quiet centre of the heart where the Lord resides. The hands either rest on the knees or control the breath with the fingers. The other basic aspects of meditation such as the gaze of the eyes, and the erect spine are maintained.

The pranayamic techniques, like the asanas, are vehicles of meditation and prayers. Inhalation or *Puraka* is acceptance of the Lord. Retention or *Kumbhaka* (from *"Kumbha",* a pot filled to the brim with water, which is thereafter silent) is savouring of the Lord in the full deep stillness of the heart. Exhalation or *Rechaka* is not simply throwing out stale breath but the emptying of the ego. Exhalation makes one impersonal and hence is a fit instrument of surrender to the Lord. It is the highest form of surrender to the Lord. Exhalation can also be understood as a cleansing process. As the breath is gently exhaled towards the heart, the heart is cleansed of evil desires and emotional disturbances. This surrender to the Lord has to be accepted, and so there is a period of stillness after exhalation for the Lord to accept this surrender before inhalation begins.

Meditation is a subjective experience and translating it into words must always fall short of reality. To use a trite example: no amount of description of how a mango tastes will ever equal the delight that the first bite into that delicious fruit brings. So too with meditation. The sure and safe techniques can be given, the state of the mind can be described, but the savour of the fruit is only granted to those who "taste and see that the Lord is sweet."

THE ART OF RELAXATION

O UR SOCIETY SEEMS TO REST upon sedatives and tran-
quillisers. The tempo of modern life is such that its
maintenance makes the taking of sedatives imperative for
most people. As the giddy pace increases, tensions build
up in our systems, our nerves get frayed, and haggard
remnants of humanity are left to seek solace in some form
of drugged sleep. This is strange, for modern men have all
the leisure at their disposal. Machines have taken the
drudgery out of life and the forty-hour week gives men
enough time to relax. The art of relaxation, however,
eludes modern men, and it seems to be something past,
beyond recall. Relaxation is necessary, for relaxation is
recuperation. The drain of energy has to be counteracted
in some way. The yogic art of relaxation known as *Savasana* puts down in precise steps how relaxation and
recuperation take place. *Sava* means a corpse, a dead body.
Asana means a posture. Savasana is thus the posture emulating the dead, and out of apparent death comes
life. Savasana is not simply lying on one's back with
vacant gaze or flopping on a foam-rubber mattress. Nor
should Savasana end in snoring. It is by far the most
difficult of yogic postures, but it also is by far the most
rewarding and refreshing one. It is a very precise method
of disciplining both the body and the mind.

Savasana begins with placing the body accurately on the floor. The place to be chosen for this should be even, clean and free of insects, loud noises and noxious smells. Spread on the floor a blanket or a rug so that the body can lie full-length on it. These precautions are necessary because a cold or an unclean floor can disturb the depth of relaxation. Next, sit on the blanket with the knees drawn up and feet together, so that a straight line can be drawn from the place where the big toes and knees meet, along the anal mouth, the navel, the sternum (breast-bone), the throat, the chin, the bridge of the nose to the centre of the forehead. Then gradually stretch one leg forward after the other so that both legs lie in a straight line in the median plane. Both the buttocks should rest on the floor evenly on either side of the anal mouth. If one buttock feels broader, place the hands on the floor downwards to either side of the hips and lift the buttocks off the floor and adjust them. With palms on either side of the hips, slide backwards to rest on the elbows. In this position adjust the buttocks again so that they lie evenly on either side of the coccyx and the anal mouth. Then make the spine convex and lower the body, vertebra by vertebra, to the floor so that the entire spine rests on the floor equally and does not tilt to one side or the other. The bottom points of the shoulder blades, like the buttocks and the hips, should rest evenly on the floor on either side of the spine. Once the spine is placed on the floor, bend the arms and touch the shoulders with the fingers. In this position gently extend the back of the upper arm towards the elbows so that the back of the upper arms rests elongated and evenly on the floor. Then lower the hands to the floor with palms facing upwards, the median plane of the wrists resting on the floor. The arms and hands should form angles of not more than fifteen degrees with the sides of the body. Unlike the rest of the body, which is adjusted from the back, the head should be adjusted from the front. Babies usually sleep with the head tilted towards one side. Because of such sleeping habits, the back of the head in most humans is mis-shaped and its centre out of alignment. Hence the head should be adjusted from the face. The chin should be perpendicular to the ceiling or floor, while the bridge of the nose should run parallel to the floor. The eyes should be kept shut and equidistant from the bridge of the nose, and move away from the centre of the forehead. The squint and the puckered forehead are always signs of mental tension. Consider each pore of skin as a "conscious eye" and delicately adjust and balance the body from within with the help of these conscious eyes, as it is difficult for the normal external eyes to observe and rectify the body position.

Briefly, the entire body should be placed with precision on the floor so that the two halves of the body lie evenly on either side of the spine. Attention to detail and precision in the body position leads to mastery of the art of relaxation. Very often the body tilts to one side and this side tilt is experienced on the stronger side of the body. It varies from person to person; in some people the right side of the body is the stronger side, in others it is the left side. The tilt is experienced as a sort of greater magnetic pull of the earth towards the stronger side of the body. Once the practitioner knows which is the dominant side of the body, that is the side exerting the greater magnetic pull to the floor, he can consciously adjust the weaker side of his body from the very start by placing it more deliberately on the floor. In this way the tilt is obviated. If the tilt occurs, there is a drain of energy in the direction of the tilt.

101

When the right and left halves of the body are evenly balanced, the positive and negative currents of the body are held in equilibrium; the energy is locked within the body, resulting in quick recuperation.

The next step in Savasana is the control of the senses and the stilling of their outward movement towards objects of desire. Savasana is a descending psychosomatic movement. It is a descent of the body and the mind as a unit within itself towards the sources of energy within oneself. Savasana is not a rigid state of stillness which, though it blocks out the external world, is still egoistical. Savasana properly performed brings on a silent state of stillness which is divine.

Savasana is not simple stillness. It is the surrender of one's ego and the receptive awareness of the divinity locked within onself. For the achievement of this state, the brain cells have to "descend" passively. The brain cells will not experience this descending movement if the senses are not controlled and the senses have not learnt to withdraw within themselves. Most of our organs of sense are located in the head and the entire struggle for control takes place on the face from the throat upwards, where the impressions gathered by the senses are experienced. Savasana is said to be complete if the breath, the eyes, the eardrums, the root of the tongue at the palate are all under control and relaxed. The beginner will observe that the organs of sense do not stay quiet. He will observe that the eyelids will flicker and the eyeballs will move upwards. These are sure signs that the eyes are tense and that the brain is being disturbed by thought waves. The appearance of saliva in the mouth and the constant desire to swallow is an indication of tension in the tongue. Tension in the eardrums can also be experienced as tension around the temples. The beginner should consciously search out these tensions, for knowing where they exist he can relax them.

To descend and relax the senses, first elongate delicately the back of the neck towards the crown of the head so that there is an upward movement of energy almost invisible to the naked eye. This flow of energy is then to be directed downwards from the top of the head by descending the bridge of the nose so that the bridge is parallel to the ceiling and the floor. In elongating the back of the neck and descending the bridge of the nose, care should be taken that a tense chin-lock does not result. So as to offset a tense chin-lock (where the chin would dig into the top of the breast-bone), the beginner must learn to lift the chin gently upwards, so that the chin is at a right angle to the floor or ceiling. This ascending movement of the chin must balance the descending movement of the bridge of the nose. Then a sense of lightness is felt on the forehead (the *Lalata Chakra*). When the bridge of the nose and the chin are held in equilibrium, the head and the brain will feel light, and the throat will feel relaxed. In Savasana the energy flows in a circular motion over the back of the head, down the nose towards the toes and then back to the crown of the head. In this way the flow of energy is kept within the body, and the dissipation of energy and consequent exhaustion are avoided. This leads to faster recuperation and refreshment of body and spirit. Once the flow of energy is correctly directed, the pupils of the eyes must be made to descend passively towards the bottom of the breast-bone (the *Manas Chakra,* which is the centre of emotions) and above the solar plexus (the *Surya Chakra*). The eyeballs should shrink pleasantly inside the sockets. A shrunken eyeball is a relaxed eyeball.

Bulging eyes reveal tension. The optical nerve must be drawn towards the centre of emotions, the *Manas Chakra,* so that in the single "eye of awareness" of the soul the physical eyes lose their identity. This "eye of awareness" of the soul is found in the *Manas Chakra.* The eardrum should be kept relaxed and the throb of nerves at the temples must also cease. The auricula, the auditory nerves and the skin of the temples must be drawn towards the centre of emotions. This joint movement of the eyes and the ears is felt as a quiet and cool movement downwards which is infinitely relaxing. The facial skin is a sensitive gauge of relaxation, but at the same time the loosely hanging folds of the facial skin should be constricted, so that the facial skin seems to separate itself from the flesh below it. The two sides of the palate at the uvula should also passively come together. When there is shrinkage and dryness in the mouth, especially at the uvula and the tongue, relaxation is experienced.

The control of breath is necessary for good relaxation. Rhythmic breathing at the beginning helps one to relax. Inhalation should not be deep, but should be of normal duration. Exhalation, however, should be longer in duration than inhalation. During inhalation as well as exhalation, the brain cells should be made to descend towards the centre of the emotions. This downward movement is more difficult in inhalation than in exhalation. For about three-fourths of the duration of inhalation one can experience the descent of the brain cells, but for the last one-fourth of the period of inhalation there is a slight movement of the brain cells upwards. This upward movement is to be avoided. Inhalation reflects the dominance of the ego, whilst exhalation denotes the surrender of one's ego to the divinity surrounding us. Exhalation empties the brain of the ego. The surrender of the ego in exhalation is accelerated when after a period of slow and smooth exhalation there occurs what might be described as "echo exhalation." This is a fine and subtle exhalation and may be likened to the exquisitely pure and delicate notes of a string instrument in the hands of a master musician, which seem to echo gently from nowhere. This "echo exhalation" empties the brain completely of the ego and results in withdrawal of the nerves and senses within onself. Conscious and deliberate surrender of the ego is hard to achieve. That is why the texts of Yoga recommend thinking upon the name of the Lord whilst practising pranayama. The practitioner then feels that the course of all energy is entering within him with each breath, while he is surrendering to the Lord his very life breath, his very ego, when he is exhaling. The Self is pure consciousness, free from thoughts, feelings and desires. The mind is the vehicle of consciousness. When the brain—the intellectual centre—is active, the mind reveals itself as intelligence. When the brain is perfectly quiet and the intellectual centre is stilled, the mind appears as the Self in the centre of the emotions. Here one is gathered up and yet suspended, empty yet perfectly satisfied, serenely balanced, neither free nor bound. There is stillness in pure awareness. The awareness of "I" is transmuted into awareness of the Creator. There is emotional stability and mental humility.

There are several signs of a well-performed Savasana. A few indications may help the beginner to test the depth of his relaxation. Yoga is not an intellectual game. It is a sharing of real experience. In a good Savasana there is a feeling of shrinkage of skin and muscles, for Savasana is after all a movement of inward withdrawal. There is at

105

the same time a feeling of elongation of the limbs and the body. Sometimes, this elongation is experienced as a twitch of the nerves. A pleasant feeling of heaviness and constriction is experienced through the whole body, but especially in the upper arms just above the elbows and in the calves just below the knees. At these four places one can experience the beating of the pulse, and the balance of the body can be tested by watching the evenness of the pulse beat. Dryness is felt in the bones and the joints. A feeling of being suspended on a thin line of awareness is also present. The best sign of a good Savasana is a feeling of deep mental peace and pure bliss. Savasana is alert surrender of the ego. In forgetting oneself, one discovers oneself.

YOGA
AND MENTAL PEACE

Y OGA, SAMADHI AND SHANTI are synonymous terms conveying the same meaning. The means and end of Yoga is Samadhi. Samadhi is the experience of shanti or peace within oneself. Samadhi means putting together, union, bringing into harmony, fixing the mind for attention on a thought, intense contemplation or meditation. Shanti means tranquility, calmness, freedom from passion, undisturbed in the objects of pleasures or pain.

Yoga is derived from the root *"Yuj"* which means to join, to bind, attach, to yoke, to direct and concentrate one's attention on, to use and apply. *"Samyoga yoga ityukto jivatma Paramatmanah."* The union of the Individual self *(Jivatma)* with the Universal Self *(Paramatma)* is Yoga.

Before understanding the communion of the individual with the Universal Self one has to know how to bring union of body with mind and mind with the Self. It is not easy to demarcate between body and mind and mind and Self. There is no cohesion in man's body and nerves, nerves and organs, organs and senses, senses and mind, mind and intelligence, intelligence and will, will and consciousness and consciousness and self. In order to bring all

107

these vehicles of men into unison, sages discovered Yoga. This vast scattered subject was codified by sage Patanjali in his treatise of one hundred and ninety-six terse *sutras*.

Patanjali enumerates eight disciplines of Yoga. These may be compared to a tree. *Yama,* the ethical principles, form the roots. *Niyama,* the individual disciplines, build up the trunk. *Asanas* are the branches, *Pranayama* the leaves which aerate the tree. *Pratyahara* is the bark. *Dharana* is the sap flowing throughout the tree. *Dhyana* is the flower and *Samadhi* the fruit. The essence of Yoga is the experience of Samadhi.

No doubt today, through advances in technology and scientific background, man has conquered ignorance but he is caught in the pride of knowledge. This pride of knowledge has brought competition between man and man, and increased the strains and stresses upon him. In order to cope with competition, speed came into his mode of thinking and action. These three, namely strain, stress and speed, made man a miserable creature on earth. His physical frame started waning, his nerves got tensed, tight and filled. He could not release his tensions. So his thinking and faculties were affected and anxieties multiplied. In order to find freedom from anxieties and restfulness in himself he switched to artificial ways of living. He became addicted to tranquilisers, sleeping pills, alcohol, various psychedelic drugs or indiscriminate sexual acts to relieve his tensions. No doubt these methods allowed him to forget himself temporarily but the cause remained and troubles returned unabated.

Patanjali, the Father of Yoga, had the foresight and vision to narrate the reasons which afflict man and disturb his peace and poise. Yoga is the only science and art which eradicates all the above causes of afflictions and disciplines the mind, emotions, intellect, will and reason so that the poise is gained in oneself to lead a harmonious life, without being affected by the past or the future, but in the present which is ever fresh. With this state of freshness man can do all his wordly duties and yet he can maintain mental peace in all situations.

Unjustified criticism of Yoga

At a conference on hypertension, the doctors were of the opinion that Yoga and meditation offer no cure for people suffering from hypertension. In the art of teaching my experiences are just the opposite. My pupils, many of whom are physicians and surgeons, benefitted by Yoga. Persistent practice is essential in all these cases. Secondly, no yogi with thorough knowledge teaches *Sirsasana, Dhanurasana* or *Mayurasana* to such patients. In Sirsasana there is a pressure on the throat and temples and respiration becomes heavy, whereas in the other two, the diaphragm is compressed which pushes up the blood-pressure. There are hundreds of asanas which are used according to the condition and constitution of the person as well as his mental situations. A wrong diagnosis or wrong introduction of medicine does cause adverse results on the patient. So also in Yoga there are certain methods to be adopted and they differ as the constitution differs.

In Yoga one is taught to unite the body, the breath, the mind, intellect and Self, and all are made to balance evenly like the string holding the pearls of a necklace together. Then one is made to create a state of emptiness (passive silence) in one's body, nerves, brain and mind through slow soft exhalation without deep inhalation. This creates in one a state of non-existence, bringing requisite serenity in the body cells. This in turn relaxes the facial muscles. When the facial muscles are relaxed, the organs of perception (eyes, ears, nose, tongue and skin) are relaxed from tension. When the senses of perception are relaxed, the brain which is constantly in contact with these organs becomes *sunya* (void). So no thinking process takes place. The intelligence which is constantly in the head throughout the wakeful state *(jagrtavastha)* is made to descend to its source which is known as mind.

In *Chhandogya Upanishad* it is said that, *"Hridi Ayam iti Hridayam"* (In the heart, the *atma* dwells, hence it is called *hriddayam*-heart). It is here that energy and intelligence take their origin. When one is active it moves towards the brain and when one is at sleep it rests at its source. Realising this dual path of intelligence, one is taught to consciously remain in the source of its seat. Then his mind too gets sublimated *(manolaya)*. This is the stability in mind. When this is achieved one is made to learn to stop the invading thoughts from entering either mind or brain. Here one is made to experience a mindless state *(amanaskatva)*. This is clarity of intellect. When one develops these qualities one does one's work not only quickly but efficiently. One has a dynamic energy but will not unnecessarily allow it to be dissipated. When a man gains this condition of mind how can he ever have hypertension? Instead of that his mind is cool and collected.

When such is the discipline and effect of Yoga, I cannot comprehend the casual remarks of so-called scientific minds, who think that they can with impunity criticise anything and everything (which is not congenial to them) existing on earth. Are there drugs for all ailments? If they fail in their treatment they brand the disease as allergic or virus diseases. If yogis fail, they make a mountain of it. Several people die of heart attacks while in bed. Could anyone prohibit them from resting in bed? If a man walks or drives carelessly in the street he is bound to meet with an accident. So also if Yoga is done thoughtlessly, anything might happen.

We are always seeking contact with heaven, but how many of us have made any reasonable contact with mother earth?

YOGA—AN ANSWER TO PROBLEMS OF TODAY

WHAT IS YOGA? It is a science which deals with perfection of the body, stability of the mind and clarity of the intellect in order that man may uncover thereby the difference between the body and the mind and transform them into a state of virgin purity so that the Self when uncontaminated by pleasures and desires may remain as pure as crystal. It shows the way to the art of right living and hence Yoga is also spoken of as being a branch of philosophy.

Though men belong to various geographical backgrounds with different historical perspectives and social environments, their basic problems, desires, pleasures and pains are the same. Yoga is without doubt the master key that unlocks the frontiers of the mind. It shows the way by which desires and pleasures which make the mind waver can be quietened. It equips the individual with the power of discrimination and the ability to distinguish between the real and the unreal, between the transient pleasures accompanied by sorrow and that which is permanent, good and auspicious.

By the practice of asanas the human system is purged of all toxic matters. The mind becomes free from the

113

shackles of the body, thus ensuring health and harmony. A healthy mind creates an impetus in man to aspire towards remaining unattached from the dictates of the body and the senses, but attached to the source of all knowledge, all actions and all emotions, that is, *Atma* (the Soul). It is then no longer one's individual ego that matters but the Universal Self. Yoga is thus the means and the end at the same time.

Can Yoga, which is as old as civilization, fit into our modern world? Technological knowledge today has advanced beyond the understanding of the average man. This knowledge has made it possible for man to land on the moon—perhaps the greatest of all wonders. Though intellectually man has advanced as high as the moon, spiritually he has become a narrower being. Man is drifting away from his fellow men. Suspicion, doubt, competition and the struggle for survival have been intensified, stresses and strains have increased, and selfishness has taken root instead of selflessness for the betterment of man. We may have conquered *Avidya* (ignorance) but we are caught up in *Asmita* (egocentric nature). Patanjali explains three human defects—intellectual, emotional and instinctive. *Avidya* and *Asmita* are intellectual defects; *Raga* (desires) and *Dwesa* (malice) are emotional defects; *Abhinivesa* (clinging to one's own) is the instinctive defect. The practice of Yoga destroys these defects, kindles in man the knowledge that is ever real, emotions that do not create sorrow but give strength. Yoga helps one to understand the weaknesses in one's fellow men and to cultivate the art of forgiveness and to surpass incidents which cause emotional disturbances.

Today man needs first and foremost physical firmness, emotional poise and intellectual clarity. *Yama,*

Niyama and *Asanas* bring physical firmness. *Pranayama* and *Pratyahara* give emotional poise. *Dharana* and *Dhyana* bring about intellectual clarity, and *Samadhi* gives the experience of that unalloyed bliss so vital to the very existence of man.

Yoga has to be done using the intellect of the head as well as the intellect of the heart. This is spiritual Yoga.

YOGA—A PATH TO
SELF-REALISATION

Y OGA IS A SEARCH for the Self and such a search is not
interested in attracting public attention.

Sri Krishna in the Gita describes the true yogi as one
who keeps tranquility of mind in heat and cold, success
and failure, pain and pleasure, evil and good. He is calm
and composed in the ups and downs of life. Yoga is
putting body and mind to the divine purpose of service
and sacrifice. Lord Krishna further states that all actions
performed gracefully and with joy are to be considered
yogic actions. Yoga then is to be understood as the uniting
or bringing together of the *Jivaatma* (Individual Self)
with the *Paramatma* (the All-Pervading Spirit of the
Universal Self) and the discovery of the ecstasy implied in
that union.

The Margas or Paths:

The *Atma* or soul is free, otherwise the search for reality
would be meaningless. However, due to ignorance of the
true nature of the soul, we dwell in the senses. To discard
this ignorance, the rishis of old pointed out various paths
to self-realisation:

1. *Jnana Marga:* the path of knowledge in which the seeker learns to discriminate between the real and the unreal.

2. *Karma Marga:* the path of selfless service without looking for the benefits accruing from such service.

3. *Bhakti Marga:* the path of love and devotion.

4. *Yoga Marga:* In this path the mind and its activities are studied and brought under control. All impulses originate from the mind which is the source of thinking and understanding. The mind itself, which is the source of desire, passion and possessiveness, should be withdrawn from the external things, made still and directed inwards, to realise the Self. The mind is in constant movement. As the mind is the king of the senses, the stilling of the mind is called *Raja Yoga.* As all cannot still the mind, Sri Swatmarama, the author of *Hatha Yoga Pradipika,* stresses that body and breath, the source of life, be brought first under control.

Body, mind and spirit have been given by God to be utilised in right living. Yoga is the science dealing with the body, the mind and the spirit. It embraces all humanity and as such is termed Universal Culture.

Lord Shiva as bestower of happiness gave the art of Yoga. As Nataraja, King of Dancers, he gave the art of dance.

YOGA AND DANCE

THE SAVANTS OF YORE discovered that the body of man is made up of three layers—physical, mental and spiritual. In order to develop these layers of body, mind and soul, rhythmically, systematically and uniformly, several arts were introduced, namely, *mallavidya* (athletics), *dhanusya* (archery), *vyavaharika* (economics), *sangitika* (music), and *natya* (dance). On a cursory observation Yoga and Dance appear to be divergent arts. When they are studied carefully, one realises that they meet at several points as if they supplement each other. Yoga is the sublimation of all emotions with a disciplined practice, whereas Dance is the artful display of emotions.

Kalidasa says in his drama *Vikramorvasiyam* that Dance, opera, ballet and drama are the sources of entertainment to all men and women of diverse tastes at one and the same time. Sage Patanjali says that the art of Yoga gives good formation, beauty, valour and lustre to the body. A careful study and keen insight of these two systems will enable one to draw inferences of similarity when they are performed and presented side by side. The differences are seen in costumes and finger movements, but the rest of the presentation and expression mostly remain the same.

Yoga and Dance sprang up from the common deity with the sole object of raising man or woman to realise within oneself the supreme peace and God realisation.

Lord Siva as bestower of happiness gave the art of Yoga. As Nataraja, King of Dancers, he gave the art of Dance. Yoga aims at the path of knowledge *(jnana marga)* and Dance at the path of devotion *(bhakti marga)*. Yoga looks to the Formless devoid of attributes or qualities *(nirguna brahma)*. Dance looks at all creation with form and attributes *(saguna brahma)*. Yoga is the path of release and renunciation *(nivrtti marga)*; Dance is the path of progress and acceptance of all creation *(pravrtti marga)*. Yoga is subjective presentation displaying posture, gesture and expression in the asanas, pranayama and dhyana. It is an internal experience and feeling of integrating the body, the senses, the mind and the intelligence with the self. Dance is an expression of thoughts, passions and actions externally. The six basic emotions of desire, anger, ambition, love, pride and jealousy are considered as the enemies for the growth of spiritual knowledge in Yoga, while in Dance they are considered companions for expressing the moods and sentiments of man's feelings. Yoga is a dynamic internal experience of oneself and Dance imitates the inner experiences of Yoga externally for one to see.

As Dance has movements like *tandava* (vigorous) and *lasya* (slow and soft), Yoga too has three movements, namely, *mirdu* (soft), *madhyama* (medium) and *tivra* (intense). The yogi uses both sides of the body evenly and rhythmically whereas a dancer's movement is one-sided with one basic emotion dominating many of his actions and presentations.

In Yoga it is important for the *Sadhaka* to treat his body as the temple of the spirit and each asana as a japa or repetitive prayer. Each adjustment makes him aware of the object of his quest and enables him to grasp the meaning *(artha)* of the subject matter of his contemplation. This in turn creates perception *(bhavana)* of the Creator, and constant remembrance of Him renews faith.

In classifical *Bharatanatyam* dance, the syllable *"Bha,"* stands for *bhava* or expression, the syllable *"ra"* for *"raga"* or melody, and the last syllable *"ta"* for *"tala"* or rhythm.

Beauty and lustre attained through Yoga will be a treasure house for the dancer for presenting dancing at its best.

The intellect needs to be humbled for the body to become
the temple of God.

YOGA AND BRAHMACHARYA

ACCORDING TO THE INDIAN HERITAGE, our society is divided into four classes based on the qualities *(gunas)* of man. This later became a caste system: *Brahma* (priesthood), *Ksatriya* (warrior class), *Vaisya* (mercantile class) and *Sudra* (labour class). Though these divisions appear to be disappearing, they unconsciously exist in all vocations. Take the example of Yoga. Even in the discipline of Yoga, a beginner has to labour hard and sweat to learn. From this stage, one moves to show off, or, as an experienced student, teaches and earns through Yoga. This state of mind is the character of the mercantile class. Then, one wants to compete with one's colleagues or teach with pride and superiority. It is nothing but the martial character of the *Sadhaka.* This is the quality of a *Ksatriya.* The final one is the *Brahmin* class where the learner or the teacher delves deeply into the field of Yoga to drink the nectar of Yoga in the form of spiritual realisation. This is the religious fervour of Yoga and if one acts with this feeling, one becomes a Brahmin in yogic sadhana.

Like the division of class, man's life too is divided into four religious orders known as *asramas* or stages of life. These orders are known as *Brahmacharya* (educative and religious study), *Garhastya* (householder's life), *Vanaprastha* (preparation to learn non-attachment while living as a householder), and *Sannyasa* (detachment from the affairs of the world and attachment to the services of the Lord).

The sages of lore having established the class and stages of life according to one's behavioural pattern, divided the span of man's life of one hundred years into four parts each running concurrently for twenty five years. They advised following the four *Asramas* to fulfil the aims of life *(Purusarthas)*.

The aims of life are also four in number. They are *Dharma* (science of ethical, social and religious duties), *Artha* (acquisition of wealth), *Kama* (pleasures of life) and *Moksa* (freedom or beatitude). Without Dharma, the observation of science of duty, spiritual attainment is an impossibility. This is observed in *Brahmacharyasrama*.

Artha, the acquisition of wealth, is to become free from the parasitic life. It does not mean to accumulate wealth but to earn so that the body is kept healthy and the mind free from wants. Otherwise a poorly nourished body becomes a fertile ground for diseases and worries. In this stage not only does one acquire money but also a partner to lead a householder's life. This second stage gives a chance to experience human love and happiness and to prepare the mind for divine love through friendliness and compassion. This contact helps one to develop universality so that one soon realises divine love. One is never allowed to shirk one's responsibilities towards the upbringing of one's children and fellow beings. Hence, there is never any objection towards marriage and parenthood. At the same time, they are considered no bar to the knowledge of divine love, happiness and union with the Supreme Soul.

126

Kama is to have the pleasures of life which depend largely on a healthy body and a balanced harmonious mind. As the body is the abode of man, it has to be treated as the shrine of the soul. Practice of asanas, pranayama and dhyana purifies the body, stabilises the mind and brings clarity in intelligence. This is the reason why the sages said that the body is the bow, asana the arrow, and their target is the core of being (Purusa).

Moksa means freedom from the bondage of worldly pleasures. It is liberation, emancipation, freedom and beatitude. This liberation is possible only if one is free from sickness, languor, doubt, carelessness, physical laziness, illusiveness, failure to maintain will power, negligence in attention, misery, despair, tremor of the body, gasping of breath and afflictions. It is also freedom from poverty, ignorance and pride. When one is free from all these, emancipation sets in and divine beauty shines. This is *Moksa*. In this state, one realises that power, pleasure, wealth and knowledge do not bring freedom or aloneness *(Kavalavastha)* and do not pass away. One learns to go beyond the qualities of *tamas, rajas* and *sattva* and frees oneself from the aims of life to become a king amongst men and is second to none. He is a *gunatitan* (above qualities). This is the path of life's flavour, worth attempting and living.

According to the dictionary, *brahmacharya* means celibacy, religious study, self restraint and chastity.

All the Yoga texts say that the loss of semen leads to death and its retention to life. By the preservation of semen, the Yogi's body develops a sweet odour. As long as it is retained, there is no fear of death says *Hatha Yoga Pradipika*.

Patanjali too, lays stress on continence of body, speech and mind. He conveys that the preservation of semen establishes valour and vigour, strength and power, courage and fortitude, energy and the elixir of life. Hence his injunction that it should be preserved by concentrated effort of will. This does not mean that the philosophy of Yoga is meant only for celibates. All the *Smrtis* (Code of Law) recommend marriage. Almost all the yogis and sages of old in India were married men with families of their own. For example, sage Vasista had one hundred children, yet he was called brahmachari because he did not indulge in sex for the sake of pleasure only. In olden times courtship took place under the conjunction of auspicious stars, the day, the time and so forth which may not coincide even once a year. That is why they were called brahmachari though married.

The concept of brahmacharya is not one of negation or forced austerity and prohibition.

According to Shri Adi Sankaracharya, a brahmachari is a man who is engrosssed in the study of the sacred vedic lore, constantly moves in *brahman* and knows that brahman exists in all. In short, one who is in contact with the very core of being is a brahmachari. By this, one sees the divinity in all and hence, becomes a true brahmachari though married.

Brahmacharya can be observed even by married men and women provided they do not abuse but rather control courtship.

Today, in the name of freedom, everyone behaves as a libertine. This libertine life is not social freedom. The five principles of *yama* are special ethics. Social freedom is not reaction against social ethics. Each one has a certain discipline to follow in society. Hence, freedom to behave as one likes is not freedom. It is liberty without discrimination. Freedom with discipline alone is true freedom.

As I see it, today a married and contented life is brahmacharya, as the married practitioner learns to love his partner with head and heart, rather than the modern brahmachari who claims to be celibate but splashes his evil eyes on women for sensual gratifications. Married people are united together whereas those who are unmarried may stray and become mere pleasure seekers.

According to the *Gita,* Lord Krsna says that moderation in sleeping, eating and regulation in courtship are the brahmacharya followed by a yogi. This is the way of a yogi's life where he blends his sadhana without casting his wanton eyes around for sensual gratification.

I decided that the quality of the skin will tell the quality of the organs inside. That is why, even today, my emphasis is on the skin.

PRANA AND PRANAYAMA

PRANA IS AN AUTO-ENERGISING FORCE. This self-energising force creates a magnetic field in the form of Universe and plays with it to maintain and destroy for further creation. It permeates each individual as well as the Universe at all levels. It acts as physical energy, mental energy, intellectual energy, sexual energy, spiritual energy and cosmic energy. All that vibrates in the Universe is prana. Heat, light, gravity, magnetism, vigour, power, vitality, electricity, life and spirit are all forms of prana. It is potent in all beings and non-beings and a prime mover of all activity.

This self-energising force is the principle of life and consciousness. It is the creation of all beings in the Universe. They are born through it and live by it, and when they die, their individual breath dissolves into the cosmic breath. Prana is the hub of the wheel of life. Everything is established in it. It permeates the life-giving sun, the moon, the clouds, the wind, the earth, and all forms of matter. It is being *(sat)* and non-being *(asat)*. Therefore, each and every thing including man shelters under prana. It is the source of all knowledge and a cosmic personality.

Prana (energy) and *Chitta* (mind) are in constant contact with each other. They are like twin brothers. That is why prana gets focused on where the mind is, and where prana is, the mind gets focused. It is said in Yoga texts, that as long as breath is still, prana is still and hence the mind is still. All types of vibrations and fluctuations come to a standstill when prana or mind is quiet, steady and silent.

By knowing this connection between breath and mind the wise yogis of India advocated the practice of pranayama, the heart of Yoga and a touchstone to climb the ladder of the spiritual world. We are all acquainted by now with prana as a self-energising force. *Ayama* means stretch, extension, expansion, length, breadth, regulation, prolongation, restraint or control. *Ayama* is a compound word springing from *Vyayama*. It consists of three words *visalata* (extension), *arhoha* (ascension) and *dairagyata* (expansion).

Pranayama consists of four parts. They are *puraka* (inhalation), *antara kumbhaka* (internal retention), *rechaka* (exhalation) and *bahya kumbhaka* (external retention).

Puraka is the long, sustained, subtle, deep, slow and rhythmic in-breath. Through inhalation, the energising ingredients from the atmospheric air are made to percolate sensitively into the air cells to rejuvenate health, enhance the span of life and make one's life fruitful.

Antara kumbhaka distributes the drawn-in energy to the entire system through the channels of nerves and blood currents; while rechaka is the way of releasing slowly the vitiated air in the form of toxins of the system through subtle, slow rhythmic out-breath.

Bahya kumbhaka empties the load of the brain, purges all strains and sresses of the muscles and nerves creating silence and quietitude.

Pranayama is not just deep breathing. In deep breathing, facial muscles get tensed, the skull becomes hard, the chest gets taut as force is used for intake or output of breath. This creates hardness in the fibres of the lungs and chest preventing percolation of breath to reach the lungs.

In pranayama, the cells of the brain and facial muscles are kept receptive and breath is drawn in or released passively. In Puraka, each molecule, fibre and cell is independently felt by the mind, made to receive the energy to soak and get whetted. No jerks are involved; gradual expansion is observed, feeling the breath reaching the remotest part of the lungs. In rechaka, the slow release of the breath provides sufficient time for the air cells to re-absorb the residual prana to the maximum extent possible. Thus, this passive observation instills full utilisation of energy, building up emotional stability and calming the ruffled mind.

Hence, pranayama is a refined art of making respiratory organs expand deliberately and move intentionally to gain perfect rhythm and balance, effort and response.

Before knowing the ways of doing pranayama, let us see what prana is. The word prana brings to my mind the epic story of Amrtamanthan where the nectar of immortality was produced through the churning of the ocean. Before going into the production of prana (*Jivamrta,* the elixir or nectar of life), let me narrate the story of Amrtamanthan. When the strength of *asuras* (demons) was uppermost in the minds of *devas* (angels), Lord Siva, Lord Brahma and Lord Indra approached Lord Visnu, the protector of the Universe, to help them in upholding the virtues which were disturbed by the power and strength of the demons.

Lord Visnu thought for a while and then suggested the churning of the ocean to bring out the nectar of immortality. He advised them to discuss with the demons the effects of *amrta* and to impress upon them to accept the offer of jointly churning the ocean, and Lord Visnu would do the rest. So the Lords went to the leaders of the demons and discussed with them the plan to churn the nectar from the ocean. They decided to use the mountain *Meru* as churner for the churning, and Lord Adisesa (couch of Lord Visnu) as the rope for whirling the mountain. This analogy can be used for the production of prana in the beings.

According to our Indian way of thinking, man is made up of twenty-six *tatvas*. They are *Paramatma* (God), *Purusa* (Soul), *Prakrti* (nature) and *Mahat* (Cosmic intelligence). This Mahat or cosmic intelligence divides itself into three parts *asahamkara* (ego), *buddhi* (intelligence) and *manas* (mind). *Prakriti* or nature has five elements. They are earth, water, fire, air and ether, and each of these five has subtle parts in the form of smell, taste, form or shape, touch and sound. Besides these, there are five senses of perception and five organs of action. All these combined make one a living being and mould one to develop with the three *gunas* of nature, namely, *sattva, rajas* and *tamas*.

Purusa or the soul represents Lord Visnu, and body the prakrti or nature. The body becomes the fountain for production and Lord of the body is its generative force.

Plants, creepers, various grasses and herbs were cast together and dumped into the ocean as raw materials so that they are churned to produce the nectar of life.

134

Mountain Meru is the spinal column and it acts as a dasher or whisker of breath. *Susumna* represents Lord Adisesa as cosmic atmosphere while *ida* and *pingala* represent the individual's breaths of Adisesa's head and tail.

It is possible that Ida represents the parasympathetic nervous system, Pingala the sympathetic nervous system, and Susumna the central nervous system. As Adisesa was used as a rope for churning, so are the inhalation and exhalation. They are the two ends of the rope which churns the rod (central nervous system) where energy is stored in seven chambers. The beginning of inhalation represents one end of rope which is gripped by the demons; the end of exhalation, the other end gripped by angels. These two ends help to churn the in-breath and out-breath to create prana.

As the churning began, the mountain sunk into the ocean. Lord Visnu, incarnated as *Kurma* (turtle), crept underneath the mountain and lifted it from the base so it would float and the churning could continue. Similarly, *atman* keeps the spine floating upwards.

The first to spring out from the ocean was the poison called *Halahala*. This was swallowed by Lord Siva. This halahala is nothing but the toxic output in the form of exhalation.

Later several gems were generated from the churning. They represent the seven constituents *(dhatus)*—namely the chyle *(rasa)*, blood *(rakta)*, flesh *(mamsa)*, fat *(medas)*, bones *(asthi)*, marrow *(majja)* and semen *(sukra)*—and ten breaths. They are *prana, apana, samana, udana, vyana, naga, kurma, krkra, devadatta* and *dhanam-jaya*. The last that sprang out was the *Amrta* or the nectar of immortality.

By the contact of these seven constituents and ten breaths, with the help of the Seer and spine, the elixir of life is produced in the body.

The five elements and seven constituents in the body act as the raw material to produce this life elixir. The earth element is the base for production and the element ether acts as distributor of energy. The element of air acts to breathe in and out. Only two elements are now left out. They are water and fire. They are anti to each other. Because they are anti to each other, the in and out breath creates fusion between these two, namely water and fire, to produce a new electrifying energy known as life force in the human system. This new electrifying energy is known as prana which is commonly termed bio-energy and bio-plasma. As prana is the self-energising force, it generates more power through the process of pranayama.

We all know that stored water is stale, while running water has a certain dynamic life-giving force. This may be at a minimum level which may not be able to produce electricity. But when the water is made to run down through the construction of a reservoir, water falls on turbines for production of electricity. The generation and distribution of prana in the human system may be compared to that of electrical energy. The energy of falling water or rising steam is made to rotate turbines within a magnetic field to generate electricity. The electricity is then stored in accumulators and the power is stepped up or down by transformers which regulate the voltage or current. It is then transmitted along cables to light cities and run machinery. Prana is like the falling water or rising steam.

The thoracic area is the magnetic field. Practise of pranayama makes the spindles of the fibres act as turbines and sprinkle the drawn-in energy to the remotest parts of the air cells of the lungs for generating energy. They are accumulated in the chakras to work as transformers. This energy generated in the thoracic cavity is like electricity. It is stepped up or down by the chakras and distributed throughout the system along the circulatory and nervous systems which are nothing but transmission lines. Hence, yogis of India discovered pranayama for making full use of drawn-in energy to fully act in the system.

Also, in pranayama, the carpet of the mucous membrane of the nostrils filters and cleanses the inspired breath. During exhalation, sufficient time is given for the system to reabsorb the drawn-in energy into the blood. In Yoga texts this is called *"Ratna Purita Dhatu"* or "The Jewel of the Blood" that is the blood filled with bio-plasma. This bio-plasma is the cause for secretion of hormones through the endocrine glands.

This full use of absorption of energy will make a man live a hundred years with clean health in body, clear health in mind and equipoise in spirit. That is why practice of pranayama is considered a great science *(mahvidya)* and art.

As wind clears the ashes and smoke and makes the wood blaze forth, pranayama, too, clears the brain which obscures right thinking and reasoning and lets the mind go towards meditation.

In pranayama, the sadhaka uses his body as sacrificial altar *(yajna kunda)*. Puraka is the offer of pouring ghee on the altar while Rechaka is the flame blazing out from the yajna kunda. Kumbhakas act as a mantra to offer all one's feelings as an oblation so that the *jeevatman* or the soul merges and dissolves in the Universal Kunda—the Paramatman.

This is how the production of prana takes place and why pranayama is necessary.

137

SIMILARITY IN TREATMENT OF YOGA AND AYURVEDA

Y OGA HAS BECOME a popular subject these days as a curative and preventative measure, but doubt arises in a common man's mind whether Yoga really cures diseases. There is no doubt regarding the fact that Yoga changes the life of a human being and thus brings health. Here, I am trying to interpret the Yoga-Sutras of Patanjali in the style of Ayurvedic treatment.

Though there are two opinions regarding Patanjali and Charaka, whether they are one and the same person or different, I see a great similarity in them. Patanjali is not less than any physician and surgeon. The only difference is that Patanjali treats the consciousness *(chitta)* and Charaka treats the body. According to Patanjali, the consciousness, the mind is the ground which needs the treatment. According to Ayurveda, the body in which the soul dwells (living body) needs the treatment.

Patanjali gives the maximum and the minutest techniques for the cures of soiled consciousness, and Charaka, similarly, provides various methods of treatment for the soiled body.

Disease is that state when one does not feel "at ease." The art of leading a life "at ease" is health.

Normally, we find life full of pressure, pain, tension, stress and strain. Man is affected by environment, social structures, life-taking competitions and never-ending struggles. He is afflicted within himself by anxieties, worries, desires, lust, anger, greed, aversion, hatred, temptations and so on. Modern living has changed simple life into complexity and affected the consciousness, and therefore it has lost its simplicity and originality. It is getting too complicated, mixed, fabricated, soiled, scattered and all-pointed.

Let us see how Patanjali deals with the problems and gives the solution, and where he comes near to Ayurvedic science of treatment. The embodied or empirical soul called *Jeevatman* has dressed and ornamented itself with intellect, ego, mind, five senses of perception, five organs of action, five gross elements and five subtle elements. The empirical soul has decorated itself with sixteen qualities, namely :

1) Happiness *(Sukha)*
2) Unhappiness *(Dukha)*
3) Desire *(Iccha)*
4) Aversion *(Dvesha)*
5) Cheerful efforts to secure the objective *(Pratyaya)*
6) Vital energy which keeps the body alive *(Prana)*
7) Vital energy which keeps the body-machine intact *(Apana)*
8) Blinking of eyes—opening *(Umesha)*
9) Blinking of eyes—closing *(Nimesha)*
10) Intellect having the power of discriminative discernment *(Buddhi)*
11) Will-power, the determination to carry on the work *(Manah-Samkalp)*

12) Power of reason *(Vicharana)*
13) Memory *(Smriti)*
14) Power of intellect to know the objective world *(Vijanam)*
15) Clear and clean knowledge of known *(Abhyavasaya)*
16) The achievement of ends: the experience and emancipation *(Vishayopalabdhi)*

This Jeevatma, however, identifies itself with its dress, decoration and ornaments and gets lost, and this is its disease. Patanjali brings back the empirical soul to the trans-empirical state.

The diseased seer identifies itself with the seen. The disease is called *vritti* (mental modifications) and *kleshas* (afflictions). The five mental modifications are :

1) Real perception
2) False perception
3) Fanciful or imaginary knowledge
4) Sleep
5) Memory

and the five afflictions are :

1) Lack of spiritual wisdom
2) Egoism
3) Attachments towards pleasure
4) Aversion to pain
5) Clinging to life

The afflictions are causes for the modifications to become diseased.

The five modifications and afflictions are basically nurtured by the three qualities of primordial matter: illumination, activity and inertia, which are known as *sattva, rajas* and *tamas.* These three qualities in different proportions activate the consciousness to undergo the modifications and afflictions. Similarly, Ayurveda holds the *tridoshas* or three humours of the body: *vata, pitta* and

141

kapha, responsible for causing disease. Almost all diseases are considered *tridoshic.*

Let me put this tridosha concept in short. The three humours of the body support the structure of the body and maintain its metabolism. The Vata represents nerve force and comprehends all the phenomena that come under the central and sympathetic nervous system. It is a dynamic, vital and inherent force that exists in the cells. It is an energy force that circulates the blood and lymph and stimulates the nerves. The Pitta maintains metabolism in the system and generates body heat (thermogenesis). It is the base for all chemical activities. It is the sustaining fire for metabolic activities. The Kapha regulates heat and preserves body fluids, lubricates the joints, builds tissues, produces energy and brings firmness of limbs.

Derangement in the function of the three humours gives rise to disease. The tridoshas in their pathogenic state vitiate seven constituents: chyle, blood, flesh, fat, bone, bone-marrow and semen. These constituents go into an inbalanced state causing disease.

When the humours are in a balanced state forming a proper constitutional structure, it is called a state of *Dhatu Samyata* (balanced constituents), and it is a healthy state of body. Similarly, according to Yoga, when the three constituents of nature are in an acquiescent and balanced state it is called *Samyavastha,* which is an expected goal. At this stage, "The self abides in its own nature" *(Patanjali's Yoga-Sutras, I-3).*

Since disease is due to a disturbance in the humours, it could be either mono-doshic, bi-doshic or tri-doshic. In fact, if one gets disturbed the other two are affected. Since the vitiation is in different proportions, almost all the diseases are categorized into five types :

1) *Vitaja*
2) *Pittaja*
3) *Kaphaja*
4) *Vatu-Pittaj, Pitta-Kaphaja, Kapha-Vataja*
5) *Sannipataja or Tridoshaja*

Hence, the diseases, modifications and afflictions are mainly of five types.

According to Yoga, the seat of sattva-guna is from head to heart, that of raja-guna from heart to navel, and that of tamo-guna from navel to feet. Whereas according to Ayurveda the location of kapha is from head to heart, that of pitta is from heart to navel and that of vata is from navel to feet.

Yoga is eight-limbed called Ashtanga Yoga, and Ayurveda also has eight branches called Ashtanga Ayurveda. The eight limbs of Yoga are :

1) Self-restraints *(Yama)*
2) Fixed practices *(Niyama)*
3) Postures *(Asanas)*
4) Regulation of energy through breath control *(Pranayama)*
5) Quietening the senses *(Pratayahara)*
6) Attention *(Dharana)*
7) Meditation *(Dhyana)*
8) Absorption *(Samadhi)*

The branches of Ayurveda are :

1) Surgery *(Shalya)*
2) Diseases of eyes, ears, nose and throat *(Shalakya)*
3) The body treatment through medicine *(Kaya-chikitsa)*
4) Treatment of mental diseases *(Bhuta-vidya)*
5) Midwifery and diseases of children *(Kaumara Bhritya)*

143

6) Toxicology *(Agada tantra)*

7) Science of prolongation of life *(Rasayana)*

8) Means of securing vigour *(Vajeekarana tantra)*

Now let us see the method of treatment according to both sciences.

Patanjali advises two remedial methods for restraining mental modifications and burning the afflictions. They are practice *(Abhyasa)* and thirstlessness *(Vairagya)*. Abhyasa is the practice of the eight limbs of Yoga, and Vairagya is reducing oneself to a state of desirelessness. Abhyasa is an evolutionary method, and Vairagya an involutionary method.

In Ayurveda there are two remedial methods: *Shodhana*, the cleansing or purifying method, and *Shamana*, the pacifying method. Shodhana is a drastic method where Shamana is a mild method. Abhyasa is also a mild treatment which can be lenient and soft while treating the patient. That is why Ashtanga Yoga is applicable to all. Neither Shamana medicine nor Ashtanga Yoga harm or show any adverse effects.

Shodhana treatment brings drastic change but at the same time is harmful as it can uproot the humours if used wrongly and frequently. If it is not utilized at all, then it also causes problems in the body; so Charaka explains that it should be used very carefully. Patanjali also warns against using Vairagya as a remedial measure, as a sudden drastic change may uproot the Sadhaka. First, he wants Abhyasa to be done positively and renunciation to be introduced accordingly with proper measures. Therefore, the doses of five types of Vairagyas are introduced slowly in five stages so they work on the body and mind very delicately but definitely. They are :

144

1) *Yatamana*
2) *Vyatireka*
3) *Ekagrya*
4) *Vashikara*
5) *Para Vairagya*

Disengaging the senses from enjoyment and controlling them with continuous effort is Yatamana. Then thoughtfully controlling the desires which cause obstruction in the path of self-realization is called Vyatireka. Now, though the five organs of action and five organs of perception are entirely withdrawn from the external world, the feeble desires remain in the cause form in the eleventh sense—the mind. To withdraw the mind from all the desires is Ekendriya. To remain completely detached from worldly and heavenly desires is Vashikara. Paravairagya is the highest form of renunciation in which nothing is desired except the soul. Like Vairagya, the Shodhana Vidhi or purifying method is also applied in five stages :

1) Emission
2) Purgation
3) Enemata
4) Enema to head
5) Blood letting

According to my understanding the Abhyasa and Vairagya are curative measures similar to the Shaman Vidhi and Shodhan Vidhi of Ayurveda.

Modern days are days of pills, tablets and capsules. The multi-vitamin pills are claimed to be equal to nourishing food by the medical world.

Naturally the mind of an average man is also trained to question in a similar manner. The question may be,

"Mr. Iyengar, is there any pill or capsule which we can take to reach emancipation?" I say, "Yes" emphatically, "Take four capsules every day without missing a day and you will be a liberated soul." These are :

1) Faith *(Shraddha)*
2) Vigour *(Verya)*
3) Memory *(Smriti)*
4) Complete absorption in the practice of Yoga with full attention *(Samadhi Prajnya)*

Take these four capsules and emancipation is at your door. This sutra has a medicinal value.

Now some may ask further, whether these capsules should be taken along with water or milk. In Ayurveda there is *Anupana*. Anupana is that which is taken along with the main medicine to bring proper and immediate effect. It is also meant for lessening the side effects of vital drugs which could be dangerous and harmful.

Patanjali calls the Anupana, "profound meditation of God" *(Patanjali Yoga-sutras I.23)*.

There is a story in the *Bhagavatam*. The Queen, Satyabhama asks Lord Krishna why he considers the Gopis his best Bhaktas. Lord Krishna says that he will reply later. One day, he complains of acute and severe chest pain. The doctors attend to him but they give the opinion that it is incurable as their medicine fails to give any relief. Then Krishna himself, being the Almighty, says that the medicine given by the doctors is absolutely a right treatment but somehow the Anupana is not correct. Naturally, the Queen asks him what they should give as Anupana: milk, juice or tulasi water. He says that the dust of the feet is the best Anupana for the disease. Naturally, all the queens are taken aback and Narada gets puzzled knowing very well that nobody will give the dust of their feet to the Lord of the Universe. Krishna sends Narada to Gokul, and the Gopis come running to enquire about the well-being of Krishna. Narada says that Krishna has an acute chest pain and needs the dust of the feet as Anupana. The Gopis, best among all the Bhaktas, immediately give the dust of their feet and tell Narada to take it as early as possible so that their Lord will soon be relieved from the pains.

After taking the Anupana, Krishna feels hale and hearty and tells the queens that this is the love of bhaktas who do not mind giving anything to the Lord. So this *Iswar Pranidhana* is the best Anupana to be taken with the above-mentioned capsules.

However, the consciousness cannot get rid of modifications and afflictions so easily as it is a chronic disease of the patient. Chronic disease makes the patient weak; he loses his power to resist to a considerable extent and becomes vulnerable. Each disease tends to be accompanied by other diseases which come as side-effects or after-effects.

Similarly, the afflictions and modifications are accompanied by *Chitta Vikshepas* (Impediments):
1) Diseases *(Vyadhi)*
2) Sluggishness *(Styama)*
3) Doubt *(Samshaya)*
4) Carelessness *(Pramada)*
5) Idleness *(Alaya)*
6) Sense-gratification *(Avirati)*
7) Living in the world of illusion *(Bhranti darshan)*
8) The inability to hold on to what is undertaken *(Alabhdha bhumikatra)*
9) The inability to maintain progress *(Anavasthitatva)*
10) Sorrows *(Dukkha)*

11) Despair *(Dourmanasya)*

12) Tremor of the body *(Amgamejayatva)*

13) Heavy breathing *(Svasa-prasvasa)*

These are the thirteen obstacles and distractions which exist to harm the chitta further.

Does Patanjali give any preventative measures? Yes. The preventative measure is *Ekatatvabhyasa,* the single-minded effort to continue with Yogic practices.

Now in Ayurveda, there are certain medicines which are meant for external application. These are known as *Bahir-Parimarjana.* They are applied in the form of oil massage, sudation (steam treatment), *pradeha* (application of ointment), *Parisheka*-poultice (affusion) and *Mardana* (massage). These are the external means to affect the inner body.

Patanjali gives equal treatment with *Chitta-Prasadanam* to bring the internal change in Chitta. Many times we have to change our behaviour and approach towards the external world for our own good. These treatments cultivate the mind to tread on the yogic path smoothly. They are as follows :

1) *Maitri*—cultivation of friendliness towards those who are happy.

2) *Karuna*—cultivation of compassion towards those who are in sorrow.

3) *Mudita*—cultivation of joy towards those who are virtuous

4) *Upeksha*—cultivating the nature of indifference towards those who are full of vices.

If this is an external means, then Patanjali gives the internal means or *Antah-Parimarjana.* According to Ayurveda, medicine taken orally or internally for cure or relief from diseases is called Antah-Parimarjana. Pari-

148

marjana is cleaning, cleansing or washing. In Ayurveda the treatment is to wash and clean the doshas, and in Yoga to wash and clean the trigunas out of which the chitta is made. The internal means are as follows:

1) Bringing calmness and quietness with the retention of breath after exhalation.
2) Involving totally with application, dedication and devotion in an interesting object, taste the essence of calmness and steadiness emanating therefrom.
3) Contemplating on a sorrowless luminous effulgent light.
4) Contemplating on men of illumination who are free from desires and atttachments.
5) Studying, recollecting and contemplating during the wakeful state, the dream-filled and dreamless sleepy states.
6) Contemplating on a thing which is conducive and pleasing to steadiness of mind.
   (Patanjali Yoga-sutras, I.34-39)

These are the various methods of concentration and contemplation utilized and applied to bring calmness, quietness, steadiness and serenity of the mind.

At this stage, the aspirant of Yoga is considered to be at the stage of well-being because the mental modifications have been made feeble, attenuated in order to undergo *Sama-Patti*. The consciousness becomes highly sensitive, choiceless, pure and stainless. It becomes crystal clear. Such a crystal-like consciousnes enables revelation of the knower, knowable and the instrument of knowing by holding them as a substrate. This is called Sama-Patti or consumation.

In Ayurveda, *Swastha* means to be healthy physically, psychologically and spiritually. Ayurveda helps to bring health of the body so that the patient develops his own talents to progress as far as mental and spiritual aspects are concerned. For this purpose, Ayurveda gives the treatment called *Rasayana* or *Ojaskar* treatment. Rasayana means the treatment which controls the ageing process, increases vitality, prevents diseases, brings health and yields long life. It is like a tonic. Ojas adds vitality and increases resisting power to combat diseases. These treatments are meant to bring *Sva-Sthyaor* equilibrium in man so that he leads the worldly life as well as spiritual life in a disciplined way.

Yoga brings the consciousness to a state of *Tatstha* and *Tadanjanata*. These are the states in which the consciousness totally remains in the object presented to it and appears completely in the shape of the object. These objects could be either subtle elements or gross elements (objects of the world) or the organs of perception or even the soul. At this stage consciousness needs some tonic. Patanjali introduces these tonics (Rasayana) for the steadiness, silence, placidity and clarity in intelligence; (Sama-Patti) in the form of Savitarka, Nirvitarka, Savichara, Nirvicham etc. (Deliberative contemplation, super-deliberative contemplation, reflective contemplation and super-reflective contemplation).

Ayurveda is not interested merely in treating the person to get rid of disease, but further it wants to establish health in the body; so rehabilitation and rejuvenation is also part of treatment to bring a full stop to further treatment.

In Yoga, Patanjali feeds a proper diet to consciousness with *Sabija Samadhi* (Seeded Samadhi). When Chitta develops the spiritual light of intelligence filled with unalloyed wisdom, glowing with truth and reality, then the question of rehabilitation or rejuvenation arises, to which Patanjali answers with the state of *Nirbija Samadhi* (Seedless Samadhi).

Chitta expresses itself in five planes to the proportions in which the trigunas exist. These planes are :

1) Wandering mind—*Kshipta*
2) Forgetful mind—*Mudha*
3) Alternate states of steadiness and distraction of the mind—*Vikshipta.*
4) One-pointedness of the mind—*Ekagra*
5) Restrained mind—*Niruddha*

The above-mentioned treatment in Samadhi Pada is for the patients who fall into the category of Ekagra and Niruddha. Patanjali gives treatment to those who belong to the first three categories.

In Ayurveda the patient is examined to assess the *bala* (strength and vitality) and *dosha* (morbidity) to give required treatment. The constitution of the patient is measured by assessing the bala and dosha, and accordingly the patient is classified into three divisions: *Pravara* (high); *Madhya* (medium); *Avara* (low). This also decides the intensity or mildness of the ailment.

Has Patanjali not done it?

Patanjali portrays distinctly different levels of aspirants as feeble, average and keen, besides the supremely enthusiastic. Here Patanjali asks the aspirant to weigh himself and decide his constitution and strength. If Ayurveda pathologically finds out the morbidity of tridosha, Yoga finds out the morbidity of triguna. Yoga gives five capsules (Shradda, etc.) and asks the aspirant to find out whether he can digest them, as they work with those for whom there is less morbidity and more purity in the triguna.

If trigunas are very much in a morbid state, the capsules have to be changed, and they are :

"Tapas Svadhyaya Ishwar Pranidhana Kriyayoga"
(Patanjali Yoga-sutras, II.1)

This capsule is called *Kriyayoga* which is three-layered or thrice coated by *Tapas* (self-discipline), *Svadhyaya* (self-study), *Ishwar Pranidhana* (surrender to God). The trigunas reach the morbid state because the web of afflictions covers them.

Afflictions, are mainly five in number :

1) Lack of spiritual wisdom *(Avidya)*
2) Egoism *(Asmita)*
3) Attachment towards attraction *(Raga)*
4) Aversion to pain *(Dvesha)*
5) Clinging to life *(Abhinivesha)*

All these change the very simple and pure nature of original mind and make it complicated. As the diseases weaken the strength of man by increasing the morbidity of tridosha, so also afflictions weaken the strength of consciousness by increasing the morbidity of triguna. In Ayurveda, the *vata* is considered to be the strongest prime *dosha* on which depends the health of a person. The *vata* creates disease in a state of agitation and aggravation, and restores health, too, when it is in a balanced state. In Yoga, it is the sattva guna. When sattva becomes weak, it is dominated by other gunas and man is caught in afflictions, but when sattva is strengthened or when it becomes predominant, man is free from afflictions.

How are the afflictions to be eradicated? *Pratiprasava* and *Dhyana* are the two methods. Pratiprasava is counter activation and Dhyana is meditation. The subtle afflictions are destroyed at the time of final deliverance

152

with counter activation, and the mental modifications are annihilated and silenced by meditation. The counter activation is *Shodhan-Vidhi* (purifying method) and meditation is *Shaman-Vidhi* (pacifying method).

In Ayurveda, the diseases are categorised in four parts :
1) Adventitious *(Agantuka)*
2) Physical *(Sharirika)*
3) Mental *(Manasika)*
4) Natural *(Svabhavika)*

The adventitious are those caused from external factors such as bites, injuries, accidents and so on, while the physical and mental diseases are commonly known to all. The Svabhavika are natural diseases which cover birth (the very birth itself and the constitutional weakness by birth), old age, death, natural hunger, thirst, sleep, etc.

Here the view is very clear, as Patanjali calls vrittis and afflictions natural diseases which exist from time immemorial, almost since the conjunction between the seer and the seen.

Now general treatment given for these is as follows :
1) Adventitious is treated surgically.
2) Physical is treated medically.
3) Mental is treated psychologically.
4) Natural is treated spiritually.

In yogic treatment, the same method is followed.

The afflictions are the root cause of Karma. The afflictions have to be eradicated only by *Karma Shuddhi* (Purification of action). The consciousness gets affected by afflictions, and the pure consciousness becomes the fabricated consciousness. This is adventitious disease which needs surgical operation. Operation is a drastic treatment; Patanjali's operation is *Pratiprasava* (counter activation or involution). The vrittis are natural diseases which need a treatment such as meditation.

Avidya, or lack of spiritual wisdom, is the root cause of afflictions. Avidya is the product of predominant tamoguna. It has to be treated. To uncover the sattvaguna, which is covered by tamoguna, the sattvaguna itself has to be operated. This operation is called *Vivekakhyati*. The instrument used to perform this operation is the Ashtanga-Yoga (eight-limbed Yoga).

Patanjali is a perfect pathologist. He does not give superficial treatments; he first takes pathological tests to find out the root-cause of the disease. Thus, he declares that it is the pleasant and unpleasant experiences of the mundane or celestial world which are ultimately painful, causing sorrow, which are the cause of disease. The painful experience is due to the contradictory functions of the trigunas, and that is the cause of disease. Therefore, the pains have to be avoided, and Patanjali takes responsibility for curing disease by applying the yogic method.

For therapeutics, four factors are necessary: the physician, medicament, the attendant and the patient. Patanjali fulfils these requirements. In the yogic path, Patanjali himself is a physician, the science of Yoga is the medicament, the teacher teaching Yoga is the attendant and the student is the patient.

The physician is expected to be excellent in medical knowledge, having practical experience, dexterity, purity. He should know all the drugs, their suitability, their multiple forms and potency. So also while treating the patient, it is necessary on the part of a Guru (attendant) to have the knowledge of asana and pranayama, the performance, the multi-effect and multi-forms to apply them as medicine.

Patanjali, being a capable doctor, knows the cause of disease very vividly, clearly. This cause is nothing else than the conjunction between the seer and seen. This union has to be avoided. Therefore, Patanjali dissects the human being to get a clear picture of *Drishya* and *Drishta* (II.18 & 19). He makes the seer (Drishta) aware of the truth that the seen (Drishya) exists for the sake of the seer to lead him to abide in his pure state of existence.

He declares that Ashtanga Yoga is the only cure of this disease. It includes all those curative measures used in Ayurveda. It is meant for cleansing the body and chitta so that one attains the state of :

1) Cleansing-Purification *(Ashuddhikshaya)*
2) Adding ojas to jnana *(Jnanadipti)*

The kindled consciousness (Jnanadipti) and the discriminative discernment (Vivekakhyati) are the state of health of chitta-consciousness.

In Ashtanga Yoga, the yama-niyama are moral principles. When one does not follow these moral-health principles, disease sets in. This disease is called *Vitarka.* Vitarka is improper and perverse thoughts. Badha is to get possessed of such thoughts. The Vitarka-Badha is a kind of infectious disease of chitta which does not allow it to keep its moral health. The cure for this disease is *Pratipaksha-Bhavanam.* This is a Shamana-Vidhi; a process of counteracting vitarka, or improper thoughts, with tarka, or proper thoughts. The proper thoughts eradicate improper thoughts and naturally the chitta gains back the moral state.

Asana is a cure for physical, mental and spiritual disease. By conquering the asanas, one can effortlessly tread on the path of Yoga, as one's body and mind totally merge or assume the infinite form of the seer. The asanas put an end to the dualities and differentiations between the trio—body, mind and soul.

Pranayama removes the veil covering the light of knowledge and increases the bala or strength of the chitta; so chitta becomes competent to tread on this path.

Pratyahara is the conquest of senses of perception. This is the health of the senses. The disease of perceptual organs is to go after the objects and indulge in them. The disease called indulgence causes indigestion. The medicine for indigestion is *Langhana* or *Karshana*. Langhana is fasting. The organs of perception have to go on a fast. Langhana has both varieties of treatment, the Shodhana (purificatory) and Shamana (pacificatory).

In Pratyahara, the organs of perception are withdrawn. The objects are vomitted *(emisis)* through the organs. The enema is given so even in the form of memory the residue does not remain. But such a drastic change may show adverse effect so the treatment of pacification is given along with the practice of asana and pranayama. The organs of perception learn to remain on a strict diet through the practice of asana and pranayama, and finally they do a complete fast.

Dharana, Dhyana and Samadhi are like rasayana. Rasayana in Ayurveda means treatment to arrest the ageing process, prevent disease, increase vitality and bring longevity along with health. Are these three limbs extending their helping hand? Dharana is focussing the attention. Dharana makes impotent chitta potent, so it is like rasayana. The chitta is made young. The diseases of chitta are prevented. Dhyana is a continuous flow of attention which increases the vitality of chitta. Samadhi is a state in which the consciousness (Chitta) merges in the object of meditation, i.e. the soul. This is a state of total consummation of chitta. The seen in its pure state remains parallel to the seer. This results in longevity of the soul abiding in its own state—in a state of Atma and not Jeevatma.

The rasayana is given when the patient is free from disease. Rasayana is not a medicine. Medicine is meant to bring health at physical and mental levels, according to Ayurveda; whereas rasayana is a treatment given to a healthy man to remain healthy. The last three limbs of Yoga, called *Trayi,* are the rasayana for those who have gained health by practising the first five limbs *(Poorvasadhana)*.

In Ayurveda, before starting the treatment of the five-fold elimination therapies (Shodhan-vidhi), the patient is prepared for elimination. This pre-preparation is called *Poorva-Karma.* This Poorva-Karma includes *Snehan* (oleation) and *Swedan* (sudation). Snehana is oiling the body using ghee, oil, etc. This is given as an oral treatment, as an oil-enema or as a skin massage, and it arrests the agitating Vata. Swedana is a treatment in which the patient is made to perspire or sweat.

The Poorvangas of Ashtanga Yoga, namely: yama, niyama, asana, pranayama and pratyahara are the poorvakarma. By these the body and consciousness are prepared to become a fit instrument undergoing changes known as restraining modification, trance modification and modification of one-pointedness—Nirodha, Samadhi and Ekagrata. The practice of the last three limbs is to bring this total transformation of eliminating the dual state in body, mind and soul. That is why these limbs are called rasayana—tonics to the consciousness.

157

Finally, the consciousness (seen) reaches the healthy state of exaltation and becomes as pure as the seer. Both being pure, remain aloof and unmingled and in the indivisible state of existence.

PILGRIMAGE
TO THE VATICAN

WHEN I WAS TO GO to Europe in 1966 to teach Yoga, my pupil, Father Lobo, suggested that I should send my book, *Light on Yoga,* to the Pope.

Father Lobo told me that I should first meet the Bishop of Pune before sending the book. I saw him. He offered me a cup of tea and we talked about Yoga. He is a fine old person, young in heart with a sense of humour. The first thing he said was, "I do not know anything about Yoga and you do not look like a yogi. You have no long matted hair or beard, no beads, no saffron clothes and no *kamandalu* or bowl in hand. What sort of yogi are you? I am sorry I cannot introduce you unless you have these qualities." I told him that his outward apearance does not make one a yogi and that I was a yogi from inside with my plain clothes. Father Lobo jocularly said to his Lordship, "Sir, he is the only yogi who rides a scooter." The Bishop was amazed to hear this remark and wanted to see the scooter. He saw it, and while talking, I offered to take him for a ride on the pillion. He laughed, and we came back into the room, sat seriously and said, "Why do you want to see the Pope?" I said Father Lobo wants me, if possible, to give a demonstration in the presence of the

Pope. Then he said, "I have seen the book and admired the work. If I had not seen the book I would not have believed you are a yogi. I shall give you a letter of introduction to Cardinal Marella who is in charge of the non-Christian world and I am sure he will do what is necessary. But, may I suggest you wear a false wig and beard and present yourself in the presence of the Pope in the traditional dress. If you promise to do so, I shall recommend your name." I laughed and asked him, "Do you approve of it?" He said with a smile, "No."

He gave me the letter addressed to Cardinal Marella as promised. I enclosed the Bishop's letter with my personal letter and a copy of *Light on Yoga,* requesting the Cardinal to forward my book and letter to the Holy Father. The Bishop of Pune wrote: "I am hereby introducing to you perhaps the greatest artist of our time, a famous Indian Yogi, whose life sketch I am giving below. May I request your Eminence to be kind enough to introduce him yourself personally to His Holiness, our Pope, who I am sure will be most interested in him and his art. Hence a quiet and kindly interview will be most obliging."

The Cardinal replied to me, "I am now in a position to assure you that I did not fail to forward to the Holy Father your book, *Light on Yoga,* together with a personal message. His Holiness has charged me to express to you his sincere thanks and appreciation for your kind thoughtfulness. It has been agreed that you will be admitted to the presence of His Holiness in an audience. However, as it is not possible at the moment to fix the day and place, you will be duly informed after you have reached your address in London."

I came to London on June 23rd, 1966, and wrote to Cardinal Marella, giving my London as well as Switzerland addresses for him to write to me as soon as an audience was granted. I received a cable on July 6th from him, saying that the requested audience was granted on July 30th. I thanked him for this and asked for the place and time. No reply came. On July 13th, I was taking off for Scotland to teach the Rt. Hon. Lord Rollo. At 10:15 am, I got a frantic telephone call from Mme. Scaravelli at Gstaad, Switzerland, stating that the Cardinal was disturbed that I was not at the Vatican to be received by the Pope, and asking me to contact him at the Vatican directly. I told her that I had written two letters to the Cardinal confirming July 30th and was waiting for a reply. The cable had definitely mentioned the 30th as the day fixed for the audience with the Pope and not the 13th.

While my host in London was driving me to the Air-Terminal, I asked him to contact the Vatican City, to read the cable received by me, ask for forgiveness and make a request for another date. At the terminal by chance I met my pupil Mrs. Harthan. I requested her to write to the Cardinal for grant of another audience. I also wrote to the Cardinal from Edinburgh expressing my distress at my absence on the 13th due to the mistake as regards the date in the cable, and prayed for forgiveness.

On July 18th I received a cable from Cardinal Marella reading: "Audience granted either on the 20th or 27th whichever is preferable to you. Cable immediately the convenient date for you." I contacted all my friends and gave them the good news. God blessed his Vicar on earth to grant me the audience and the gates of heaven opened for me as the doors of the Vatican opened. I left London on July 26th for my historic mission.

I arrived at Rome at 4:30 pm and my pupil Alberto Scaravelli was at the airport to receive me. We reached his home and phoned the Vatican and were told to call on the Cardinal at his office at 9:30 the following morning. So on the 27th we journeyed to the Vatican in a car which had to be pushed and pulled to start the machine. At 9:30 am we were at the entrance of St. Peter's Church and it took us more than forty minutes to locate the office of the Secretary of the non-Christian World. We were shunted from place to place and at last we were given the gate pass to go inside. But we had to give the car number, driving licence number and name of the person who was driving the car.

A nun present there took us by the lift to the third floor. At the entrance a priest was waiting to receive us, who, after speaking in Italian to my friend, handed me a sealed envelope and a cable sent by the Brighton pupils c/o The Pope. I opened the letter and read that the audience was granted at 11:30 am at Castel Gandolfo and I should proceed there immediately, a distance of seventy-five miles! Before going to the Vatican, I had almost expected that the audience would take place earlier than anticipated and had prepared myself to proceed to Castel Gandolfo in case a demonstration was demanded. Then I opened the telegram which read, "Salutations from your Brighton Yoga pupils, thinking of you all, especially Christopher Columbus!"

We then proceeded to Castel Gandolfo. In Rome one should be adept at driving. The traffic moves like snakes and they take whatever position possible to take the lead. It requires skill to overtake cars and get your way, otherwise you are stuck and hooted at by others. We eventually reached Castel Gandolfo, the summer residence of the head of the Catholic world. Thousands and thousands thronged the Castel Gandolfo to get a glimpse of the Holy Father. The gatherings there are like many sacred places in India where thousands and thousands gather for *darshan* in temples on important occasions. The traffic was controlled by the police and we were asked to park the car in the parking areas. We had to go half a mile to find a place, and then we walked around the beautiful lake surrounded by hills. We had still ten minutes to spare. As we had not had coffee or tea since morning, we went to a restaurant, had an expresso coffee and proceeded slowly towards the Castel Gandolfo considering how I should bow and talk to the Pope.

We came near the gates; two colourful guards in yellow, orange and dark blue striped uniforms stopped us and asked for the appointment letter. I presented the letter, and they allowed me to go in. I asked for my friend's admission. They flatly refused as the audience was for me alone. So I had to leave my friend behind. With sore heart I asked my friend what he intended doing. He said that he would wait for me outside in a cafeteria. I went in.

I was directed to go on to the right and to follow the steps. I did as directed, and I found a big assembly hall like our darbar halls. Guards standing on the doorsteps in their beautiful uniforms received me, noted my name in the register and led me to the hall. Nearly two hundred people were there. Looking at all the people I thought that mine would not be a private audience. People from various parts of the globe came to have the *darshan* of the Holy Father. I was the only Indian with my *dhoti* and *kurta* and shawl, waiting to be received by the Pope.

After twenty minutes the guard came and took me to the adjacent room. There I was asked to sit on the first chair. Then he went back and called some others till there were ten of us. Two or three minutes later I was asked to stand in front of another door and others were asked to stand too. In a few seconds my eyes glittered to gaze at a man—the great Pope—with long yellow robes and a white cap on his head. He was followed by the guard and then the secretary and the interpreter. I was moved by his simplicity and bearing, though he was guarded like a King. I folded my hands and bowed to him. He moved with warmth and kindness towards me, caught my hands firmly and said, "I love India and Indians. I liked your book. You are indeed a professor and a director. What more can I say to a person like you who possesses such an art? I bless you with my heart and I wish you well. I hear that you have done very good work in your art and again I bless you." I asked him whether he would give me an opportunity to demonstrate my art. His interpreter put it into Italian and the Pope answered that though he would love to see it, there was no time for him to do so. "I have seen the book. It is wonderful," he said.

I then presented him with a few books of Sadhu Vaswani and a pure sandalwood walking stick. He gave the bundle of books to his Secretary, and holding the stick in his hands he moved his fingers on it, smelt it and said, "Wonderful! Nice! Good!" He gave it to the Secretary. Then the Pope said, "I would like to give you a souvenir of our meeting." and looked at the Secretary, who handed him a box. The Pope opened it and in it was a bronze medal. On one side was his profile with an inscription: "Palus VI Pont Max MCML XIV and III (his third year of reign)" and on the reverse side was the city of Rome with *"Manus Dedvest Me"* meaning "My hand leads me." This he presented to me with a smile and firmly holding my hands he said again, "I bless you for your work." Again I asked him to permit me to show what I practise. He said he loved it but there was no time to see it. When I parted

164

from the room he again shook hands with me and placed his palm on my head. He moved forward and I was taken by the guard to the lift from where His Holiness came. As soon as the lift went down the guards received me at the entrance, opened the doors of the lift and led me to the gate. There the guards presented me a guard of honour and led me out of the gate.

Thus ended my momentous journey to the Holy City of Rome where God's chosen representative lives on earth.

EXTRACTS FROM ARTICLES

by B.K.S. Iyengar

IS YOGA FOR ONE AND ALL?

Yoga is a fine art, and, like any other fine art, it too seeks to express the artist's abilities to the fullest possible extent—but with one difference. Artists need instruments like a violin or a painting brush or ankle bells as aids to the expression of their arts. A yogi's sole instruments are his body and his mind.

Yoga is a science, for it has a highly evolved technique based on well-tried principles. It is a science which shows how to commune with the body, the mind and the soul. It thus establishes a highly intelligent communication, or rather a perfect communion between the body and the mind, and the mind and the soul. It thereby brings a thorough understanding of one's nature so that one lives a profoundly positive life. Such an individual is at peace with himself and with his fellowmen.

Yoga is based on physical, mental, intellectual, moral and spiritual discipline.

A true aspirant must, after attaining emotional and intellectual stability, endeavour to identify himself with the *purusha*, the soul, through the path of meditation. Only then is a *sadhaka* raised from the human level to the

Divine. Then the sadhaka surrenders all his actions and "the fruits thereof" to the Supreme Force—the Lord.

It is only then that this great and noble art can assist in eradicating the impurities of the body and make it a fit instrument for enjoyment of life without abuse to lead one towards enlightenment.

ON FOOD

The type of food taken is important for the asanas. It should be neither too hot nor too cold, nor excessively pungent, sour, salty or bitter. Our outlook on life is determined to a large degree by what and how we eat. If each morsel is taken to enable us to serve the divine better, then one is along the right path. Whereas it is true that character is influenced by the food we eat, it is equally true to say that the practice of Yoga changes the food and eating habits of the aspirant. The sages tell us that Yoga is not for him who sleeps too much or keeps awake too much. Moderation in one's living habits are the rule.

ON THE EFFECTS OF PRANAYAMA

The practice of Pranayama brings illumination, as it purges the all-powerful brain and forces it to surrender to the seat of consciousness. Thus the impurity and the ignorance of the ego, which covers the self, are destroyed. In the movement of withdrawal, the senses are made passive, and act now as friends to guide the aspirant to the gate of peace. The regular practice of pranayama rids one of fear, develops strong will power and clarity and correctness in thinking. The mind is steadied, becomes stable, and fickleness is eradicated. Then the imposition of discipline is no longer forced but this is a natural urge for Sadhana.

ON SAMADHI

Samadhi is a feeling of existing in a state of complete peace and oneness with the universe. Here the ego is annihilated. One exists without the awareness of "I-ness."

There is no consciousness of mind, breath and movement, of anything, in short, except Infinite Peace and Joy *(Ananda),* which the senses cannot perceive.

This experience of bliss is the last stage in Yoga— that of Samadhi. Then this instrument, the self, is a fit instrument for God realisation. In all fields creativity means forgetfulness of the "I" consciousness. The musician can bring forth delicate and subtly divine sounds only by forgetting himself. The poet, too, distils the quintessence of language, and the artist presents the wondrous world of line and colour only by transcending the self. The yogi, too, is creative within himself, and the experience of this new creation touches a state where neither time, cause nor effect touch him. His forgetfulness of self is at the same time a sense of oneness, the awareness of an integrated personality. Body, mind and self are integrated as one, and in this unity purity and wisdom shine forth, combined with humility and simplicity. Such a person shines like the sun, which is impeded by no barriers or limitations. Not only is he illumined, but he illumines all who come to him in search of truth.

If, by the grace of God, a man born blind is granted a glimpse, for a moment, of the beauty and grandeur of the world, who would be able to measure his ectasy? In the same way, too, one glimpse of the Divine is worth all pain and hard work implied in the practice of Yoga.

YOGA AND DHARMA

Yoga is one of the foremost and most refined forms of

Indian art, based on an extremely subtle science, the science of the body, the mind and the soul. It is the wealth of wisdom that enables an insight into one's innermost being as it shows the right way to live. Is it not the highest philosophy which is a part and parcel of any true *Dharma,* as Dharma is universal?

Dharma is that which supports, sustains, upholds those who have fallen physically, morally or spiritually, or those who are falling, or those who are about to fall. It has no denomination and no frontier. It is that which is revealed and realized through divine inspiration.

Dharma is a code of conduct prescribed by the Vedas as one of the four ends of human existence. Dharma is the guide to living in the right direction.

Asrama-dharma still holds sway on society irrespective of colour, creed or nationality. There are four stages in a man's life. The first is *Bramacharya*—the period devoted to the study of the scriptures. The second is the stage of *Grhastha,* or the life of a householder—a harbinger for family and society. The third is the stage of *Vanaprastha,* or preparation of the mind for retirement from objects of the world. And lastly is the stage of *Sannyasa,* or renunciation of the material world in order to pursue the spiritual goal. It involves Chitta with a view to focussing on *Isvara,* the Lord and the Architect of the Universe.

The *Purusarthas,* which are ends pursued by man, are *Dharma* (duty), *Artha* (prosperity), *Kama* (pleasure) and *Moksha* (liberation). Dharma indicates the way of life, and Yoga takes one to the art of living a perfect life. Both Yoga and Dharma are refined after thorough discipline, defining each movement in action, thought and words for the betterment of the individual as well as humanity.

Dharma has its own scientific techniques like Yoga, in order to move from *Avidya* to *Vidya* (from the darkness of ignorance to the light of knowledge), from *Apurna* to *Purna* (from the incompleteness of death to the fullness of immortality). Man is blessed with hands, heart and head which correspond to *Karma* (work), *Bhakti* (worship) and *Jnana* (wisdom).

IMPORTANCE OF SARIRADHARMA

"Sariramadyam Khalu dharmasadhanam" of Manu and *"Nayamatma balahinena labhyah"* of *Kathopanisad* amply illustrate the great importance of physical well-being, not only for enjoyment *(bhoga)* but also to be free from disease *(roga)*. A weakling cannot realize *Atman;* neither is sadhana possible without peace in the body and poise in the mind. In order to have both poise and peace, the *Yoga-dharma* has been placed in the first order. Yoga has no nationality, caste, time, age, sex or dogma. As it is for all men on earth, it is no doubt a universal culture. Dharma is the culture of the self, and so is Yoga. It makes its *Ksetra,* i.e. the field or the body, pure and holy for the *Ksetrajna (purusa,* or the self) to dwell in.

Yoga is divided into *Bahiranga-sadhana, antaranga-sadhana* and *Antaratma-sadhana. Bahiranga-sadhana* comprises ethical practices in the form of *Yama* and *Niyama,* physical practices in the form of *Asanas* and *Pranayamas. Antaranga-Sadhana* is emotional or mental discipline brought to maturity by *Pranayama* and *Pratyahara,* while *Antaratma-sadhana* is brought to maturity by *Dharana, Dhyana* and *Samadhi.*

One who pursues the knowledge of the self should not neglect the body. Is it not abuse of the self if a part of the self, namely the body, is neglected? Is it not necessary to be completely aware of the body so that one is totally aware of the self? By practising Yoga, a sadhaka gets the light of the self which leads towards God-realization.

The observance of Dharma also leads towards true realization where life and death are experienced as one. Yoga, too, brings the consciousness to a state of stillness with no fluctuating, no divisions and no dualities in the subjective or objective thinking, experiencing the state of stillness and silence. Both Dharma and Yoga lift the sadhaka from the state of being to the state of becoming, so that one lives in the state of pure, unalloyed Being.

As Yoga leads from the cult of the body to the culture of the Self, from individual to society, from society to the world at large, so Dharma, which is like a gigantic tree sheltering the whole of humanity, leads towards the path of righteousness; so that he who follows Dharma drinks the nectar of spiritual fragrance, the culmination of Dharma or Yoga.

THE NEED FOR YOGA EDUCATION IN SCHOOLS AND COLLEGES

Yoga is character building—the development of a character such as to ensure unity and harmony of the body, the mind and the soul—a well-integrated personality at peace with himself and with society.

"Education" derived from Latin *educare* means "to educe" or "draw forth" or "unfold" the latent or potential— that is, to develop the talents and gifts of the individual. In short, it is the drawing out of the best qualities of a person.

The daily practice of Yoga helps one to achieve a perfect understanding of the intellect of the body, for the body also has its own intellect. This knowledge of the working of one's own body is based on direct experience.

The pliability of the intellect and its capacity to learn from new experience leads one to true education as distinct from an education which depends upon information from books and lecture notes.

Yoga is a subject that has to be experienced, not merely discussed or argued about. Even if one wants to discuss it or argue about it, one has to experience it.

Through Yoga one attains not only physical well-being or 'toning' of the body but emotional stability and firmness of the intellect as well. Hence Yoga is an art which disciplines and develops the body, the emotions and the intellectual faculties, its purpose being to refine men.

It is a science, since it is a systematic study based on the principles so pithily expressed in the aphorisms of Patanjali and also in the other books on Yoga such as the *Yoga Upanishads.*

It is a philosophy, as it studies the principles of right conduct and shows thereby the road to right living which has a backing of centuries of experience.

One cannot emphasize enough the need of Yoga for our students. India is rapidly becoming industrialised and urbanised. We are thus heading for an era of speed, stress and strain. Such a life makes heavy demand on our nerves, which are but indivisible branches of the brain. When the nerves collapse, anxiety and neurosis of one kind or the other sets in. The individual becomes a nervous wreck. "Prevention is better than cure" and Yoga is the "prevention." It ensures strong yet elastic nerves that can face a good deal of hectic activity with equanimity and poise. It is, if you like to so put it, a natural tranquiliser and, what is even more important for a poor country like ours, it can be taught without heavy financial investment or equipment, a large hall or a building and the rest of the paraphernalia. It could be done at any time, according to one's convenience. Why, it could even be suited to the needs of the undernourished or the over-fed.

In fact, after years of teaching Yoga I feel so strongly on the subject that I would insist on withholding the award of a degree to a student unless he is found fit not only intellectually but physically too. At the same time I would not consider an athlete properly qualified unless he is also intellectually developed.

What I wish to emphasize is a harmonious all-round development of the student in the body, the mind and the spirit, a well-rounded personality with a strong character. Only such students can build a healthy, just, honest, self-reliant, independent and, therefore, a healthy and a happy nation.

THE IMPORTANCE OF ASANAS

What is it that keeps us from pain and sorrow? Health of the body, mind, and soul alone can make us live happily from birth till death. Health alone can enable us to die nobly and majestically. Health is not a commodity which is gained by swallowing pills. It has to be earned by hard work and discipline. One has to exercise in order to keep the muscles, the organs, the nerves, the glands, the flow of blood, and the systems of the body in proper condition. The entire human system should be well-regulated like the rising and the setting of the sun. Then the mind becomes free from the shackles of the body, unattached from the dictates of the senses, and becomes attached to the source of all knowledge, all actions and all emotions, that is *Atma* (the soul).

The body is the only capital that the Soul possesses and it has to be taken care of, whether it is used for pleasure of the body or realization of the Self.

Today we live an artificial life, have artificial foods, stimulants for sex, and tranquilisers for sleep. Yoga asanas have stood the test of time; they stimulate the system as well as tranquilise it as the occasion demands.

Asanas restore the balance in the system, making the body fresh and clean. Asanas have to be performed with even, flowing energy and with dynamism, creating new avenues and hopes as mankind is ever dynamic and looks for further expansion in knowledge and experience. Asanas should never be done mechanically, for then the body rusts and the mind stagnates.

If *Sirsasana* is done accurately and precisely no weight of the body is felt and the brain gets the sharpness. If *Dwipada Viparita Dandasana* is done, it not only makes the brain sharp, but alert and active. If *Sarvangasana* is done, the brain remains sober with no negative or positive changes in the brain (both are evenly balanced) whereas in *Halasana* or *Uttanasana* the brain becomes empty, silent, non-creative and one hundred percent receptive. If *Setu-Bandha Sarvangasana* is done, the brain becomes full, non-oscillating, silent and one hundred percent positive and creative. When *Paschimottanasana* is done, the whole physical body feels the peace and poise in each life cell. If *Baddha Konasana* is performed, the bodily desire for sexual union diminishes, while in pranayama the mental desire for sexual union diminishes. Like this, each aspirant can trace the effects of asanas by religiously performing them with an open mind to see what comes.

There are two ways of doing asanas, either with *ajnana* (without any thought behind them) or with *prajnana* (with fullness of thought). While performing asanas, the spine, the arms and fingers, the legs and toes, the skin, the fibres, the membranes of nerves and muscles, the organs, the intelligence, even the very Self, should be

175

sharp, mobile, alert, alive, observant, and receptive. Activity and passivity must go together to get the best effect from each asana. And that is Yoga—Union, or total integration while performing the asanas.

As a healthy tree alone bears healthy flowers and fruits, only accurate performance of asanas gives one a healthy personality, peace to the mind, and poise to the body. Perform asanas with uninterrupted awareness and undivided attention *(vivekakhyati)*. Do not perform asanas mechanically, with the mind wandering elsewhere. Perform with total movement and involvement. Penetrate the intelligence from one end of the body to the other, vertically, horizontally, circumferentially as well as crosswise. This will bring uniformity and harmony to the body; it will sculpt the body to bring out its latent beauty. Just as a goldsmith beats and melts the gold to remove impurities, the yogi performs asanas to remove toxins that accumulate in the body. It acts as nature's gift, dissolving all types of complexities and enables us to come to simple living and high thinking.

Perfect performance of asanas does not bring one to the state of body consciousness alone. It rather frees one from the limitations of the body and sets one free, sublimating the mind with the Self. As a devotee surrenders his or her all at the feet of the Lord, the practitioner surrenders, merges, and becomes one with the asana. There is then no difference between the knowable, the knower and the knowledge. There is only the experience of that which is true, good and beautiful.

The asanas affect not only physical, physiological and biological changes, but also psychological ones. The aspirant does not take up the practice of the postures for the sake of sensual pleasure or showmanship. Rather his practice is directed towards life and in the spirit. It is fallacious to believe that the maintaining of a posture in comfort for a given length of time means mastery in Yoga; for a sitting posture alone will not eradicate the scores of evils and infirmities man is heir to. Nor is health to be mistaken for mere existence. Health is the delicate balance in harmony of body, mind and spirit, where physical disabilities and mental distractions have vanished and the gate of the spirit is open.

The most important effect of performing asanas is to bring the mind closer to the core of being, as it naturally likes to remain attached to the body, senses of perception and organs of action.

According to Patanjali, the mastery of the asanas leads to freedom from dualities. The duality between the body and the mind and of the mind and the soul vanishes and results in tranquility. To live in the Infinite is the result of Yoga. This happens only when the aspirant's attempts become effortless *(Sahajavastha)*. Though he gains in health, strength, firmness and lightness, his knowledge becomes more sharp, yet at the same time humility increases as the ego slowly dissolves. Thus the practice of Yoga makes possible service and sacrifice.

INTERVIEWS & COMMENTS

PERSONALITY THROUGH YOGA

(broadcast on All India Radio, in 1958)

Mr. Pocha: We all know that Yoga can play an important role in building body, but this evening I have a very fascinating aspect of Yoga to discuss with you. The subject is "Does Yoga help in building an individual's personality also?"

Mr. Iyengar: The subject is indeed fascinating but first of all for my benefit could you tell me what you mean by personality?

P: I shall have to give you a very common definition of personality. By personality I mean that attractiveness in an individual which commands attention and respect of the people towards that individual. The man or the woman may not be handsome or beautiful but he or she may attract attention. It does not necessarily mean beauty.

Iyengar: Thank you. I take it that your definition of personality does not mean external appearance only. The personality is thus an integrated whole. If so, I can say with confidence that Yoga plays a very important role in developing such a personality. Here I might say a few words about what Yoga is. Patanjali, the Father of Yoga, in the Yoga sutras says: *"Yogaschittavritti Nirodhah,"* which means controlling all the activities of the mind and bringing them into a single pointedness. That is Yoga. It is a science dealing with the mind. Mind is the mirror of the soul, because the soul is reflected through the actions of the mind and the body. You will agree that it is more difficult to control the mind than the body, because the mind is more subtle. The mind is easily attracted towards external objects. If I might say, to draw the mind back into internal thought or internal world is Yoga.

P: Before you proceed further may I ask what you mean by internal thought or internal world?

Iyengar: By internal world I mean the knowledge one acquires as to what is happening inside our system, which is the internal universe or you call it knowledge-space. Man has higher aspects in life besides material achievements. In spite of advancement of science and technology, material satisfactions do not lead us towards true happiness and joy. The mind always holds on to the senses for pleasures and pains. It is easily drawn towards the external objects through the senses. To draw in and study our reactions to our thoughts, words and deeds is the internal world. The *Kathopanishad* has the following parable. Our senses are like horses, the body is the chariot, the mind the reins and the charioteer is the soul or the spirit. If the reins are let loose the horses run wild and end in disaster. Similarly the mind wanders when undisciplined towards the external world. To discipline and control it is what the science of Yoga teaches. By such discipline the energy is saved, which is used for right living, right thinking and right understanding of oneself. In short I say that it teaches the true ART OF LIVING. This is the internal thought.

P: Well, I think I get some idea. But then how does Yoga influence our minds and where does our personality come into it?

Iyengar: The body is the temple of the spirit. The body is the effect and the mind is the cause. If the cause is in the right path, the effect also is in the right line. For example, if the body is healthy, the mind also becomes healthy. If the mind is not healthy, the body does not function properly. Watch, when a man or person gets annoyed or irritated very easily, his nerves are disturbed, thus his bodily activities are also disturbed. Take the case of a sick person; he is more irritable, has less poise than a physically fit individual. So developing the body is a means towards disciplining the mind. But both these disciplines help one to develop personality.

P: Do you mean to say that if I have a very strong mind I can develop my body without the exercise?

Iyengar: That is possible, but this would apply to a very few individuals, those who can control the body through their mind. What we are interested in at present is that the common man should develop his body, and through this, the mind and his soul. The normal common man had more of the animal instincts in him, whereas the other instincts (humanity and divinity) remain dormant. Realising this, Patanjali, though he started with the controlling of the mind direct, later elaborated the "Kriya Yoga" (The Yoga of action) in the second chapter for the common man. He termed the eight stages of Yoga as *Yama, Niyama, Asana, Pranayama, Pratyahara, Dharana, Dhyana and Samadhi.*

These are again formed into four categories as ethical, physical, mental and spiritual. For a common man to curb his animal instincts he has to build up a healthy frame of body by asanas and pranayama (i.e. breathing exercises). By these the body is kept in a healthy state for higher aims in life.

Also it is not considered possible to have a healthy frame of mind without moral character. So Yama and Niyama are essential. The practice of Yama is non-injury to others by thought, word or deed, to be honest to oneself, truthfulness, chastity and non-covetousness. These are social virtues. Niyama forms the individual virtues. Purity from within and without, ardent penance for a cause, contentment, studying scriptures which deal with evolution of life, and surrendering of all our activities to God.

P: Thank you, but you have not mentioned anything about the development of the mind or the exercises that lead to it.

Iyengar: Well, now let me come to the point. It is called pratyahara in Yoga. That is restraining the senses. We should know the causes for the afflictions of the mind. Sage Patanjali has analysed that *Vyadhi, Styana, Samshaya, Pramada, Alasya, Avirati, Bhranti Darshana, Alabhda Bhumikatva, Anavashtitattva* accompanied by *Duhkha, Dourmanasya, Angamejayatva, Svasa-Prasvasa.* That is, weakness of the body and mind, dullness, not being able to form decisions, carelessness, illusions, laziness, instability, suffering from pains, diseases and despair, even the very breathing he says are the distractions from which the mind has to deviate. So the sadhaka after the above stated practices, develops to cultivate *Maitri*—friendliness towards people, *Karuna*—compassion towards inferiors, *Mudita*—joyfulness and *Upeksa*—indifference towards vices and virtues, pleasures and pains. When this is gained will he

184

not have a balanced mind? When the body is healthy, is one conscious of it? Are you conscious of your tip of the ear or tip of the nose unless there is a wound? So also when the mind is brought to a state of stillness what remains? The "Self," is it not? (When a fuel is extinguished from the fire, do you still see the fire or the flame?) So also when the *Vasanas* or desires (the fire) are extinguished, the mind is transformed towards knowledge and illumination. When you achieve such a state, there can be no greater glory nor greater joy. It is a state where the body, the mind and soul are one. That gives the personality the power to attract and no external beauty is considered. When you are aware in that state there is no place for dualities.

P: I do understand how by developing a healthy body one builds up a subtle and healthy mind. I can quite see your point that the mind and soul will reflect through one's body and naturally that is your personality, but now I would like to know how long does a man require to practice these yogic exercises to develop such a personality.

Iyengar: This doubt is as old as civilization itself. Realising that this very same doubt would occur to one and all, sage Patanjali explains *"Satu Deerghakala Nairantarya Satkara Sevito Dridha Bhoomihi."* If there is long uninterrupted practice without any disturbance, with a single-minded effort and determination, then you are the Master. Actually the progress depends upon individual ability, practice and perseverance. Some can develop very quickly. Then there is the other class of people whose progress is slow and they are those who are mentally under-developed and here the progress is slower. But when the mental attitudes are cultivated and practice is

185

intensive, the progress is bound to be quicker. One thing is certain, that no labour is lost, for whatever is gained is a permanent gain.

P: Is it possible for a man to learn these exercises without a teacher?

Iyengar: It is possible but not very advisable. There are certain exercises which cannot be done without an instructor and if undertaken without full knowledge may injure the body as well as the mind. Though it is possible for children to learn from books, do we not send them to schools? Why? So that they can follow the right method. The same thing holds good in the other fields.

Let me tell you how it may endanger the system. Take the breathing exercises. Breath is an indirect method of controlling the mind. If the breath is rythmic, the mind is in tranquility. When a person had lost his temper, his breath is fast. While he is in a state of joy, his breath is fine and deep. This I am giving you as an example to show how closely these two are connected. Even the authorities say, *"Yatha simho gajo vyaghro bhavedasyashanai shanai."* As you tame a lion, an elephant or a tiger very slowly and gradually, tame the breath. Still further the scriptures say: *"Pranayamena yuktena sarva raga ksyo bhavet. Ayuktabhyasa yogena sarva roga samudbhavaha,"* that is, if breathing exercises are done properly all the diseases will vanish otherwise all diseases are invited. By reading books one may do beyond one's capacity and invite danger. So is it not better to have the guidance of a teacher?

P: I see Yoga being a special type of exercise, is it possible for a teacher to teach more than one person at a time?

Iyengar: I think so. In my opinion it is possible for a teacher to give mass training. As a matter of fact I introduced Yoga for the masses when I trained students of different colleges and schools.

P: What time is it necessary to devote to these exercises every day or every week for acquiring this knowledge? Once one becomes perfect is it necessary to continue these practices?

Iyengar: *"Yoganganusthanat-ashuddhikshaye jnana deeptir avivekakhyate."* Through practice of Yoga the impurities of the body and mind are destroyed and the light of knowledge and wisdom dawns. Is there an end to knowledge and understanding?

P: What is the age limit? At which age may one start to learn Yoga? Can a man or a woman start at any age? Do the exercises differ for men and women?

Iyengar: Yoga can be practised by men and women of any age, whether weak or strong, young or old. In my own experience, I have taught Yoga to children from the age of five, to men and women of eighty. I recently taught Yoga to the Queen Mother of Belgium who is eighty-one. This shows that Yoga can be done by one and all. Only it has to be done according to one's age, circumstances and constitution. There is no different method for women. Only a few things are not permissible. That is all.

AN HOUR WITH SHRI B.K.S. IYENGAR

by Arvind Mulla

The West with its scientific mind has already understood the efficacy of Yoga, while in India the obsession with the supernatural rather than the therapeutic aspects continues.

Arvind Mulla: Is Yoga a science or art?

Iyengar: Yoga is both. Where there is a "technique," there is science. Yoga has its own technique of physiological, psychological and supramental well-being of man. So it is a science. Like a musician who plays with his instrument, the student or adept in Yoga plays with his body, depicting various animate forms of nature. Like the sculptor fashioning out a sculpture, the yogi chisels his body and mind and expands his consciousness into the universal.

If you accept the view that there is no art without philosophy, in which the practitioner is drawn to the shrine of divinity within himself, it is the art of living truly. Yoga does not express a view on life. Rather it is a way towards right living. Hence it is a science, an art and a philosophy. Yoga is a science of character-building or right conduct.

AM: Do you think a scientific approach towards Yoga will lead towards better understanding?

Iyengar: Science, no doubt, is a great boon to mankind. The extraordinary technological progress has yielded many benefits to man. Nevertheless, comparatively speaking, in the domain of the intellect, mind and consciousness—realm of the psyche—physical sciences have their own limitations. The importance of Yoga lies here. Mischief and mistrust belong to the field of the psyche. Hence, I feel that a scientific approach to Yoga (a corollary to the basic issue discussed in the first question) has a vital contribution to make towards the creation of a climate of better understanding.

AM: But, sir, to an ordinary mind Yoga means swallowing nails, drinking acid, gulping down snakes, walking on water and the like. Do you subscribe to this view of equating Yoga with magic and miracles?

Iyengar: Like anatomy, Yoga is a practical science dealing with human development. There is no question of miracles. What appears as a miracle to an ordinary person might be the manifestation of an established law in the realm of nature. Miracles have their own value in rousing the curiosity of men. However, Sage Patanjali, the Father of Yoga, warns the student of Yoga of the danger of *siddhis* or the power to work miracles.

Walking on water, swallowing nails and other such feats are all possible. These powers are the result of certain specific sadhanas. But these are all passing phases in the process of man's development as an integrated being. It is the maturity of body, nerves, emotions and intellect which is important to acquire perfect consciousness.

AM: Are you a hatha yogi or a raja yogi?

190

Iyengar: I am neither a hatha yogi nor a raja yogi. I am only a Yoga practitioner. It is not correct to demarcate Yoga into such artificial divisions as *karma, bhakti* and *jnana* except for theoretical purposes. The word *hatha* is composed of two letters, *ha* and *tha. Ha* is the sun or positive electricity, and *tha* is the negative electricity or the moon. The union of the two generates bio-energy. That science is hatha Yoga. *Raja* means king or soul. Raja Yoga also leads to Self-realization. Yoga as such is the science of an itegrated, balanced personality in which the intellect and the emotions are well blended.

AM: What, according to you, are the basic requirements for the practice of Yoga?

Iyengar: Patanjali speaks of *shraddha* (faith), *veerya* (courage), *smriti* (memory), *samadhi* (meditation) and *prajna* (uninterrupted awareness) as the basic requirements of Yoga. *Hatha Yoga Pradipika* mentions self-knowledge as the requirement of Yoga. Probably it means the urge to know oneself. I think the "will to do" is the *summum bonum* of Yoga. As one progresses in Yoga, character also improves. Fundamentally what is required is the tenacity of purpose, determination to work hard and complete faith in what one does.

AM: Is celibacy essential for practising Yoga?

Iyengar: Sir, I am myself a married man and a father of six children. That should answer your question.

AM: What about dietary discipline?

Iyengar: Geography has much to do with diet. Climate and such other factors influence the diet of people. But here are some basic guidelines. Do not eat if saliva does not spring from the mouth when food is brought before you. Secondly, when the brain alone speculates about the choice of food, it means that the body does not need food. Even then, if you eat, it will be non-nourishing. It will be an abuse of food.

Our mind is born of subtle elements of food. From this point of view, non-vegetarian diet may not be conducive to the development of the spiritual aspects of Yoga.

AM: Mr. Iyengar, you must have been practising Yoga for over forty years at least. May we know the basic situations that led you towards Yoga?

Iyengar: For my present position in relation to Yoga, two factors are responsible: first, my ill health in 1933, and secondly my devotion to Lord Venkateshwara. Later, in 1946, I and my wife had prophetic dreams suggesting an intuitive push into the field of yogic practices. Thereafter, with my Guru's (Shri T. Krishnamachar of Mysore) blessings, I used to practice for ten hours every day since the year 1935. Now yogic practices have become a part of my life.

AM: During your practice of Yoga, you must have come across different physical maladies and mental illnesses. Would you name a few, giving the time taken to cure them? What psychological changes do you find amongst your students as a result of Yoga training?

Iyengar: To mention but a few ailments cured by me through yogic practices: arthritis, slipped disc, polio, war injuries, injuries due to accidents, insomnia, glandular malsecretion, appendicitis, heart trouble, nervous breakdown, prolapsed or displaced uterus, virus infection of the spine, sinus trouble and nephritis.

I have treated these ailments in India and abroad. During my last visit to Mauritius, I was consulted about a case of cancer of the uterus. I suggested certain yogic postures and the operation became so easy that the doctors were amazed. After the operations, the doctors insisted that the patient continue the Yoga exercises under my direction, as they enabled her to regain her bladder control. A similar case was treated by me in London.

As regards the duration of yogic exercises as a cure, it may take a month or a year, depending on several factors such as the constitution of the patient and the degree of cooperation from the subject.

The last part of the question should be addressed to the students themselves. However, I can see the influence of yogic postures in their health and vitality in general.

AM: Then, according to you, Yoga has therapeutic value. How far is this aspect recognized in the world of medicine?

Iyengar: As I have already told you, doctors in the West have already recognized the therapeutic value of Yoga, mainly because the patients as well as the doctors have a scientific bent of mind. Unfortunately, in India the concern is more with the supernatural rather than the therapeutic aspects of Yoga.

AM: Is Yoga a mission or a vocation?

Iyengar: It is neither. I am attached to Yoga and still I am at an experimental level bettering the postures and the pranayama and dhyana practices in their minutest detail. For example, take *Sirsasana*. Is it possible to lessen the load at other places? Can we maintain the extension of the pose without straining the brain cells? Can we relax the brain, and to what extent? And so on and on. Or take pranayama. How to inhale, how to exhale? What are the things to be observed? How should we place the fingers on the nostrils to get the maximum benefit?

AM: Please tell us the technique of Transcendental Meditation.

Iyengar: Meditation is one. There is, according to me, no such thing as Transcendental Meditation. Raising of consciousness from one set of conditionings to another is the objective in meditation. When all conditioning ceases to operate for the meditator (the subject), then there is no meditator separate from the object (of meditation). The postures for meditation are simple, either *Padmasana* or *Sukhasana*. where eyes are drawn towards the seat of the mind (cardiac centre) with the spine erect and the brain quiet.

AM: What is your opinion about teaching of Yoga in schools and colleges of India? What do you feel about the teaching projects in foreign countries?

Iyengar: The teaching of Yoga—its theory and practice—is an excellent ideal. Unfortunately in India we glorify the past rather than the present. Brawn is ignored and brain is encouraged. Imbalance and bad health result. So, for a happy and healthy generation of tomorrow, Yoga should form an essential part of education.

At this stage it is necessary to distinguish between Yoga and other types of physical training or mass drill. How many of the students like physical training? I had the pleasure of introducing Yoga in Pune schools and colleges in 1937. I also taught Yoga in the National Defence Academy at Khadakvasla as an experimental measure.

As regards foreign countries, the Adult Education Scheme of the London County Council has introduced Yoga under my supervision. Since 1967 every year I train teachers to conduct classes under this scheme, and unless I certify no teacher is accepted or allowed to teach Yoga in these classes. In July 1971, my pupils at Brighton started the B.K.S. Iyengar Yoga Institute to teach Yoga and train teachers for Yoga-teaching in England.

AM: Yoga has entered the international sphere. But is not Yoga exclusively Indian?

Iyengar: Sir, can any science accept such narrow thinking? Is there American electricity or Russian cancer or European tuberculosis? Yoga might have had its origin in India but it belongs as much to a man in Moscow, Sydney or London.

Yoga is for all men, women and children irrespective of race, colour, sex, language or religion. Yoga after all aims at a union of individual consciousness with cosmic or universal consciousness. In this sense, Yoga as a way of thinking, feeling and living is truly international. To limit Yoga to the boundaries of one nation in these days of moon-landing is the denial of universal cosmic consciousness.

In order to do good you have to come out of your own soul,
your own self, is it not?

A VISIT WITH
B.K.S. IYENGAR

Importance of Alignment

Iyengar: I first used a prop in 1948 when I was not getting Baddha Konasana at all. I started using bricks, the heavy stones which were available in the street. But the ideas to use props really struck me in 1975 when the Institute came into existence, and I was planning what to put into it.

It wasn't until then that the idea struck me that alignment is the most important thing. Yoga is alignment. This word was there theoretically, but no one explained what it means. Everybody also said that asanas are only physical; they have nothing to do with the spiritual. That idea was also in my head and a means to guide me. I had to accept all kinds of stupid and wise statements given to me by people, then sit at home and toss them over. I asked myself, what is right, what is wrong; should I take this one's word or that one's word? I began to look at photographs of people, drawing lines between their way and my way of doing it, chest to chest, hand to hand, elbow to elbow. The poses were there, but not aligned. In head balance, the head was in one place, the nose another place, the chest another place; one leg was turning. I wondered why there was this difference. Where was that alignment that Yoga talks about when it says one has to be balanced?

In order to know what alignment is, it is important to realize that the centre portion of the body is the median plane in each and every part. If you take your finger and divide it down the middle, you get the median plane. When we stretch, are we in the median plane on either side, or are we overstretching from the median plane on one side, and understretching on the other side? If there is overstretch somewhere, there must be understretch elsewhere. The median plane is the God! It is what brings you to the art of precision. From the outer part, inner part, front part and back part—you always, have to measure how much you are extending from the median plane. There is no overstretch; you are balanced exactly in the middle.

On the Skin

Carol Cavanaugh: Could you talk about why the skin is so important?

Iyengar: When I did Yoga in the early days, I perspired tremendously because of the diseases I had when I was young, which were never treated. The smell of my perspiration was unbearable. In my heart of hearts I knew that I was definitely unhealthy, otherwise, why would it smell? I didn't follow the old theories; I felt that if you are sweating you should sweat. When I noted the water gradually changing, my attention went to the skin. I asked myself what is the skin's duty while performing asanas; is it just an anatomical cover of the body, or is it an organ of perception? The skin has to be expressing something within; how could it alone produce this smell? I thought about the skin. I would feel that while doing a pose there was no response, no action. I wondered why. Is my skin connected to my body, or is it outside of my body? If it is connected, then it should move also. So, let me learn with skin movement. When I started moving the skin, I realized that ancient people said the skin is an organ of perception. I soon noticed that the smell began to disappear. I would feel patches of skin and say this skin is thick—why? When I started working on this skin, it became thinner. I decided that the quality of the skin will tell the quality of the organs inside. That is why, even today, my emphasis in on the skin.

CC: You said in class that the flesh is anatomical and the skin is an organ of intelligence.

Iyengar: Yes. According to Samkhya philosophy, the five senses, the organs of perception, are connected to the qualities of the elements—earth, water, fire, air and space. These five senses are meant to feel the body temperature, the reactions to the poses, where heat is created, where it is not, when I am moving, and whether space is created in each joint. I take all these qualities of the elements as a source of understanding when I am doing poses. That develops me more and more.

The *Gita* said that theoretically the skin is the field, the intelligence is the fielder. The agriculturist acts as a fielder and produces something by cultivating a field. I use the body as a field and the intelligence as the fielder, to find out where the field and the fielder meet together, the body and the intelligence. I started balancing the intelligence on the anatomical body. Flesh is an anatomical system; the skin is an organ of perception. It is sensitive, unlike the muscles. If there is a formation of pus or something, it tells on the skin. Otherwise the disease remains hidden.

Role of the Diaphragm

CC: One of my favourite things that you say is that the diaphragm is the mediator between the physical body and the spiritual self. How?

Iyengar: The diaphragm balances our physical and mental body. When people have a catastrophe, depression, sorrow and miseries, they say their solar plexus is gripped. Why? What is the medium for our existence? It is the diaphragm. If the diaphragm is cut, can a man survive? Although it is a physical organ, you can see that it has tremendous bearing on the mental state. It is the only muscle which makes you draw the vital energy. When there is fear or sorrow, the breathing is heavy because the diaphragm does not take an aligned movement upon inhaling or exhaling. We pant and wheeze. Everything affects the diaphragm first. Someone comes up to you and screams, "I will stab you!" You hold the diaphragm. On the other hand, when you see the setting sun, or an old friend whom you have not seen for years, think of how you stretch the diaphragm. In Yoga we learn to develop the elasticity of the diaphragm. Pranayama plays a very important role, as do the asanas. In olden days people suffered from mental diseases; today there are stress diseases. They suffer the same. Why? Because there is no elasticity. Tension and pressure make the diaphragm harder. "I ought to be like that." "I have to be competitive in life." "Come what may, I want to take that challenge." Although they take the challenge from the head, where does it grip? It starts from the diaphragm. The diaphragm is the window of the soul. And since it is, the more tension you have, the more this door is closed. If the diaphragm is spread, it takes any load, whether intellectual, emotional or physical. If you shorten it, harden it, it has no room.

On the Medical Aspects of Yoga

CC: I would like to ask you a few questions about the medical aspects of Yoga. If you have an injured part of the body, most medical people will say to avoid using that part. Your approach is to make a point of working that area.

Iyengar: That is true. Suppose you have an injury to your heel. In Yoga there are two systems—a stimulative method and an irritative method. Other systems of exercise have no stimulative method to rest the injured part. If a runner has torn a muscle, he cannot run. If he does, he ends up in the hospital. With Yoga, there are movements which stimulate the injured part so it heals. There is a healing touch. We say to go ahead because the poses supply blood to those areas, helping them heal faster. Western doctors use ultraviolet rays to improve ciruclation. Yoga does the same thing. The poses bring blood to an area by stretching and blocking other areas. Supppose you do Trikonasana, for example. If you do it on the right side—because of the contraction on the right side and the extension on the left—the blood which is moving on the left comes here and is squeezed. So when you do it on the other side, the left side squeezes, because on the right side there is a freedom of stretch. It just flows. That's why we emphasize do this, do that. A weight-lifter develops his biceps and triceps; he develops his muscular body. But how many people ask how to develop the liver or the spleen? Your muscles become hard, but how do you get your liver in good shape? No way but Yoga, is it not? Yoga poses are gravitational movements which bring blood to flush an area, making it healthier. Gravitional forces have a tremendous effect. Whenever I teach, I bring attention to maximizing blood circulation, because unless and until the circulation improves, the organ will not be healthy. This is known as supplying the energy through the blood current to various areas, so the cells may become healthier.

CC: Are there any physical conditions that Yoga cannot cure?

Iyengar: How can I say that? An effort should be made. Even if there is five per cent progress, that is a success. You have seen how I work with children with genetic defects. Even if their progress is one per cent, I should consider it a great success. Yoga, being the art of action, has to bring an effect. I may not bring the maximum effect. Sometimes the seed may take two days to sprout; sometimes it may take one or two years. Perseverance is the key.

CC: We often hear people in Yoga talk about strengthening the nerves, a concept not often discussed in Western medicine. I wonder if you could talk about that?

Iyengar: No, it is not strengthening the nerves. It is the endurance of the nerves. The power of endurance depends on nerve cells. Nerves carry what is called bioenergy, supplied by the current of blood, like electricity. If there is a storehouse of this bioenergy in the nerve cells, then a person has tremendous patience. Their nerves are strong and can take it. If there is stress and strain, the person is spent like a man with no bank balance. The bioenergy system is eaten away by intellectual thinking, brooding. We draw all that energy from the storehouse, and we collapse. Because of the various stretches given through each asana, the blood current flows to each and every part of the body. Whatever energy is needed is supplied by the blood current. That is why pranayama is also essential. Without the respiratory organs, the blood is not supplied to the system.

Yoga does not eat away; it supplies. That's the beauty of it. When you do head balance, the blood is circulating to the head. When you come down, you feel completely refreshed. When you do *Setu Bandha Sarvangasana* on the chair, the blood is supplied to the chest. Naturally, when you come down you feel as if you are in a state of peace, of poise.

On Yoga and Mental Health

CC: Do you think people can reach a balanced mental state without Yoga?

Iyengar: It is very difficult, because of what I already said about the nervous system. Nerves are the unconscious mind; our brain and mind are the conscious intelligence. When the conscious intelligence is weak, psychiatrists will guide a person, but when the nerves have collapsed, they cannot supply energy, and shock treatment or sedatives may be suggested. In Yoga, there is tremendous feeding of the nerves to store energy in the nervous system. Then there is no possibility of the mind breaking.

I have seen people meditate without knowing that. There you get an imbalance. When people are imbalanced, not stable. . . in Western countries they give them medication. . . eh, meditation. Medication or meditation, these are the only two ways they know! Meditation is an introverted art, but they are already negative, so we have to make them an extrovert. They need the asanas and pranayama, which are extroverted arts. If an introverted person goes to meditation, they will become more diseased; that is why failure comes. Yoga says an extrovert should become an introvert; an introvert should become

203

an extrovert. When a person knows what extroversion and introversion are, he is complete. To a negative person meditation is a negative approach, so he collapses more and more. That is why we have to study Yoga—to know when it should be adjusted. Even Yoga can bring disease. A wrong practice, a wrong method adopted at the wrong time, will lead to various complications, or a right practice at the wrong time will create problems to the practitioner.

On Psychological Aspects of Yoga

CC: We know that incorrect practice of Yoga can cause physical problems. Could it also cause difficulties in the psychological state?

Iyengar: Yes, yes. The first thing is irritability. Because they read books, they say, "I have improved in Yoga; that's why I am irritable, because I don't like worldly matters." But they don't realize their own mistakes, they don't go into them. I ask myself, "Why, when I was not irritable yesterday, am I today? How can that happen? Something is wrong, my nerves are disturbed." As my nerves are disturbed, they become shaky inside, which creates that irritability. So I work; I say, "Let me see tomorrow. Let me see how I did it yesterday. Can I repeat that?" If I again feel the irritability, that means I have done the wrong practice. Just as you have to climb steps one after another, in Yoga you have to climb according to your capacity, constitution, strength and pliability. How much clarity do you have, how much confusion? If there is confusion, how can you run on ahead? Go slowly; get confidence. You have to think all these things. Then, Yoga is a friend; otherwise, it is a foe.

CC: How has Yoga changed your psychological state?

Iyengar: I had tremendous power to endure the pain as well as the pleasure. I used to go the depths of pain when I was doing poses. I had to struggle. But in that struggle I found out the range of pains which came to me, and I absorbed all those things. After absorbing, only I knew what is right, what is wrong. If I get a little pain, I will not run away from that pain. I say, "Why did that pain come? Is the pain on the other side also? If the pain is not on the other side, why is it paining on the first side?" My logic commences at that moment. When I understand myself, I know what happens to others. That's why I am so quick. If someone says, "I am getting this pricking pain," I say, "Your hand is placed wrongly." I correct the problem immediately. Unless I had suffered that, how would I know?

On Role of a Teacher

CC: How do you see your role as a teacher? What are you aiming at when you walk into the classroom and see a group of students in front of you?

Iyengar: No, no, no. One good thing is that I don't aim at all. But when I start working, I ask if it is possible to bring these people to my level in a shorter period than I took—that is the only reason why I am strong in class, but to others it appears as aggression. Why should they waste their time as I did in my earlier days—not knowing what alignment is, what rhythm is. My brain was thinking and my body forgetting, or the body remembering and the head thinking elsewhere. All these things I had to face in my early days. Is is essential for everyone to go through that? Why not show a direct path and go?

CC: When do you think a student of Yoga can start to teach? Are there certain characteristics that need to develop before a person can begin?

Iyengar: Confidence, clarity and compassion—these three are sufficient. Clarity, because if I have to teach, I should be clear in what I know. Even if I know ten poses, I should be clear in those ten poses, so I can say I know these ten. If somebody can teach you twenty better than I, you'd better go. If something is new, I will not try it on another person; I will try it on me and face the consequences, but I will not take a risk on others. That's why I can talk confidently; I can give confidently. I know to what degree a raw body will give. I imediately calculate that a certain movement will give such-and-such a person a certain feeling. Because my body is so sensitive, so elastic, I have to overstretch to get that extra feeling. I have to struggle more than others. I have to penetrate deep inside. I get clarity myself, then I give.

CC: Do you teach Westerners differently from Easterners?

Iyengar: No, not at all. That is a misunderstanding. But, of course, for your people, whose intellect is too strong, I always tap that intelligence to use it on the emotional area. Our Easterners are very lethargic. I have to behave like a slave driver with them. If I were like a lazy Indian, I would probably not have come to this level. Having worked so hard, I know how much effort it requires to experience this. Here, in India, they are emotionally good; they can bear the pain. Though they go on saying I have a pain here, I have a pain there, they will not cry. They will only complain. Western people want to solve everything intellectually, even the poses. An emotional disease has to be felt emotionally. These are emotional diseases, so I have to think emotionally what things to give to this person. I cannot solve intellectually. I can intellectually think and emotionally act; here emotion stands for compassion, friendliness and dispassion. I have to think of what area affects him. What is the feeling? How does his mind behave? I have to feed those areas.

On Creating Awareness

CC: You explained in class one day why it is that you slap people in class, and how that brings awareness. Could you repeat that?

Iyengar: Actually, the word is not "slappping." The dull part is very, very insensitive. With all the power of their intelligence, students may still not observe that the part is weak. I go and give a certain movement according to the demand of the skin, ribs or muscles. If it is too dull, too broad, my fingers also become broad. According to that instinct, I immediately adjust to give sensations to them. In that sensation, I create action, and they get the pose. Do you follow me now?

CC: Yes, I've had direct experience of your method. (Both laugh)

Iyengar: You may be intelligent, but cannot use it because you cannot penetrate that area. Why waste forty or fifty years? Learn quickly to observe these things. But if I allow you, it may take a long time. I am creating intelligence in you now. Previously I was making you do it. That is not creating intelligence. It is only showing that I can do more, I can teach you more. I have made a constructive change in my teaching method, so you can learn and become an original person in your practice. I have been doing this for the past two or three years. I am giving a link in the chain, making you understand that the knowledge grows in you subjectively, rather than coming objectively from me. I am making everyone become more and more sensitive. Previously I had to work like a donkey to build this up, to create interest in each and every one. Today, the interest has come in you. Now what is my job? It's not necessary to create further interest. I have to ignite the fire in you by making you understand yourself, more than by my showing you. My little touch creates intelligence in you. You start working from that point, remembering that Mr. Iyengar touched you there.

CC: Do you have anything more you want to say?

Iyengar: Yoga is a light which, once lit can never fade out. The more you do, the brighter the flame burns in you. Yoga is a fountain for all things in the world. It has been given to us, but we do not know how to make use of it. When we know, the whole world will be revolutionized.

Excerpted from "A Visit with B.K.S. Iyengar" by Carol Cavanaugh. Reprinted, with permission, from *Yoga Journal,* July/August 1982. Copyright © 1982 *Yoga Journal* August 1982.

B.K.S. IYENGAR
TALKS ON YOGA

Karin Stephan: Mr. Iyengar, you've worked with Westerners for over thirty years; in what way do you feel that the Western person needs Yoga?

B.K.S. Iyengar: For the simple reason that though they have tremendously developed their sense of comfort, they have had to use their limbs less and less. Due to this lack of movement in the joints, the nerves start constricting, and passages in the arteries become narrowed, so that the diseases start increasing. Not only the West, but also the East had to adopt Yoga. At one time those from the East had to struggle very hard to keep up the movement of their bodies to maintain a certain amount of good health because they were under-nourished. But as the comforts started coming to them as well, their health also started taking its toll. So Yoga really has become an essential part and parcel of our lives, not just as an exercise but as essential as food and rest are to the system. Of course, Yoga is not exactly an exercise, but as a layman we must understand these postures where each and every joint is thought of, made to feel, made to function.

Secondly, Yoga is an all-around exercise. Here when I say all-around, I am not speaking from the physical, psychological, intellectual and mental level. Nothing can be forgotten in Yoga, whereas in other types of exercises emphasis is given to one part or the other. But if you take Yoga, you can really call it holistic because it works from the physical field to the field of the spirit. In that sense, it is an all-tonic exercise: nothing is neglected. Yoga is going to play a tremendous role as science develops.

KS: Do you feel that Westerners tend to be more apathetic, more lethargic than the people of India?

Iyengar: No, not lethargic. You see, unfortunately the West, having developed tremendous objective knowledge, has not resolved the problems of human suffering. Emotional diseases—such as high blood pressure, diabetes, impotency and depression—are only dealt with in a mechanical way in the West. But that's only handling a part of the human being. Even sex life is thought about intellectually, but it works not only from the head but also from the heart. So there is a tremendous necessity to blend and balance the intellectual and emotional centers of each human being. Intellectual development is a vertical development, like reaching the moon, but horizontal development is how we behave humanely, compassionately with one another. And yet today it just goes mechanically like computers and automobiles, but the human touch, the human feeling, has gone away. Yoga is a subject which brings this humane awareness back, and that's its beauty. We're all victims of emotions more than anything else, so being the victim of the emotional side, Yoga then plays a very tremendous role because one has to work from the very core of one's being, the source of one's consciousness. From there the action sprouts out, and the emotional center is touched by the practice and teaching of Yoga. But one has to develop this aspect of intelligence, what you call the emotional center. Yoga is a key because whatever one says, science has not tested the emotional harmony of a person when he practices Yoga. Yes, they have tested the blood pressure and found it has gone up or down, but what about that internal feeling?

If all of my pupils, when they have finished and experienced the joy they got out of Yoga, make up their minds to go out of their way to help humanity through Yoga with compassion, I am sure the initiated too will have the same feeling of joy. Like this, the world will be full of contentment. This subject has been lost in the West, as they saw only on the intellectual level and developed vertically, but now they are trying to develop horizontally and are beginning to see the true value of Yoga and meditation.

KS: Mr. Iyengar, I often heard you speak of Patanjali, that you wanted to look at him again. Could you comment on your perception of him?

Iyengar: You see, for example, how everybody speaks of Yoga as a philosophy and that it has nothing to do with the healing aspect? But if you go back to the second sutra of Patanjali, he gives what I call a mental shock treatment. Patanjali, in fact, never spoke on the philosophical level, but gives the therapy: *"Yoga chitta vrtti nirodha"* (Yoga is the cessation of the fluctuations of the mind). *Vrttis* are the thought waves which change from second to second, and that is what we have to attack. So is Yoga a therapy, or a philosophy?

Then he says, "Wherever you have contact of your mind, your mind rests there; it cannot go into the spirit." And where does it rest? He has given the examples: disease, languor, illusion, doubt, avariciousness, sensuality. He gives lots of examples such as sorrow, heavy breathing, or trying to reach a goal and stopping in the middle, or after acquiring a certain state, being complacent in it. He also said those things are illnesses. So those feelings keep the mind in contact with that idea of a disease: "I've got high blood presure; I've got heart palpitations; I've got acidity." So one's mind is nearer the problem; it does not see elsewhere. So in order to treat that, he gives various therapies: concentrate on certain points; concentrate on whatever object appeals to you, or do pranayama; do all the eight aspects of Yoga, or concentrate on a light, or think of an ideal person. So he gives several ways which are known as therapy and various means to each individual to find out for himself which of the therapies suit him.

Then it is all acquired by the practice of these eight aspects of Yoga and the various means which he gives— such as friendliness, compassion, gladness—so there are all these healthy ways he gives. In those healthy ways, he says, you will experience your mind as being like the even surface of a lake. Though there are lots of currents underneath, your consciousness in that state will engulf your field (the body) without any fluctuations. When you reach that state—the purity of head, heart and mind—then nothing but peace flows in it, and this peace is the highest nectar of life. To experience that elixir of peace in each and every cell, as if consciousness is resting without any disturbance, like water spreads on the floor to find its own level, so in the body the consciousness spreads everywhere. And when it spreads everywhere, it means that that person is absolutely free from pains, sorrows, prejudices, cleverness and all those things. So that is known as the river of peace which flows in you, and that is the effect of Yoga. For me it is very important now, because there is unhappiness, both physical and mental, and not one person can say he is one hundred per cent happy, one hundred per cent healthy.

KS: Do you understand why you chose to take the burden of other people on to such an extent?

Iyengar: No, I did not take the burden on my own self. Somehow or other circumstances or environment pushed me to take this responsibility. Whatever came, I had to go with it. That made me give out all my affection in such a way that it appeared, for any observer, as compassion. If I have to bring my child up, I have to be strong; I have to find out whether the child is working or not, whether he's growing up or not. So all that we want in our own children, twenty hours a day, is their health and happiness, for their growth. So in that case, parents sometimes have to use that force that they use only with love and affection. So the same way with me. All my pupils do not belong to me, but when they come to me, I have to take that step, and it is my duty to see why they have come, in order to get some happiness. It may be a physical problem to be relieved, or it may be a spiritual problem. They come with some hope. If I give them that hope by hard or soft means (probably they get it sooner if I use the hard means) then I feel that I have done my job well. So that is how I see the face of God. And secondly, you should know that God exists everywhere, whether we see him or not, and every human being is a part of this divine force. So even if I lose my temper, I am serving that God which is within the body of that student. And that is why I go out of my way in all of my patience which you have observed, to have my students go beyond their capacities, because God exists in their hearts too.

KS: Yes, by demanding so much of us, you are challenging us to be our very best, which doesn't happen very often in one's lifetime.

Iyengar: That is why one day I told you that emotional expansion of teachers has disappeared. They are very petty. They've got small eyes, small minds, but they expect big things. In order to do good you have to come out of your own soul, your own self, is it not? Anyone who protects himself or herself, how can he or she serve people? We have to give our lives as teachers. In order to serve the God in you, I have to come out of myself. If each and every one thinks like that, the society will be different; we will all be different.

KS: So in a way what you're saying is that basically our sicknesses are first spiritual?

Iyengar: No, sufferings are not spiritual first. There are different types of diseases. What, for example, do you call allergies?

KS: Allergies are something that create a reaction such as sneezing. . .

Iyengar: But why do they call it an allergy? Because there is no name for it. The causes are not known. They just say you are allergic to this, to that. But why are you allergic to certain things? Our tradition says, "This is your fate, where your past lives come in." The West would not agree with this point of view, but the East believes it. They say this is our past evil karmas which are playing their role now. This is one kind of disease. The other is due to outside forces, such as that coming from the five elements: a cyclone, or something which disturbs the harmony and creates mass destruction. These are really, of course, outside the individual's power. But what comes from within each individual, which many people think is

214

spiritual, is not really. It is our mind that does it to us—that is what Patanjali gives us as the first sutra, *Yoga chitta vritti nirodah*. Because the mind is wandering, hankering for many things, it cannot remain stable, so whatever it sees it wants, and wants to enjoy it. That is man-made disease, not spiritual disease, and the only way to combat it is through Yoga.

KS: Because if we create it ourselves, we can also undo it?

Iyengar: But how do I know this? People have different ailments, different psychological fear complexes, and how do I work for them? I have to work with them physically. I can't say, "Your mind is weak so you do it." Because when you have a certain psychological weakness which is taken by the heart as if it is going to burst, there must be some physical weakness somewhere for you to elaborate on it so deeply mentally. So we say that there is a seed of the physical in there. Through Yoga we work with physical weaknesses using certain postures, by which the student develops confidence. That is what the Western people call a feedback system. So we make our own blood, our own vital energies, circulate vigorously through the required parts of the body. If a person is suffering from the liver, it is up to the Yoga teacher to see that the student works in such a way that the liver directly receives circulation and energy. In order to hit one area, you have to go into that part by blocking the other areas so it circulates more—this requires tremendous affection to go into that.

KS: Do you feel that you pick up the physical problem in a person as soon as you see them?

Iyengar: Yes.

KS: Instantaneously?

215

Iyengar: Yes.

KS: So that everyone who walks in your door—you have a definite feeling for their particular problem?

Iyengar: Why did Patanjali use the words physical disease as his first words? Why not mental disease? He was a better scientist than today's scientists. Wherever there is a weakness, your mind is attached to that, so you cannot think of the soul. The moment the weakness is taken off, the mind thinks of the higher feeling. Till then it cannot.

KS: And this is why you feel that many people who do spiritual things without working through the body are hypocritical.

Iyengar: It's going to be a failure. It's bound to be a failure. Like meditation in Yoga is the same as a university degree in Yoga, but without the foundation. So without foundation, what do they get? Sensual quietness, but that sensual quietness is not going to eradicate disease. The senses have to be interpenetrated—if they don't interpenetrate each and every cell, one cannot be healthy. As I said in the classes, each cell has to feel the joy and satisfaction of having done its job. Then only is there what you call total happiness, not like, for example, when one says, "I'm happy, though I'm constipated." If he's happy, why did he use the word *though?* That means something is pricking inside. "I do get sleep, but my eyes pain." Haven't you heard people saying things like that? There must be something wrong in the eye, so that is happiness? That is what Yoga psychology is about. When he finishes that sentence, what words is he using? That is the clue for us that such and such a man has got a physical problem which we have to handle.

KS: So you're picking things up on all kinds of levels.

Iyengar: That even the patient will not be aware of. Unconsciously he says the word and that word gives the clue from which we develop the hypothesis and then we go into that without questioning. So the more I ask him, he changes his cause but unconsciously when he comes, we know it has started from there—like the branches of the trees going in different directions. His intellect goes in different ways, but the first few words give the clue to the cause of his problem that we have to work on.

KS: I think I remember you referring to yourself once as a gardener. So you have an image—do you see yourself as a gardener, a potter, a doctor?

Iyengar: Yes, as the farmer pays tremendous attention to the tree—how to clean it, how to keep it healthy, what to do, what not to do, is it not? He removes the weeds so that plants may not be destroyed by the weeds. So in the same way, weeds are created in the form of diseases. So each individual is a gardener in the garden of this divine body—so he has to cultivate, to fertilize as we use the word today. These are the words we use to bring that total attention to peep into the inner bodies more and more. Once that person knows the inner body, we know the causes of his weaknesses which can be brought out. Then, as I said, that river of joy, that river of enlightenment just flows without any obstacles.

KS: Can you feel even from behind you?

Iyengar: When I'm teaching, I'm nothing but fire. And the Fire of Yoga is to get rid of impurities. So when I'm there my job is to see that the body is purified, so the fire is burning in me, more than in you people.

KS: But this is an instinct that I think you have specially. . .

Iyengar: You can't call it instinct. It is intuition. It has been changed. Instinct is like animals. I haven't got that feeling because I've already conquered the instinct and turned it into intuition. So that's why one can see from the back. From instinct, you cannot see.

Excerpted from an Interview by Karin Stephan conducted in January 1983 and published in full in the *Iyengar Yoga Institute Review*, June 1984

A COMMONWEALTH INTERVIEW

(An excerpt from an interview Mr. Iyengar granted to students from the Victoria Yoga Centre, Canada, and Sydney Yoga Centre, Australia, in November 1985 and which was published in the *Victoria Yoga Centre newsletter* in May 1986)

On Teaching Yoga in the West

Mr. Iyengar: India is a hot country, even in winter; here a little rest does not disturb the body. The blood current will continue to flow to the extremities due to the weather conditions, so we can offer a little more explanation. Many Western countries are very cold; there if the explanations are too long, the warmth of the body disappears and it takes time to recharge that body. This is one way one has to adapt between the East and the West.

In the West, the teacher should be careful to see that the warmth of the pupils is maintained. When the body is cold even if the correct technique is given, the body cannot accept it; all explanations lose their charm. You have to demarcate how much you can explain whilst maintaining the body's warmth, and continue from there next time. But I am seeing that teachers try to explain so much in one day that they exhaust themselves as well as their pupils. Teachers should break their sentences, see whether their

219

words have been digested or not and whether the system has absorbed the instruction. Give it time. Then add a few more words.

In the West teachers are not differentiating between untrained beginners and someone who has been practising for years. They are all listening to the same instructions, but with an untrained student the teacher should say, "Stop now—because you're a beginner, you cannot take it." This has to be known.

When we give an intense course there is no uniformity in our dealing with the groups. We give these courses on condition that you have practised sufficiently to take our points, but many who come are very raw and haven't got much experience. Old students, new students—how soon we can see the difference! The intense course is too much for some. So we also have problems, but by looking we know exactly that we have to give points for the beginners and for toned up bodies.

Teachers should observe how much the pupil can absorb. The teaching is of absolutely no value unless the pupil can receive it. When we run classes we give our technique and present how the poses should be done because we know the subject, but at the same time we see what mistakes are happening. This is known as feedback. Teachers in the West must develop this feedback, capture the weaknesses of their pupils and build from there. That will make the teacher a good teacher, and also help the pupils—understanding will come slowly. Maturity in the pupils will come as the teachers mature. That is what I say is lacking and when that develops, I say "Wonderful!"

We teach asanas as living anatomists. Although many western people have an intellectual knowledge of anatomy and physiology and can name the different parts of the body, they don't really understand their functions. Only asanas can teach this. His leg is long, your leg is short. We cannot depend on anatomy alone to teach Yoga because it does not give the whole picture.

Analysis and experience should go together. Teaching is analysing, analysing the students—their mental calibre, their physical calibre—then discovering how to bring their deficiencies in par with their mind or their mind in par with the body. Sometimes an ignorant man does better than an intelligent man. Why does this man without brain present well? Why does this man with such understanding commit a mistake? Compare the bodies. That is known as factual intelligence from which you can gain the methods of teaching.

Yoga Centre: That's the science of Yoga.

Iyengar: Yes, that's the science of Yoga. I know the asana, I know the technique of the asana; but I also have to know how this technique is going to help the individual.

On Rhythm and Cycles

YC: In the Intensive, Geeta's explanations are very clear and I've appreciated the focus on each step and the progressions. She is really emphasizing the correct order of practice. Are you taking more time to emphasize this ?

Iyengar: Correct order means rhythm in the body, otherwise there is no rhythm. For example, take music, when you go to a high pitch in music, can you come suddenly or do you come gradually?

YC: Gradually.

Iyengar: Ah, now you have understood. When you go to the ascending order, don't you go scale by scale? When we finish the work we send the pupils away with joy because we bring them back to the normal.

In order to serve God in you I have to come out of myself.

For example, can you do back arch immediately?

YC: No.

Iyengar: You gradually build up to the back arch. After the back arch can you suddenly come back to forward bends? They are known as cycles. We can group these cycles but for certain persons they may not work at all, so we have to show another way according to their body. You know that in cars they have four or five gears. Can you change the gear without coming to neutral?

YC: No, you'd grind the gears.

Iyengar: It's the same in Yoga. We lose our tempers when we see people come and suddenly do the back arch, or suddenly they go back over the rope. What happens without coming to the neutral poses?

YC: Injury.

Iyengar: We are showing that cycle. You have to experiment on several people to know the ill effect and the bad effect. That's why we change immediately if something happens.

Take that girl in your own group who has been suffering since childhood with cough and cold, I changed the whole system for her. Only yesterday she said "Now I feel life is coming." I told her that she would have to stay here six months to get her life back, but she is only here for the three week intense course, so I cautioned her, "Don't listen to anyone else for six months but just continue with what I have given you. Don't change anything, and remember the cycle. With the same cycle, gradually increase the time and the endurance will come. Even if it's stale, you have to continue. Don't take a risk." That is known as rhythm. There should be rhythm in Yoga. In music unless there's tone and tune, do you listen to that music? What is body, after all, but an instrument

223

and the vibration is the sound, the tune? The vibration in my body must synchronize in my movement. That is why poses are done in a certain order.

For example, we recently started a class for beginners upstairs; I gave them a syllabus to use in my absence whilst I was in London. First, the teacher should demonstrate the pose two or three times, then stand and take the class. If the pupils have not understood, show it again twice more, and then the third time do it with them saying, "Look at me. Look at my leg. Look at my hand. Look at my other leg." In the beginning the teacher has to work thirty minutes and the pupil only twenty minutes. After one month the teacher will be working twenty minutes, the pupil will be working twenty minutes. After four or five poses have been taught, the first pose will be shown once and taken also once.

When I am doing the pose with my pupils my practice improves, and I know what to teach them next. As I am explaining I am looking at them to see what is missing. Capture one or two mistakes then teach the same pose tomorrow giving only one or two points—major points, not minor points. Until we bring the gross mistakes to the surface, we should not touch the finer ones. Gross points are important. You have to make the gross body a foundation to correct the finer points. Later, these finer points will give you the idea of rhythm and cycle.

Now, what is neutral? If you do a back arch, you can't immediately do forward bends. *Bhradvajrasana* is a neutral gear. How many people know the neutral gears? Three or four standing poses and in between you are made to do *Uttanasana*. It is a neutral gear. I am telling people now to trace the neutral gear. When they make a mistake, I bring them back to the cycle again. I also measure overdoing or underdoing the cycle. This prevents injury to any part of the body.

People say that I am an aggressive teacher, but I am an intensive teacher not an aggressive one. Do you mean to say that if I was of that type so many students would have followed me? These are political games that other people play which I have taken with grace, that's all. Nobody has practised the way I did. I never changed my methods. If I was wrong I would definitely have changed. I have seen the wrongs of my teacher and I have seen the wrongs of others, so they were all my teachers because I said, "Let me not do what they have done."

Once it so happened that my Guru was teaching a great lawyer—an old man who had some very great problems—and he said to me, "You have come from Pune. You have got young blood. I know that you can work better than your Guru. Can you show me?" I said, "Yes, but my Guru has to give me permission; otherwise I don't touch. How can I teach when my Guru is teaching you. My Guru has to give me permission." I saw what was being taught and I knew exactly what I could add, because of my practice—I was practising then, I am practising now. The moment I stop I will lose the intensity and have to depend on "don't do this" and "don't do that." Fear complexes will come to me. I have no fear at all because I am still practising.

This is the ethics of the teacher; explain less and do on your own bodies. For instance, when you say "legs straight," do it yourself and find out whether your own leg is straight. If not, this will amaze you and you will learn to use less words but to see the facts.

The rhythm is essential, then no dangers will take place. If someone does complain, ask what they did and then play with your own body until you understand how she or he did it and you know how to correct. Then the cycle will come to you. The cycle is important.

A teacher may be telling pupils to keep their feet straight but instead of looking at the feet will be looking at their faces. If I say "chest," I look at the chest. The teacher should co-ordinate his eye with his terminology. You go on explaining about the hand in full arm balance yet the legs are collapsing. When the legs are killing, how can I explain about the hands? I have to look up and down and see what is happening overall, not just forget and go on with the same point.

If you can put all this together then you will understand how to remove and lessen the pain. Cycles are a must. One link can pull the chain down. We have hundreds of links in our body: three hundred joints, seven hundred major muscles, and many other muscles around those major muscles helping them to function. One muscle is dependent on the other. We have to come to the basic end root to find where this muscle is holding. Then you will become a good teacher, the art will have a strong foundation which cannot be shaken because you have a grip of the art. This is what I want.

Intellectually you are all very good, but what about emotionally? Human beings live 90% emotionally. Can you stay one day in the Himalayas in a lonely place alone? It is a known fact that we cannot because we are all living emotionally. Mind is connected to the emotional feelings; brain is intellectual feeling. A balanced personality is one where the emotion is connected with the intellect and the intellect with the emotion. In Yoga, when we are doing the postures, we have to connect the intelligence with the emotion, emotion with the intelligence, and synchronize these two with the body. We have to use the poses, otherwise the mind becomes empty.

On Meditation

What is the difference between asanas and meditation? Don't you experience calmness and tranquility in a good head balance? Don't you experience serenity when you are resting very well in *Sarvangasana, Halasana* or *Setu Bandha Sarvangasana* on the prop? Then you also do meditation. In the asana you are connected and at the same time detached.

Meditation, as it is ordinarily taught, leads you to emptiness. There is a disconnection between the body and the soul and in between there is emptiness. But when you do *Halasana*, the mind is not distracted from the body or from the soul, and that is known as fullness.

People with emotional disturbances cannot meditate immediately but they can do Yoga. Haven't you seen that many people cry when they do *Savasana?* Those people cannot meditate at all. They become empty and fearful because there is no connection with where they are. They are up in the air, in suspense like a suspension bridge.

YC: When the emotions are out of balance then they can't meditate.

Iyengar: Ah, they cannot—asanas are more effective, Patanjali said: *"Prayatna saithilyananta samapattibhyam."* (II.47) and *"Tato dvandva nabhighatah."* (II.48)—By relaxation of effort and meditation on the Infinite, posture is mastered. From that (mastery of posture) there is no assault from the pairs of opposites.

Patanjali would have been a fool if he had said that these asanas are only for physical Yoga. *"Dvandva"* means split: in asana the dualities disappear. In medita-

227

tion dual personalities set in and create a fear complex. I can't face it! I can't do it! Whereas in Yoga it is not loneliness it is aloneness. Aloneness, fullness—everywhere you are there. You are in contact but alone. Hatred does not come in Yoga: "Oh I am far advanced. I don't want family. I don't want children." That feeling does not come in Yoga, in my method. Asanas bring the mind closer to the self without losing the contact with the external world, whereas in meditation, people get completely lost. They can't touch the internal world, they cannot come back to the external world and that is the problem.

That is why Patanjali has given meditation as the seventh stage, but today everybody starts there because that's the easy way. Patanjali has explained very well that an unbroken flow of thought without any feeling is meditation. It is not said anywhere that you have to close your eyes and sit in a corner.

The *Bhagavad Gita* says you have to keep your body as firm as a rock; from the centre of the anus to the throat, you have to draw a straight perpendicular line. You have to sit in such a way that there is parity between the centre of the anus, the throat, the front body, back body, side body. This is the art of sitting for meditation or pranayama. In pranayama the head is kept down whereas in meditation the head should be exactly in the centre of the throat so that it will not fall forward or back. Without using the body, how can you meditate? The *Gita* explains how one has to sit, but today they say "use any comfortable pose and meditate." After five minutes the person stoops forward and that becomes comfortable pose—so meditate on that. (laughter) Is it not a fluctuation? You have to learn why you stooped. Learn that deliberately.

228

When I sit, I am observing the behaviour of my cells. I am studying my own emotions. I am studying the working of my intelligence. Asanas lead to fullness, tranquility with fullness, not tranquility with emptiness. That's the difference.

On Teacher Training

YC: How should we approach training teachers?

Iyengar: Training teachers has to be considered in a different way altogether. I gave you the clue already—that the mature teachers should come together and have an apprentice course for themselves. Souls are not different, so we should not give much importance to our personalities. Instead of saying, "I am better than he," say, "Let me see what I can learn." I don't believe in a teachers' training course as it happens in the academic field such as bachelor of education. They give a class, and marks are given. You cannot take Yoga that way because Yoga is subjective; you are in contact with the person. As you come into the contact with the student whilst teaching so in an apprenticeship course the teachers should come together. You have to chart what is missing, what is not missing; how to link your teaching and their teaching together and form a uniform method which will act as a guide for those in training who will teach later. With Yoga you can't just give a teacher training course and say, "I have trained you, now go and teach." Where is the base for them? You have to give the base; and then build up from there. Give freedom in that base. Go at any angle, but always come back to the base. Train teachers who will be the cream.

First teachers of experience should come together and work themselves, then junior teachers should be called for a workshop and asked to conduct the class. "I give you a base, can you conduct a class within this base?" Then you can measure whether they are going beyond the fundamentals which you have given. If so, bring them back and remind them, "No, you are going too far away. I told you to teach from this base." When a musician is teaching, he says, "No, you can't jump there; come here, come to the scale." You have to find out whether they are coming to that scale. Then when they go, they go with clarity and without fear complexes.

It is an apprenticeship course when senior teachers come together and guide junior teachers. After guiding them make them conduct classes, see how they conduct, then wait. In the West they want to become teachers quickly. You have to tell them that there are pitfalls from becoming a teacher too soon before you have learned these things. After one year they will be a better teacher than if they began teaching immediately.

YC: I'm interested in why people start Yoga.

Iyengar: Because they cannot find relief from any other method. The gateway for human health is the respiratory system and the circulatory system. When you do *Setu Bandha Sarvangasana* the lungs expand automatically. In my method the process of breathing is increased indirectly even without teaching pranayama. That's why pupils find relief. The chemicals of the blood change, which gives them health.

For anything, a motive is necessary. So a cause is there—a cause in the form of pain, a cause in the form of suffering which makes people come to Yoga. The real religious practice commences afterwards. First we have to help them find relief, then we have to encourage them to get attached to the real art and science of Yoga and to live this art. 99% of the people who come are motivated only to get rid of their pain, and we have to work in that area alone. Don't injure them—even if you don't give relief right away it's all right, still you are safe, because when they can bear the pain that itself is progress. First give them bread, then they are stuck with that.

On Asana as Prevention and Preparation

YC: You talk about using your teaching for prevention.

Iyengar: It's a one hundred per cent preventative, sir. No question arises at all. It's a hundred per cent preventative, physically, mentally and spiritually. Suppose by the grace of God spiritual light falls on you; if your body cannot take it, tell me?

YC: Devastating!

Iyengar: Ah, devastating! I have to make sure that my nerves will be strong enough to take the light, the spiritual light easily.

Can we all live like that everyday, full of generousness in whatever work we do?

QUOTES AND COMMENTS

From B.K.S. Iyengar during his visit to
Southern California in 1984

From a speech he made at a party in his honor in Los Angeles:

Today you will see that for hours we were all together as a single soul which we call Yoga unity. Can we all live like that every day, full of generousness in whatever work we do? Let us have that delight which gives dessert to the soul, not to the stomach. Yoga gives this pure nectar—the art that gives real nectar to the entire system, the body, mind and soul. Not to stop for whatever comes in your way, so that you always drink the pure nectar forever. I hope that all of you come together and please allow this tree of Yoga to grow to such a size that it bears tremendous fruits of health, happiness and joy.

Following a student demonstration in San Diego:

The body is the envelope of the soul. If any of us neglect the body or abuse the body, we are abusing the very inner core of the body—the soul. If the soul is to remain free, the body and the mind have to remain free from the shackles of diseases, from mental ill health, or whatever it may be. Health cannot be earned without strength. Health cannot be purchased in the market. That's why the asanas have to be done without stop.

The body is a big self, the mind is a smaller self, and the self is the subtlest of the soul. As such, these three cannot be separated from each other. The intelligence, the mind, and the body are made to act, to think, and to function evenly. Then, the big self (the body) and the smaller self (the mind) merge as two rivers in the ocean of the soul. This is the meaning of Yoga. The experience of that state is the goal of Yoga.

Why do we do the asanas when we hear from many people that self knowledge does not require these postures? Asanas have two functions. They activate the brain to perform. Then, after performing, the brain receives knowledge thrown from the body and the brain reflects. This means posing and reposing going together. What is posing and reposing? As we are posing, we have to learn the art of reposing which is known as activity in passivity, balancing the activity and the passivity of the body, the mind, and the intelligence together.

While we are performing the asanas, the fibers (spindles of the flesh) send messages to the skin. How is the skin receiving the message from the flesh? If the muscles are too hard and if they hit the skin, the skin becomes insensitive and cannot receive the message from the body. And if the skin is too tight, then the flesh does not come nearer to the skin because it becomes insensitive. So while posing, while performing, you have to create tremendous space between the inner layer of the skin and the heads of the spindles of the flesh so that they communicate to each other and send a message to the brain. This is known as reposing, whether the communication received from the skin is right or wrong. Then, the brain guides the pose whether it's done well or not. This is how the asanas have to be done.

Why should the asanas be done? What is the technique? In common feeling, common life, the mind is very near to the senses. The communication between the senses and the mind is faster than the communication between the mind and the self, the inner being, the core of our being, the core of our existence. While performing the asanas, many of you must have felt the delight, the joy, the pleasure. Probably you may not know consciously why that bliss, why that joy is coming. While performing the asanas, due to the tremendous extension, creating vastness in the body, space is created between the senses and the mind, and the mind goes slightly far away from the body. Thus, the distance decreases between the soul and the mind while performing the asanas and the space increases between the mind and the body. That is why we feel the delight. By regularly doing postures, it takes a long time for the senses to send messages to the mind regarding attachments or desires. After finishing the asanas, for a half hour or an hour you have that delight. The mind is far away from the contact with the senses; but after some time, the mind and the senses come nearer. That's why the yogis say, "Go on practising." Continue your practice so that the mind is far away from contact with the senses, so that it will be connected to the self, so that it may move nearer to the self, so that the mind and the self may become one. That is why we are doing the asanas. It is for this purpose only that the asanas were introduced, not as a physical exercise, not as contortions. Many yogis say, "Why do you give pain to your body?" If the body is affected, I ask them, "Why do you give pain to your 'self'?" It is easy to say from the platform, "Be detached." Only one or two can be detached, not all of us. As we cannot be detached so soon, these asanas were given so that the mind can be drawn slowly and detached from the senses.

The divine marriage is between the element of body which is mutable, which is changeable, and the soul which is immutable, unchangeable and which is also existing within you. These two, having a divine union inside is the effect of asana. The body, the mind, the intelligence, which are the vehicles of the self get married to their lord, the self. That divine marriage is felt, and is experienced as eternal bliss which is unalloyed. Then we need not shout for peace.

If we have peace within us, peace will follow with others, too. Then the world is also in peace. To get that unalloyed bliss, please take to Yoga.

As long as there is the tremendous energy which these poses give you, there is no fear of death at all.

I am pleased that if I see so many people showing interest in this art, I think I have done some service to humanity. My pupils too, have worked hard to prove the value of this art to humanity.

As long as there is the tremendous energy, which these poses give you, there is no fear of death at all.

The FLOWERS

OUR BROTHER

by B.K. Doreswami and B.K. Vedantachari[1]

OUR FATHER WAS a retired headmaster in the Primary School at Naraspur near Bellur. He had no possessions and was not able to educate us beyond the High School. Our father had thirteen children. We are nine now with five brothers and four sisters. Sundara was born in the village of Bellur in Kolar District, Karnataka State, on December 14th, 1918. Our maternal uncle, Josyam Srinivasachar, a great astrologer of those days, had predicted that this boy born in the constellation *Bharani* has a great future and would shine as polestar of the family. Our father had great belief in this prediction for this boy.

Fate had it that our father passed away in his sixtieth year when Sundara was only nine years. This had a spell of gloom on the family. We had to bear great hardships to make both ends meet.

In his teens, Sundara had an attack of typhoid and was admitted into the Government Victoria Hospital, Bangalore. It became enteric and he lost the power of speech. We had lost hope of his recovery in spite of the assurance held out by the doctors. Much to our relief, after some months of strict diet, he was able to recover. But he became bony and while walking, he faltered due to weakness and terrible loss of weight.

Our brother-in-law, Shri Krishnamachar, a great Sanskrit scholar and an adept in Yoga, became Yoga tutor

241

to the late Maharaja Sir Krishnaraja Wadiyar of Mysore. The Maharaja, realising the value of Yoga, established a Yogashala in the Jaganmohan Palace, Mysore and appointed our brother-in-law as its director.

Sundara had completed VIII Standard. Our brother-in-law had come to Bangalore and he took him to Mysore where he completed his matriculation. By force of circumstances, young Sundara learnt the alphabets of Yoga under the guidance of our brother-in-law. By hard work and keen interest he picked up the art of Yoga with commendable proficiency which attracted the royal attention and he was encouraged to propagate the art of Yoga.

Sundara visited Hubli, Dharwar and Pune in 1936 and 1937 to teach Yoga. This inspired him to study Yoga seriously and paved his way to becoming a great Yoga teacher.

We deem it fit to recount his past to express our delight on the event of his sixty-first birthday.[2]

By his resolute perseverance, indomitable courage and drive, he gradually rose to position of eminence and glory. He had to struggle very hard for several years to obtain even minimum requirements in life.

Since he was unmarried and his activities many, we decided to have his wedding as quickly as possible in order to reduce the physical strain and bring cheerfulness to his mind. Our intentions bore fruit and he was married to a noble lady, Rama, in 1943. She was largely responsible in moulding his career in face of great adversities of life. She was a very good housewife. We were always treated with cordial hospitality by Rama and Sundara whenever we visited Pune, though their household was very modest during their years of struggle. She conducted the home with commendable efficiency. She exhibited perseverance and courage in fighting against emotions and desires

242

natural for a young wife. She infused added interest in him to go ahead in Yoga with dedication and practices. At no time she became an obstacle in his path. He travelled much and established the great Indian art with a scientific and modern outlook wherever he went. She bore him five daughters and a son who are all strongly dedicated to Yoga and doing the meritorious work. Providence was rather unkind and our brother lost her in his brim of life especially when she was most needed. How can we all, who knew her, forget such a noble, magnamimous and kind hearted soul? Admirers, friends and pupils of Rama, Sundara, Geeta and Prashant founded the Yoga Institute and named it after her. It is now known as **Ramamani Iyengar Memorial Yoga Institute**. It is unique in its plan and construction—a symbol of the Yoga system. It has become a centre of learning Yoga, and attracts men and women from all over the world.

Light on Yoga by Sundara is the outcome of his research and experience. It has been translated into many languages. He is relentless in his teaching and this is reflected in the book which has no parallel. He gives minute attention to all students alike and tries to make them perfect in the art.

To crown all these, Sundara is simple in his ways and humble in approach. His nobility, kindness, benevolence, large-heartedness, sympathy and philanthropy are household words today.

We are really proud of our gem of a brother. We pray God to bless him with long life to continue his noble work and dedicated service as a true karma yogi.

1. In India first comes the name of the village where one is born, then father's name, afterwards Christian name and last the community to which one belongs. (B.K.S. Iyengar).
2. The completion of 60 years and entry into the 61st year.

I was a little nervous about this. She looked so frail.

IYENGAR AND THE
QUEEN OF BELGIUM

by Smt. S.B. Taraporewala

In 1956, Menuhin introduced Iyengar to the Dowager Queen Elisabeth of Belgium. She was eighty-four years old at the time, and asked him to teach her *Sirsasana*—the headstand.

"I was a little nervous about this," Iyengar admits. "She looked so frail." But the Queen Mother was adamant. "If you can't teach me to stand on my head," said the royal lady, "you can leave." "From her manner of saying it," said Iyengar, "I could sense that this lady was strong-willed and had immense self-confidence." He had no option but to carry out the royal behest; he proceeded to instruct her and in time the Queen Mother of Belgium stood on her head in a perfect Sirsasana.

Just before starting a Yoga demonstration at the Queen's residence, Iyengar greeted her with a *namaskar,* and explained that this was the Indian form of greeting. She brought her hands together hesitantly, and returned the greeting, but asked what was wrong with the Western custom of shaking hands. Iyengar replied, "That is just a way of expressing your ego: I am a great person—you are

245

a great person. By folding our hands, we say in all humility, the divine in me salutes the divine in you." The Queen thought for a while, then said with a smile, "Let's do it both ways."

The Queen, a gifted sculptress, made a bust of Iyengar, had it cast in bronze, and presented it to him. Today, it is one of his most prized possessions, and has been installed in the Yoga Institute.

The Queen's Farewell

While in Gstaad, in 1965, Iyengar received a call from the Dowager Queen Elisabeth of Belgium. She had suffered a paralytic stroke and urgently needed his help. He flew to her aid, and within a few days taught her to regain some movements, so that she could once again hold a fork in her right hand. She was happy, and said, "That's good, but clumsy."

When Iyengar went to take leave of her, she held up her right cheek to him, saying, "Kiss me." He did so; she held up her other cheek saying, "The other side too." As Iyengar kissed her, tears rolled down the cheeks of the ninety-two year old Queen. She had taken very much to heart her parting with her Indian Guru.

A short time after they parted, the Queen died.

I never cease myself to be inspired by the sight, by the
spectacle, of a man who performs with no instrument.

Menuhin

WITH NO INSTRUMENT

by Yehudi Menuhin

Introductory speech before Yoga demonstration in Sanaan, Switzerland on the 15th August, 1966.

THIS OCCASION is for the benefit of a children's school in Bellur, in the State of Mysore, in India. It is an example of the faith, of the devotion that Mr. Iyengar has for his birth-place, for this Indian village. He never forgets his birth-place, and the more they need him, the more he remembers them.

This little village had had no school, and there have been at least sixty children who have not been taught to read and write. Perhaps by now we have all some misgivings about these things—reading and writing like all other things can be used to good advantages and to bad. Fortunately there is still sufficient innocence in India to believe that reading and writing are really only good and can only be good. In India the written word is only known, or has only been known, for thousands of years as the holy word, the word of the scriptures. They know as yet relatively little of the cheaper uses of literacy, but this will be a school which will fulfil the need of the village and will fulfil Mr. Iyengar's faith in his people.

I never cease myself to be inspired by the sight, by the spectacle, of a man who performs with no instrument. I need a violin to express myself, other people need all kinds of instruments, presentation of introductory words. He doesn't even need that. He doesn't need anything except what he has made of himself, what he is himself. Through his body, through his discipline, through his thoughts, through his art, through his purity, and in the best sense of the word through his simplicity, he has achieved a completeness of body and soul, a completeness of balance, completeness of relationship with his fellow men, which leaves nothing to be desired. Any one of us can meet him and feel that we have met a good man and a friend, a kind man, and goodness and kindness do not come without preparation. Without inner preparation you cannot ever be kind, without knowing something about yourself and having made yourself into something worthwhile, because if we do not use ourselves we might as well not be here at all. So Mr. Iyengar uses himself in a way that I think few of us have achieved. Some of us have achieved it in the communal sense, others have achieved discipline in a particular craft or art, but few of us have achieved discipline of himself. This is the greatest thing I can say of Mr. Iyengar and his art. I leave the rest to Mr. Iyengar to demonstrate.

You are going to see a man who is as dedicated to his art as any of us musicians or other people can be, but it is an art reduced to the very simplest, in a sense, yet of the most complicated, because it requires no instrument at all. It requires but the instrument you are born with, your body. There is no formal choreography, no script, no rules as it were laid for form, but all the rules of the choreographer and of the artist and the writer are inherent in the body itself, but to perfect this art requires a lifetime of patient and persistent effort towards trying to perfect this instrument that we are given.

Mr. Iyengar is a man like all of us. He has a family in India. He is devoted to his country and his people, and he is a young man. He is in that respect not like those remote sages of old, whom you can still see in India, with long white beards, orange robes with beads, and who are rather forbidding. He is a very warm-hearted and friendly person, but when it comes to his art he is exacting, tenacious and as fanatical as any artist must be. We have a lot to learn from him, a lot to learn from what his art has to tell us, because we in the West for the most part miss those very things he can show us—control over ourselves, ability to use what we were given to the best advantage to remain healthy and well and balanced to an old age.

CONTRIBUTIONS TO KNOWLEDGE BY MR. B.K.S. IYENGAR

by Bruce Carruthers, MD

How can i begin to describe the impact which the teaching of Mr. B.K.S. Iyengar has had upon me? Long imbued with Western scientific approaches to the body-mind and its functioning, I could scarcely believe my ears and eyes as Mr. Iyengar addressed processes and parts of me which I had been taught to believe didn't and couldn't exist, and obtained resonating responses. For Mr. Iyengar, in his books and teaching, is concerned with integrating the whole human being, not just those parts which can be efficiently and accurately approached with scientific instruments.

Science can be regarded as a method of generating objective knowledge in which the distinction between the knowing subject and the known object is clarified and stablized, with the systematic exclusion of all subjectivity from the field of the known. Its success depends on the prior distinction and separation of subject from object and on the reduction of all subjective entities to their objective correlates. Thus it offers a reduced view of human being, shorn of its subjective attributes. In the flows which constitute a human life as experienced concretely, prior to any reflection about it, science can "see" matter and energy, but it can't "see" purpose, value, will, intention, or consciousness, since these latter are methodologically excluded from its view. Thus science, while an excellent means of getting to know the objective attributes of human being, cannot be used to contact the complete person or to foster the integration of all his parts.

Yoga, on the other hand, is a method of discovering knowledge where each aspirant comes to know the self, the complete human being that he is and can become, prior to any analytical distinctions between this or that side of himself. Yoga *simplifies* the context of being a human so that the aspirant is his own body-mind field as he works with dynamic postures, breathing, and meditation. But it does not *reduce* human being to its objective or subjective side. Thus Yoga allows the self to contact its own vital flows of matter, energy, consciousness, purpose, mood, will, tendency, value, and meaning, at a level where these interpenetrate to form a unified continuous process, the flow of life. The knowledge generated in this process is obviously not a system of objective or subjective concepts, but is more direct, unmediated knowledge in touch with its own sources, those deep taproots, vital currents which found the very project of obtaining knowledge in the first place.

It may be said that by staying at the level of the lived body, yogic self-knowledge forfeits the clarity, precision and public accountability which was obtained for scientific knowledge by its reduction to objectivity. On the other hand, yogic self-knowledge retains its contact with human values, purposes and meanings, its intimate relation to human life, ethics and spiritual growth, relations which scientific knowledge forfeits.

It is the genius of Mr. B.K.S. Iyengar to have shown how clarity, precision and individual accountability can become features of yogic self-knowledge, generated at the level of the living integrated human being without necessitating any disintegrating split into subjective and objective. Such knowledge must be directly experienced by each individual pupil in the process of doing Yoga, and is only incompletely communicable to others. The clarity and precision of this knowledge come from clarity and precision in doing the asanas and pranayama. It is this which Mr. B.K.S. Iyengar has given the world—the discipline, the means of practising asanas, pranayama and all the limbs of Patanjali's Yoga with great clarity and precision. He has also given the means of applying individual standards of excellence to gauge progress or lack of it in the practice of Yoga.

Fears that this introduction of clarity, precision and individual accountability (attributes of objective knowledge) to Yoga would automatically reduce the integrated practice (e.g. asanas and pranayama) to its objective correlates (e.g. physical exercises and breathing exercises) are obviously unfounded. By increasing the competence and awareness with which asanas and pranayama can be done, Mr. Iyengar has amplified their effectiveness as each pupil learns to contact himself with greater and greater depth and thoroughness, with increasing integration of his self with his Self. As his pupils are stimulated to generate their own knowledge-by-doing, they realize the rewards of working—that agonizing, frustrating, gratifying, delighting progress towards the perfectly balanced state of unity which can include *all* the limbs of Yoga.

How does Mr. Iyengar attain this clarity, precision and individual accountability in a context of integration? He consistently, persistently addresses his pupils at the level of whole integrated persons. He asks them to work with simple well-defined abilities, readily available to them, which retain their synthesis. For example, he asks his pupils to direct their *conscious energy* to specific sites of their own body-mind. Now consciousness is subjective, of the mind, while energy is objective, of the body. Together they form a mind-body, knower-known *unity* capable of generating clarifying knowledge. He asks his students to use this probe to systematically contact all the parts of their body-mind field. By the precise placement of the body parts and of their activities in asanas he ensures that his pupils generate specific vectors of energy, matter, awareness and intention. He ensures that these vectors have specific relations to goals, along with a specific balance between will and acceptance, mood and meaning, pride and humility. He welcomes the growing awareness, the broadening and deepening integration of all the parts in a unity of being and the increasing Self-knowledge of his pupils. He encourages synergic perception, the unified use of several channels of sensation (such as seeing plus kinesthesia plus hearing) to gain clarity and depth of awareness. By ascertaining the capacity of each of his pupil's ability, he ensures that they work to their individual limits and he challenges them to expand the boundaries and depths of the field of their body-minds. His language is often exhortatory, stimulating flows of feeling, emotion and new sources of energy as his pupils stretch to their endurance limits, learn greater precision of movement and develop proper attitudes towards their working. He sets standards by example, so that his pupils can begin to understand the depths, the potential of an asana.

What are the results of this working? The growing number of his sincere pupils throughout the world *know* how splendid the results can be if they accept Mr. Iyengar's challenge. Dramatic changes are often seen in those of Mr. Iyengar's pupils who have chronic diseases. Treatment of the "objective" side of their disintegrating illness had often achieved a partial benefit, but was vitiated by its failure to address the patient as an intact person. What happens when such a pupil's whole being becomes engaged by Yoga under the tutelage of Mr. Iyengar forms a remarkable sight. The whole person truly blossoms and leaves his disease far behind as he copes more and more handily with all aspects of his life in the course of working for authentic freedom.

Thus Mr. Iyengar's contributions to knowledge have been immense. *Light on Yoga* and *Sparks of Divinity* continue to illuminate the world. This contribution will be extended as *Light on Pranayama* begins to circulate. But he also gives each of his pupils an additional precious gem—direct contact with the creative source of his or her own knowledge. This is Mr. Iyengar's contribution to the *genesis* of knowledge.

IYENGAR—AN ENIGMA

by Col. D.I.M. Robbins

THERE ARE MIXED FEELINGS in the world of Yoga about Iyengar. Everybody knows this, not least, the members of the British Wheel of Yoga. Whilst Secretary General of the Wheel, I was grappling continually with conflicting views which came my way about his system, which was either physically and mentally insulting or physically and mentally out of this world. During his visit to London in June '76 I was invited to one of his advanced classes, but only as an observer. I found it then quite impossible to assess him. Although he discussed his style vigorously with me, I had insufficient grounds on which to judge. I watched him thumping students with hands, feet, and boomps-a-daisy. While I felt no rapport at all with him, his students seemed to. It was all very odd, and I left feeling disquiet and resentment about "Iyengarism."

I met him again in December '76, when I was a representative at the International Yoga Teachers' Congress at Panchgani, India. There were many outstanding Yoga masters present. Dawn meditation was followed by Hatha Yoga classes (the right order?). I determined to submit myself to Iyengar. He welcomed me to his class with an almost wolfish relish which did not bode well for me. It was not long before I was singled out for his personal brand of attention. A sympathetic, long-term Indian student of his muttered that I should regard this as a compliment! The criticism and ridicule to which I was subject was puzzling at first, because I am but an amateur, despite pretensions to having taught Yoga in Germany and London. I was taken apart systematically and sometimes quite violently. But strangely I found myself going along with all he did. A class companion of mine was Dr. Bhole of Lonavla. He was subject to an equally rough dosage. But all was done with an expertise which was difficult to fault. Both of us persevered to the end, though many delegates retired from the fray after one session. I never found myself resenting his methods. They both amused and intrigued me. Each day after two hours of intense physical and mental effort, I walked out more aware and on air. I was "brought up" by Sir Paul Dukes, a Master of Yoga, a martinet, and an old colleague of Iyengar's. I have to admit that Iyengar is about the most effective teacher I have experienced in over twenty-five years of serious Yoga study. His Guru was his relative, the esteemed Krishnamachar, father of Desikachar. But Iyengar has developed on different lines from these two. I can now see and understand why. We should reflect that there are many paths to the ultimate goal.

Iyengar does not consider he is aggressive, but he revels in being intensive. He considers himself a man of destiny who has risen from nothing to become a Master of Yoga—par excellence. He interprets the *Sutras* of Patanjali according to his own peculiar instinct and understanding. He lives by them. The discipline of Yoga is paramount in his life and in his teaching. He brings the whole mind and intelligence to bear on the accomplishment of each asana. To do an asana mechanically or in a slipshod and unthinking manner is anathema to him. It brings swift retribution to the hapless student who is caught out. He believes that a body which does asanas with little effort and no tension is in grave danger of stagnation. Each day he cajoles that little extra from the body, subjecting it painstakingly to the microscope of the mind. Through the practice of Yoga asanas should come a state of humility. This he illustrates by his individual "bringing down to earth" of each student. The more advanced the pupil, the better Iyengar can show how little that student really knows. It is a traumatic experience for all. Iyengar may not be tactful, but he is certainly "factfull!"

Only once, whilst passing beside me during *Sirsasana* he murmured, almost grudgingly, "well done, sir!" I felt the same sense of accomplishment which a recruit must feel when his Regimental Sergeant Major condescends to say how clean his boots are! Later, when the Congress ended and Iyengar bade me farewell, he could not resist slapping me heftily. He went on to say he considered me a sincere student. The nerve of the man! How does he get away with it? What is his charisma? I believe it is due to his lifetime of dedication to true Yoga. Although many believe that he denigrates all but the asanas, they are not right. Iyengar believes wholly in Integral Yoga. He understands the purpose of and need for meditation. He reveres the ultimate goal of the union of the body with the mind and the spirit. He is a good man. I shall be ever grateful that my sessions with him have helped me to a new humility, and a better understanding of the subtleties of mind, intellect and will. He knows the value of pranayama to a true yogi and how it confirms the power of life. When each asana can be performed as a mantra, he believes every asana becomes a spiritual posture.

How can one helpfully summarise the man and his subject? Iyengar is controversial because "He is too physical." But he believes fanatically that the body must be conquered before it can become divine. "He ignores the spiritual." But where is the evidence? "He is an egoist of the highest order." But even he must have his special problems. "He is harsh and aggressive." Yes, he manhandles students, but there is no record of him personally damaging anyone. The Guru purges the *chela,* but with compassion and understanding.

So where do we go? The only danger I can see in "Iyengarism" is where his students seek to imitate him, instead of following in his steps. It is the sychophant who tries to ape the Master slavishly in all he does, in word and deed, who does the damage to Yoga, to unfortunate pupils and to Iyengar himself.

For me, Iyengar, for all his ego, has a correct attitude to Integral Yoga. His instinct is sure. He will always be Iyengar and I suppose this is the enigma.

B.K.S. IYENGAR
—A TRIBUTE

by Joyce Stuart

AFTER FIFTEEN YEARS of interest, mild practice and continued search in the field of Yoga, light was brought in the form of the book, *Light on Yoga,* by B.K.S. Iyengar. Our background of search had led us to many wonderful people all of whom added to the knowledge of Yoga which initially was started by a book on breathing. When one is sincere in anything the Lord seems to make it possible to gradually widen the knowledge and understanding.

The Lord truly guided my footsteps to place myself at the feet of the Master in London. One goes to such a meeting inevitably with preconceived ideas not only of oneself but of the situation generally. Just one three-hour class with B.K.S. Iyengar chopped all these ideas down to their proper perspective and brought this seeker literally to her knees. With the body barely able to move after the intensity of the onslaught it had undergone, the mind was light and felt free. The soul, right from that first moment, was placed at the feet and in the hands of this great Master. Time cannot be measured, but it appeared then that it had taken many lifetimes to find this shining light.

A return to South Africa brought with it the urgent necessity of passing on this complete personal revolution to others. Much thought went into how to adjust classes to what was for us so completely different an approach. There had been no awareness of a lack of the real aspect of Hatha Yoga, for classes had been held for years with many people gaining benefits from what little we had to share with them. The only possible way was to stop the old method entirely and start from scratch on the new. The response was quite amazing, and as the personal practice increased so the awareness for others grew. South Africa at this stage was extremely "Yoga" conscious, much publicity being given to all aspects and in a number of cases the wrong one.

Having had a taste of the nectar of Shri Iyengar's teaching, it seemed essential to repeat this experience as soon as possible and to allow others to experience this wonder. With literally hundreds of people throughout the country teaching Yoga, many with little or no experience, it seemed that the more people who could experience the true aspect of this science from an adept the greater the total benefit must be.

Much water was to pass under the bridge, much correspondence to take place, much disappointment to be undergone and yet still remained this tremendous urge to return to the feet of the Master. Eventually in 1968 eleven Yoga enthusiasts were airbound for Mauritius. With the help of Swami Venkatesananda, two beach cottages had been secured for us on the island. They were not ideal by any stretch of imagination and much adjustment had to take place to enable the group to occupy one of them. Only the spirit that emanates from such great souls as Shri Iyengar and Swami Venkatesananda could have made those three weeks, despite all the difficulties, into the enriching experience that it was for all. At the end of the time on the island to almost weep at parting, shows the magic of the teachings of Shri Iyengar whose instructions are not just for the body but the mind and spirit too. As one husband remarked when meeting his wife at the airport, we all glowed. This was not just health but an inner light which had been kindled by the Master.

For him, the spreading of his art is perhaps the basis of his love for his students, for there is no holding back here. Whatever knowledge is there is given freely, with joy and spontaneity. The basic principles are firm, the moral fibre inflexible and the heart overflowing.

It took two years before we were again on our way to Mauritius. The Master, out of the goodness of his heart, had agreed once again to meet us there after his strenuous European tour. The group this time consisted of twenty-four people, most of whom taught Yoga, and of whom six had been on the first course. Hotel accommodation had been arranged at Le Morne which must be one of the most beautiful places not only on the island but anywhere. The joy of meeting once again our Guru cannot be described. It was like coming home. The lithe body, sparkling eyes, infectious laugh, talking eyebrows, hands and feet make the heart beat faster.

Our lesson with the Master handling twenty-four people, only six of whom he knew, was indeed unique. It was obvious then and continued to be a source of wonder throughout the course, that this great soul had not in any way stood still in the two years since we'd met. On the contrary, with postures that had become even more unbelievable, a technique for teaching had evolved still further. Who can ever forget the precisely aimed blow which gave awareness to the exact spot that was dead? Or the joy that filled one's being when, having striven with everything one possessed, the words came, "That's a good one." The understanding comes that every word addressed to an individual is said for a definite purpose. If anyone comes to Shri Iyengar with false ideas and values, it seems to take just one day for him to assess this and from there the lessons in all forms take place. The penetration, the insight which brings to the surface all the weaknesses of the individual, has to be experienced. Has anyone tried to explain the taste of sugar? A whole saga could be written on the knowledge of Shri Iyengar which comes from the intensity and devotion given to his own practices. Everything is verified before being handed on to others. So often we were left shaking our heads and gasping at the subtlety of just one movement which altered the whole aspect of the asana. Many of the teachers said they just wouldn't know how to go back and face a class in the light of this Master.

If it is possible, perhaps this mastery was demonstrated even more in the teaching of meditation, pranayama and relaxation. There is an expression, "All this and Heaven too," and perhaps these late afternoon gatherings for the purpose of learning pranayama provided this experience. For some this was the first time the spine had been put straight in a sitting position, and after twenty minutes of this effort the body becomes so stiff it can hardly move. Perhaps this too is a technique in itself, for only if the body can be subdued and controlled can the mind hope to grasp the more subtle details necessary in pranayama. So much is written in books on this subject but it becomes evident that without guidance it is impossible to experience even a glimmer of what should take place. And here indeed the Master provided just that. For the writer one glimpse into the stillness was given. That glimpse was sufficient to make her understand how complete the surrender must be and to see the necessity for more and more practice. It brought with it too, an involuntary prayer of thankfulness to the Lord in the form of B.K.S. Iyengar in allowing these three weeks to take place in Mauritius.

Let us pray that this human soul whose God-like qualities bring us closer to reality may be with us for many years to guide, encourage, laugh at and with us and yet inspire us. Let us go down on our knees and thank the Lord for B.K.S. Iyengar.

THE MAN OF ACTION AND PERFECTION

by Madhu Tijoriwala

EVERY SATURDAY, whatever the weather, if you wish to find a man catching the morning Deccan Queen from Pune for Bombay it is Shri B.K.S. Iyengar. His Bombay classes are conducted on Saturday afternoons and Sunday mornings. He catches the Manmad Express to return back to Pune in the afternoons. The return journey is a very tedious and long one. The strain of the journey and conducting two classes in fairly quick succession is not less. But he is game for that.

Once a pupil enquired of him whether with the emergence of the Institute in Pune as a centre of all Yogic activities, he might give up coming to Bombay to conduct his classes. Prompt was his reaction: "So long as I have life and energy in me I shall never stop conducting the Bombay classes. I love my Bombay pupils. Many of them have been devoted to me for many years and despite the trouble involved in travelling to and from Bombay I love to meet my Bombay pupils."

And his present-day schedule is more strenuous. After coming to Bombay he sits, with three or four pupils for two hours, finalizing his draft on *Light on Pranayama.* Thereafter he conducts his afternoon class. After a coffee break he works on the papers with his pupils and then goes to his hotel where he works before taking a night's rest.

On Sunday morning after conducting his class there is a tea break. After a short period of rest in *Savasana* and a light and quick lunch, he sits for his book *Light on Pranayama* till the time arrives for catching the five o'clock train for Pune.

He is a man so determined in his decision that he does not swerve from that decision once it is taken.

What are the secrets of success of Guruji B.K.S. Iyengar in Yoga and in life? It is his conviction that Will must prevail over Matter. He has courage and confidence in himself which he instils in his pupils. He has uncanny insight, and his psychological approach helps him to understand people. His resourcefulness is great, and he can make circumstances and material at hand suit his purposes. According to the *Bhagavad Gita,* Yoga is dexterity in action. Guruji B.K.S. Iyengar exemplifies this saying of the *Gita,* for he can get the maximum amount of work done efficiently in the limited time in his busy schedule.

There is no love of amassing any wealth. Whatever he gets he distributes. There are many known and unknown acts of charity in which he freely and without any restraint indulges. However, the best charity is in imparting knowledge to one and all who come to seek knowledge. Judged by this standard one cannot find a more charitable person than Guruji. According to the *Svetasvatara Upanishad,* the first fruits of the practice of Yoga are: health, little waste matter, lightness of the

270

body, a pleasant scent and absence of greedy desires. All these are found in Guruji.

Yoga is equanimity and keeping one's balance of mind. It means the disciplining of the body, the intellect, the mind, the emotions and the will. It is the poise of the soul which enables one to look evenly at life in all its aspects. Years of discipline of Yoga have generated courage and fortitude in Guruji. The Gita tells us that death is certain for all that are born and rebirth for all that are dead, and that one should not grieve for what is unavoidable. This teaching entered into Guruji's bloodstream and enabled him to face bravely the deaths in his family.

In 1958, the Bombay class had arranged a picnic to Elephanta on a Sunday morning, when both Guruji and his wife Rama specially came down from Pune to attend it. What most of the pupils did not know was, that prior to starting from Pune, he had received word that his beloved mother was dying at Bangalore. He did not disappoint his pupils. After the Elephanta trip, he and Rama went on to Bangalore and met his mother who passed away within a few hours of their seeing her.

Guruji was in Bombay during the last weekend in January 1973 when Rama had been removed to hospital. A phone call was received from Pune by one of his pupils that Rama had breathed her last. Guruji was persuaded by three of his pupils to leave for Pune immediately and not take the Sunday morning class as he intended doing. He was told that Rama's condition was serious. As they were approaching Pune, Guruji was told about his wife's death. There was a mist over his eyes for a moment. Then he remained calm and collected. He consoled his sobbing children and since then has been both mother and father to them.

There was a similar incident lately on August 15th 1978, when a joint session of the Bombay and Pune classes was held at the Institute to have photographs taken for a proposed brochure by a professional photographer from Bombay. After the strenuous session was over, he insisted upon the pupils having refreshments and also lunch at the Institute. As the Bombay students were leaving, he told a senior pupil that a phone call had come in the early hours of the morning that his elder brother had passed away at Bangalore, and since then he and his family had not slept. The secrecy was kept with a view not to inconvenience the expert photographer from Bombay who came to Pune in spite of his very busy schedule and also the Bombay pupils who had gone to Pune for the occasion. It was only after the programme was concluded that he left for Bangalore. It requires a good deal of courage, fortitude and equanimity to be able to carry on the work in hand when one is struck with a bolt from the blue in the form of news about the sudden death of one's elder brother. Even in the midst of great personal loss, Guruji kept his equanimity and had consideration for others, thus providing for his children and students an object lesson they will never forget.

Guruji's physical courage is accompanied by his sense of balance and proportion. He posed in *Sirsasana* for a photographer of LIFE magazine at the edge of the roof of a skyscraper in New York. On another occasion he did *Sirsasana* on a rock at Yosemite valley in California, under the spray from a nearby waterfall. During a visit to Mahabaleshwar in 1973 he stood on his head and did difficult balancing pases like *Natarajasana* and *Mayurasana* on a ridge at Kate's point, against a strong wind with a sheer precipice of 4000 feet just behind him.

272

He is a strict disciplinarian in the class. A person is not bound to accept him as his teacher if he cannot put up with his rigorous teaching; but if one chooses to accept him as his Guru there is no alternative to learning with speed and sincerity. His courage can best be seen when he meets a challenge. When people with various diseases incurable by medical or any other treatment come to him, the best in him comes out and the Master pours in his life blood to teaching and curing his pupils. He gives far more than a pupil could even think of repaying him. Once a serious-minded pupil gets in, he cannot get out of it for his life.

Many a time questions arise in our minds. Why we should bother to undergo such a vigorous training? Does this system of training give any benefits at all? Answers will be given by those who have undergone training with him. The pupil's stamina increases. He acquires confidence. His power of concentration increases. His process of thinking becomes clear. He learns to work with speed and efficiency. He gets a greater degree of equanimity. The nerves become strong and the pupil is able to face the challenges of life better. What a pupil cannot achieve on account of his weak will, he achieves by the strong will of the Master. His approach to life is positive. He does not tolerate pessimism or defeatist mentality.

The sense of balance and proportion in Guruji provided grace of movement and keen interest in other sports and fine arts. He has taught Yoga to artistes of world renown and to sportsmen, and they have become better performers. In his youth, Guruji had contacted the famous dancer Uday Shankar and had offered to teach him and his troupe Yoga, and in return to learn dancing from him. Fortunately for the world of Yoga, the offer was not accepted.

The Guru in the class while teaching and the Guru outside are two different persons or two extremely contradictory phases of one person's life.

Outside the class it is difficult for a stranger to realise the greatness of Guruji. He dresses in a very simple way. He mixes with every one without disclosing his real identity. While travelling in planes to and from India, if anyone inquires of him as to what he does, his prompt and short answer is that he is a Yoga teacher. Nobody can make out that he is the world's most-sought-for Yoga exponent and has widely travelled round the world almost every year for the last thirty years.

In the class he roars like a lion. Outside the class he is meek as a lamb. Those who have seen him conducting classes only can never realise how mild he could be outside. Once class is over one finds him bubbling with fun and joy, with great zest for living and ever ready to embark on new adventures.

Can anyone cheat him in class? Impossible. Can anyone cheat him outside the class? It is not only possible but probable.

His innocence and good-heartedness is reflected in his spontaneous laughter. At a given moment he may express his dissatisfaction at a pupil not doing the asanas properly and the next moment he will say something which will make the whole class split into laughter including himself.

How does he deal with family problems? Is he as strict with family members as he is with pupils in the class? Certainly not. He gives liberty to each of them. What if they go wrong? His solution is that each one should question whether what he or she is doing is against his or her own conscience. This way each member of the family acts in a manner that is not against his or her own conscience. There are no occasions when he has to speak even harshly to anyone. His is a very closely knit family.

In connection with his sixtieth birthday, his pupils from all over the world, his friends and admirers decided to celebrate the occasion suitably. When the suggestion was put to him, he promptly reacted that no celebration was required as he believed in living a simple life. When it was pointed out to him that this occasion would aid the cause of propagation of Yoga he agreed to the suggestion.

Guruji is fearless, pure and innocent in heart. He is charitable. He can control his passions. He practises spiritual disciplines. He is staight-forward and truthful. He harms no one. He is mentally unattached to the things of the world. He is compassionate towards all. He abstains from useless activity. He has faith in the struggle of his higher nature. He can forgive and endure. He is clean in his thoughts and action. Such qualities are his birthright. Thus he answers almost all the divine qualities referred to in the sixteenth chapter of the *Gita*. He also answers many of the qualities of a *bhakta* (servant of God) referred to in Chapter XII of the *Gita*. He is friendly and compassionate to all. He is free from the delusion of "I" and "mine." He accepts pleasure and pain evenly. He is free from attachment. He is content with whatever he gets. Being a devotee as described above, he is dear to God.

Considering the many varied and colourful facets of his life it can truly be said of him that he is—

"A man so various that he seems to be
Not one, but all mankind's epitome."

275

IYENGAR
—THE GUIDING LIGHT

by Smt. Freny S. Motivala

A N ANCIENT CHINESE PROVERB says, "Great souls have wills, feeble ones have only wishes. Wishing makes an idle dreamer, but putting backbone into the wish makes the doer." And that is what Iyengar is—a remarkable man of dynamic action and iron will!

When you build in yourself the total harmony, says the Divine Mother, perfect beauty can express itself through your body. Indeed, Iyengar has built his body that is beautiful in form, harmonious in postures, supple and agile in its movements, powerful in its activities and resistant in health and organic functions. This is a colossal achievement, considering that before he started Yoga, he was a sickly boy suspected of suffering from tuberculosis, with a chest measurement of 22".

Sixteen years ago, I started Yoga with this master for my spinal injuiry, as the best of orthopaedic surgeons failed to give me relief. For a complete cure, an operation was promptly suggested. All the doctors in one voice had forbidden me to do forward bendings of any kind, lest I would be a cripple for the rest of my life. Hence, when

Iyengar tried such postures on me, I was petrified and informed him of the doctor's advice. In a firm voice the master inquired of me, "Do you wish to follow your doctor or do you wish to follow me?" Supreme confidence in his tone was enough for me to surrender without any reservations and I have never regretted my decision. Somehow, I knew instinctively that I had found "the light" that would guide me correctly.

Apart from getting completely cured of my back trouble, I have derived countless other benefits throughout my association with this lovable teacher. He has helped me to see life in its proper perspective and realise where true happiness really lies. Both my husband Sam and I were anxious to share this great blessing with those who were less fortunate. And that is what launched us on our teaching career in 1966.

Very often Iyengar seems like a slave driver in the class, trying to draw the maximum out of us. Actually, I feel that when he expresses confidence in our ability to accomplish something, he strengthens that ability and we are pushed beyond the frontiers of the mind. Good health and success depend on the functioning of the glands—so to begin with, our sweat glands are the target of his attack. He actually makes you slog, but his pupils are more than happy to sweat it out with him.

He believes that the only way to conquer fear is to face it and with him around, you can never run away from attempting a difficult asana. By hook or by crook, he will get us to do it. He imposes his will on ours and the impossibility becomes a thing of the past. A gleeful look comes into our eyes, as we realise that we have achieved something, not entirely by our own effort, but more due to his grace.

My thoughts go drifting back to the time when once I came to class with a broken ankle, thinking that I would be a passive spectator, happily listening to the pupil's moans and groans. I went up to him to give my excuse, which would have been good enough for any Master—but not for him. He astounded me with his sweeping remark: "Your ankle may be injured, but the rest of your body is not," and so saying he gave me a tight slap on my back and pushed me in the class. As I hobbled on my feet to join the others, pathetic looks from the pupils were thrown in my direction, but none came from the Master. Soon I realised to my amazement, that there was so much I could do, in spite of the affliction. From that day onwards, I learned never to take the escapist attitude.

"You all want to learn Yoga, but you are not willing to accept the challenge that comes," says Iyengar. We can see that those who take the plunge and persevere are the ones who have gone a long way, no doubt with his help and guidance. He impresses one with his exceptionally dynamic personality and sincerity.

When he is teaching, he does not consider it his work. For him, it is a way of life. Like a true *karma yogi,* he gets totally involved in his work and enjoys himself heartily, because he is making his contribution to the individual in particular and to the world at large. His work is his own reward. It seems he is thankful to the Lord for having bestowed on him this splendid art. His teaching is a source of continuous discovery. The creativity and the brilliance in it is remarkable. He is supremely confident in his knowledge, which he has acquired by his own effort. I once heard him assert—"No one can cheat me in Yoga, but in other matters I may get cheated." Like any great artist he is a seeker of perfection.

279

He tests people by asking them to do what they are reluctant to do. He sees their perseverance and from that judges their sincerity. To a sincere seeker, he gives of himself freely and wholeheartedly. All he demands in return is total attention, total surrender and total dedication.

Many a time he blasts your ego and of course his criticism is ever so painful to the mind. It is said, "He has a right to criticise, who has a heart to help." Those who know him well, realise that Iyengar's heart is ever flowing with the milk of human kindness. Throughout these long years of my association with him as his pupil, I have seen him bring about unbelievable cures of major as well as minor ailments. Surprisingly, when the doctor has failed in many cases, he has succeeded.

Guruji is a great sport in every sense of the word. He is fun-loving and adventurous with an open and daring mind, ever ready to try out anything and everything—a tough minded optimist with a pleasing disposition. He has a very healthy and positive approach towards life and living and spreads sunshine wherever he goes. He is also a man with subtle qualities, which make him calm in adversity. I will ever remember his reaction to the news of the extremely sad and sudden demise of his wife, whom he cherished dearly. The unpleasant task of conveying the message to him fell on our shoulders, as he was in Bombay over the weekend. When he was told, he remained perfectly quiet and peaceful, as though devoid of all emotions and then a few moments later, with total surrender to the Divine Will, all that he said was, "I can bear anything that comes to me in the form of adversity, it is only my children I am worried about." At that moment I immediately recalled what I had read in the *Bhagavad Gita*,

Chapter II, about the "Man of Perfection" *(Sthita Prag-nya)* and how he remains calm and composed, full of internal strength, under all circumstances.

Guruji's physical, mental and spiritual strength is phenomenal. In his teaching as well as in his own *sad-hana* (practice), he sets us the highest example. Having seen "the light" he is trying his utmost to throw this powerful beam in our direction. Often times he even sacrifices his health for the sake of his pupils. Can there be a better love?

> "There are many kinds of love,
> As many kinds of light.
> And every kind of love,
> Makes a glory in the night.
>
> There is love that stirs the heart,
> And love that gives it rest,
> And the love that leads life upwards,
> Is the noblest and the best."

OUR GURUJI

*by Mrs. Kalyani Namjoshi,
Prof. Kulahalli & Mr. Mahadevan*

G*uru Gita* IS A DIALOGUE between Lord Shiva and his Consort Parvati regarding Guru, meaning the dispeller of darkness. It sings the praise of Guru, his role and glory.

*Ananandmanandakaram Prasannam
Jnana Swarupam Nigabodha Yuktam
Yosindramidyam Bhavaroga Vaidyam
Srisadgurum Nityamaham Namami*
(*Guru Gita*—93)

"Guru is bliss incarnate, the bestower of bliss, radiance personified, the very embodiment of knowledge, spiritual guide, king among yogis, worthy of praise and reverence, destroyer of worldly afflictions—to such a noble Guru I bow daily."

Hindu tradition contains a moving description of the glory of the Guru, the Guru's true form, feeling for the Guru and devotion to the Guru. The Guru has been recognised as the very embodiment of pure knowledge.

Thousands of years of unbroken and pure tradition of Hindu philosophy owes its vibrant form to the tradition of Guru-disciple relationship. Because of this tradition, the Hindu philosophy acquired dynamism, evolved and expanded, became a force for all time to take one to the experience of the noumenon. The life of Guruji, who has revived the profound Patanjali Yoga, in spite of the disruption of tradition, has been consecrated by the touch of the noumenon.

In today's fast-changing world, man is in search of imperishable, permanent happiness. But the more man pursues happiness the more it eludes him. Indian tradition recognizes four main paths that lead one to lasting happiness. These are: the path of Knowledge, the path of Devotion, the path of Action and the path of Yoga.

According to Patanjali Yoga: *"Yogah Chitta Vritti Nirodhah"* (Pada I, Sutra 2). Yoga is the restraint of the modifications of the mind, i.e. it is Yoga of stilling the mind.

How to secure permanent happiness through the path of Yoga has been stated in the most convincing way in the dialogue between Lord Krishna and Arjuna in the *Bhagavad Gita* (Song Celestial)—an unparalleled and universally extolled work. Arjuna asks :

> *cancalam hi manah krsna*
> *pramathi balavad drdham*
> *tasya ham nigraham manye*
> *vayor iva suduskaram(6-34)*

> "For the mind is verily fickle, O Krishna,
> it is impetuous, strong and obstinate.
> I think that it is as difficult to control
> as the wind."

Krishna, the Lord of Yoga, has beautifully explained:
asamsayam mahabaho
mano durnigraham calam
abhyasena tu kaunteya
vairagyena ca grhyate(6-35)

"The Blessed Lord said:
Without doubt, O Mighty-armed (Arjuna),
the mind is difficult to curb and restless
but it can be controlled, O Son of Kunti
by constant practice and non-attachment."

Yoga is hard to attain, I agree, by one who is not self-controlled; but by the self-controlled it is attainable by striving through proper means. The mind travels faster than light. It is subtle and mercurial, hence difficult to control.

Guruji, while elucidating the yogic approach for making the mind steady, observes that Yoga which brings balance and harmony in the body, mind and intelligence is a complete science. This science has been expounded by Patanjali in terse but profound sutras. This yogic path has been a boon to the whole mankind. Today's fast-paced life with its stress and strain makes the mind of man restless and enfeebles the power of discrimination. The unsteady mind, the wavering intellect and the body through which they live are the result of fear, anger, weakness, numerous complexes and diverse diseases. Yoga is a science that deals with all the the three planes of existence. Yogasanas benefit not only the body but also bring about desirable changes in the mind and intellect of man. This has to be experienced rather than debated. Yoga is an experiential science. It is a complete science that supports and nourishes the qualities of health, self-confidence, balance or equanimity, discipline, honesty and character, thus enriching the whole personality.

The asanas are the gateway to Yoga. While explaining the quintessence of asanas, Guruji observes that for effectively gaining the benefits, asanas should be performed with intensity, intelligence and devotion. Rooted in the mind of man is the inseparable relationship between pain and fear. Asanas give one courage to face sufferings. Mind is not only fickle, it is also moving and evolving. To counteract fickleness of mind and unsteadiness of intellect, one has to bring about a proper co-ordination between body and mind. To effect this, one has to focus the attention or mind on both gross and subtle movements of the body. Thus the mind and body movements become synchronised. If the body is in one position and the mind is wandering away, the mind will never become one-pointed, steady and quiet. By constant practice of asanas, mind is cultured to keep pace with the body and gradually it becomes steady and still like the serene and waveless flow of the Ganga.

For success in Yoga, as stated in the *Bhagavad Gita,* Guruji exhorts us to inculcate two principles. These twin principles are *Abhyasa* (Study) and *Vairagya* (Renunciation).

Abhyasa is the effort to remove the heaviness (impurities) in the body, mind and intellect. Abhyasa makes one dynamic. It is a psychological and basically a deliberate effort. One's practice becomes Abhyasa when it is done uninterruptedly and over a long period of time with sincerity, purity, devotion and a spirit of surrender; otherwise the practice does not qualify to be called study. This kind of study or Abhyasa leads one to Vairagya. Vairagya leads to steadfastness and has a great influence on the senses. It weans the senses away from their objects of enjoyment, turns them inward and sets one on the path of self-realization. With the study of asanas, renunciation sets in. This sprouting of Vairagya further strengthens the Abhyasa. Thus Abhyasa and Vairagya progress together strengthening each other at every step.

Guruji's successful and fruitful life is due to his regular and devoted practice. In spite of many bodily ailments, discontinuation of education brought on by adverse economic conditions, and deprivation of proper Yoga guidance on account of only a brief association with his Guru, Guruji has emerged as the foremost, incomparable exponent of Yoga only because of his determined, devoted, long and uninterrupted practice. To simplify the learning of Yogasanas and to enable even the diseased and the debilitated to gain the full benefits of Yogasanas, Guruji has evolved aids and equipment which are a monument to his expertise and creativity. People from all parts of the world come to Guruji with various problems and diseases. He discerns quickly from the structure of the body, its movements and tone, not only the present diseases but also the latest ones likely to surface in the future. That is, instead of just treating the reported complaints (symptoms), Guruji goes to the very source of the problem and removes it root and branch. Thousands are leading a healthy and creative life thanks to Guruji's guidance.

Practice, development and dissemination of Yoga thus became the goal and mission of Guruji's life. Because of this he had to bear unimaginable poverty and humiliation that no ordinary man could ever withstand. If we turn to the pages of history, we notice that all over the world, benefactors of mankind were made the butts of ridicule, humiliation and derision. Guruji is also no exception to

287

this. He bore personal slights under the most adverse circumstances with rare fortitude and equanimity. But to combat indifference to Yoga, propagation of wrong notions, misunderstandings and shortcomings of Yoga, Guruji made herculean efforts without being overwhelmed by personal suffering and problems. Once the mind becomes steady and resolute it does not waver under unfavourable circumstances. As the flame of a lamp burns steadily even in a storm, so mind too, even under inhospitable conditions, is stilled and remains steady on its path.

Renunciation is non-attachment, and to realise renunciation and freedom from the senses, it is not necessary to become a recluse and to forsake family life. It is the greatness and beauty of the tradition of the Indian seers or rishis that a yogi of the stature of Yagnavalkya was a householder. He presided over a university community consisting of sixty thousand pupils. Even at that time he was a great yogi and has been recognised as such. Our Guru's eminenence in Yoga and his profound reflections on the various aspects of Yoga *(Yama, Niyama, Asana, Pranayama, Pratyahara, Dharana, Dhyana and Samadhi)* leave no doubt in the minds of his pupils and other serious students of Yoga that his life too is like that of the yogis of yore. Otherwise the kind of mastery gained by Guruji is difficult to come by. One feels profound gratitude that there is no Guru like our Guruji.

Guruji's life is an open book and there is nothing secretive about him or his work. He practises together with his pupils. He has resisted the branding of his system of Yoga as Iyengar Yoga. He is like one of the ancient seers. His Yoga is universal; it is not a cult. Guruji has one more thing in common with the great seers—the continuance of the tradition of Yoga in his family. Vasishta's lineage is very well-known for this. Guruji's daughter, Geeta, and son, Prashant, both wholly devoted to Yoga, certainly ensure that Yoga will continue to be taught with purity and intensity.

When Guruji flies into a temper and scolds to make the pupil's practice firm and intelligent he reminds one of a stern dutiful father. When he handles the sick and the weak with care and compassion, he reminds one of a mother. When he expounds Yoga in simple language and elucidates the hidden subtleties of asanas and pranayama, he reveals himself as a born and devoted teacher. Guruji is verily the confluence of the three sacred rivers—the serene motherly Ganga, the turbulent Yamuna and the invisible spiritual guide, the Saraswati.

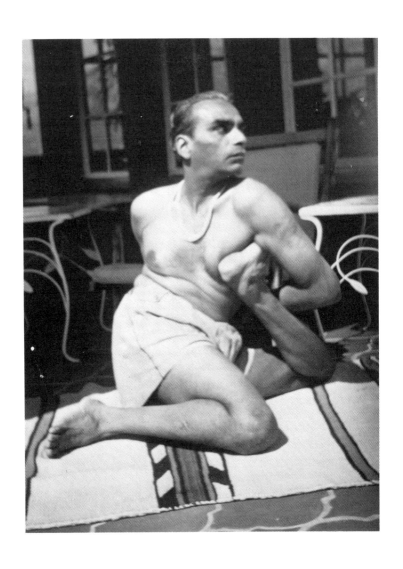

Position God for every asana, then reach towards him.

THE EVOLUTION OF AN ACHARYA

by B.I. Taraporewala

T HE WORD *evolution* has several meanings. It means any process of formation or growth; development, a product of such development; something evolved. In biological sciences, the word means the continuous genetic adaptation of organisms and species to the environment by the integrating agencies of selection, hybridization, inbreeding and mutation. The word also means a motion incomplete in itself, but combining with co-ordinated motions to produce a single action, as in a machine. It means a pattern formed by a series of movements. It means an evolving or giving off, of gas, heat or other forms of energy. An obsolete use of the word in the science of mathematics means extraction of roots.

The words *evolution* and *evolve* have to be considered with two other words, namely *involution* and *involute*. The word *involution* means the act or an instance of involving or entangling, involvement; the state of being involved; something complicated. In biological sciences, it means a rolling up or folding in upon itself; retrograde development; degeneration; regressive changes in the body occurring with old age. In mathematical science, the word means the raising of a quantity or expression to any given power. Used as an adjective, the word *involute* means involved, intricate or complex, curled or curved inwards or spirally. In botany, the word means rolled inwards from the edge, as a leaf. In zoology, the word is used to describe shells as having the whorls closely wound. When used as a verb, it means to roll or curl up, become involute; it also means to return to a normal shape, size or state.

Who is an *Acharya?* A look at a standard Sanskrit dictionary provides an insight into the personality of an Acharya. According to the dictionary, an Acharya is a *Guru,* a *siksaka* and a *mata pracharaka.*

Guru is used both as an adjective and as a noun. As an adjective, Guru means heavy, great, difficult, long, important or momentous, best or excellent, respectable, haughty or mighty. As a noun, Guru means father, ancestor, elderly person, a teacher, the head, the ruler, and also Beihaspati—the preceptor of the gods. A Guru is one who removes the darkness of ignorance and brings illumination.

A *siksaka* means both a learner and a teacher. The word *mata* means a thought, an opinion or an aim. The word *prachara* connotes wandering a path, a manifestation, a pattern of behaviour or custom. Mata pracharaka implies a propagator of a way of life, who travels widely, spreading his ideals and message with zeal.

Fuse together the meanings of the words given in the Sanskrit dictionary, and you have some glimpse of what an Acharya is.

Let us try to find out the reasons why Yogacharya B.K.S. Iyengar's teaching methods arouse interest, enthusiasm and acceptance in every continent among peoples with widely varying ethnic and cultural backgrounds. It is because of the universality of the message of Yoga which he propagates. Yoga takes in its sweep the totality of the human personality—physical, emotional, mental, intellectual, ethical or moral, and spiritual. The range of Yoga covers arts, sciences, and principles of philosophy which have stood the test of time. Years of *tapas,* keenness of observation, analysis, application of detailed knowledge of the human body and unrivalled experience in dealing with patients suffering from physical and psychological handicaps and discipline are the foundation of his methods.

Yoga is the mother of various forms of art. Art is the quality, production or realm of what is beautiful and of more than ordinary significance. The foundations of all arts are the principles or methods governing any craft, skill or branch of learning. Art is skill in conducting any human activity, or as the *Bhagavad Gita* expresses it, *karmasu kausalyam*—"skill in action." Art is the method of expending the minimum of energy to get the maximum of results, and the skill of knowing where to deploy forces of energy; how to conserve energy and avoid its wastage. Art is knowing the latent capacity of things and beings and how to bring out those latent qualities to the surface for all to see, and how to release hidden or locked-up reserves of energy by patient application of highly specialised knowledge.

Music is the manipulation of the world of sound, the acquisition and maintenance of pitch, resonance, rhythm, melody, harmony, point and counter-point, balance, nuances, variations and improvisations resulting in symphony. Yoga is like music and it is a measure of Yoga-charya Iyengar's mastery over his own body that he amazes his pupils and audiences around the world with the balance, grace and fluidity of movement of the body in seemingly impossible positions. More than that is the skill of imparting and passing on the benefit of his unrivalled and highly specialised knowledge and experience to his pupils around the world. Ignorance has no beginning, but it can be ended. Knowledge has a beginning, but it is endless. Acharya Iyengar's knowledge continues to grow. With every session, his pupils learn something new; something original is shown, something hidden is revealed, some new skill is taught, some new principle or source of action and balance is pointed out. As he expresses it, "It is as if the body has a thousand eyes spread all over it. Open those eyes and observe every shade of movement, repeat and consolidate the newly-acquired skill. Have a sense of total awareness of the body from the pores of your soles to the pores of skin on the top of your scalp and your finger-tips. Have total attention everywhere, then the body will not waver. There will be steadiness and balance, stability and grace, and you will become the embodiment of the asana—fused in time and space and in precision." Is it any wonder that he ranks among his pupils some of the best-known musicians of the world?

Each asana has its own architecture and follows the principles of architecture. The triangle is amongst the lightest and strongest of geometric forms. It is one of the main building blocks of various geometric forms. Four triangles make a square, five a pentagon, six a hexagon, and so on. The geodesic dome is made up of numerous triangles. One of the basic standing poses is *Trikonasana*—the pose of the triangle. Acharya Iyengar explored this basic asana in depth and produced a slide show explaining the nuances of the asana and its benefits. The views of the body, presented from the front, back and sides, show how every little element affects the entire posture. You see the cause and effect of the stretch of the skin, the underlying muscle and the joints. You see how wrong movements like contortions of the face or tightness of the throat and tongue cause drainage and wastage of energy. You see how movements of the eyes affect the movements of the entire body. You see how precision in performance of the asana leads to conservation and increase of energy. You see how the movement of the skin in one direction and the movement of the underlying muscles in the opposite direction bring about refinement and precision in the pose.

The idea of the flying buttress and the steeple of Gothic architecture is embodied in *Virabhadrasana I*. The precision of the placement of the bent front leg, the evenness of the stretch of the inner and outer ankles, the perpendicular shin, the correct placement of the bent leg thigh parallel to the floor, together with the stretch of the rear leg from the groin to the heel, leads to lightness and balance in the pose. The stretch of the arms from the pelvic girdle to the finger tips relieves the breathing. Endurance comes when the throat and the tongue are kept relaxed while performing the asana.

The part of the body which is most difficult to adjust in asanas is the head. This is so because the placement of the ears adjusts the balance of the body, and the movements of the eyes regulate the tension of the body. It is Acharya Iyengar's firm conviction that the standing postures lay the firm foundation for the other postures, because they teach the pupil how to use his knees and ankles. It is the mastery of control over the movements of the knees and ankles which determine the correctness of the posture in *Sirsasana, Sarvangasana* and other inverted poses. Sirsasana is an abdominal exercise, apart from being an exercise in balance, and this balance is controlled by the stretch of the knees and ankles. "First learn how to balance yourself on the floor when your feet are firmly planted on the ground, before you learn how to balance yourself on your head with your feet in the air," says the Acharya. He believes that the pupil should first learn the mysteries of his own body which he can see, touch and feel, before the pupil begins to delve into something intangible like his mind, intellect and soul.

By disciplining the body in the performance of the asanas, you gradually learn how to tame your breath, then your emotions, then your mind and later your intellect. When you watch a class of beginners, you will find illustrations of the five states of mind and of awareness. Some pupils are so bemused that they cannot absorb the teacher's instructions. Their minds wander elsewhere. There are some pupils who do a particular thing correctly and forget all other instructions and get confused. They do not know which is the right side of the body and which is its left side. They cannot understand which is the upward movement and which is the downward movement. They become disoriented when the normal level of the body is altered. There are some pupils who will absorb some instructions and create unnecessary strain by violent movements of holding their breaths and so become tired and dispirited. By constant and repeated practice done devotedly, without distraction or interruptions, some pupils learn mastery over a few asanas. As their practice improves, so does their comprehension and concentration. They gradually acquire awareness of what is happening to themselves and to the world around them.

They absorb instructions and learn total awareness. Their bodies automatically and instinctively adopt the correct postures. They become better disciplined. They find that a greater volume of work gets done in a relatively shorter span of time. By constant contact and absorption of Acharya Iyengar's teachings, his pupils learn one of the definitions of Yoga given in the *Bhagavad Gita,* namely, "Skill in action." It is rare, if not impossible, to come across teachers like Acharya Iyengar, his eldest daughter, Geeta, and his son, Prashant, who can get more work out of their pupils within an allotted span of time. Mastery over movements of the body gradually leads to maturity over breath. This in turn brings about control over emotions and then the mind, which is the king of emotions. This leads to clarity of thinking and intellect, which in turn leads to sound judgment. Gradually the pupils grow and mature from a careless state of mind into a care-free state of mind. They learn how to get totally absorbed in their chosen work and they learn how to relax also.

Raw recruits in the armed forces are gradually put through drill formations till they grow into a homogeneous and cohesive unit and acquire a reputation of being crack troops. So also the pupils of Acharya Iyengar acquire reputations as disciplinarians and teachers in their own right. The Acharya believes that though the design of the human body remains unchanged, each individual body is different, having its own peculiar set of weaknesses. He studies the individual anatomy and adapts the asana prescribed to the environment by modifying its performance with devices and implements like walls, doorways, chairs, weights, wooden blocks or ropes and belts. It is a process of selection and mutation or modification of the asanas so as to provide maximum relief to pupils suffering from peculiar ailments or combinations of ailments. A pupil may suffer a combination of ailments like high blood pressure and diabetes, which is like combining fire and ice. If one ailment is treated in a normal manner, the other ailment gets aggravated. Acharya Iyengar will devise asanas which are incomplete in themselves, but by combining with co-ordinated motions produce a single action, namely, relief to the patient by eradication of the ailment. He extracts the disease from its roots and makes the ailing body of his pupil give off its noxious content, so that health is restored to tired and aching limbs and organs. He brings about a "disunion of contact with pain and sorrow," which is another definition of Yoga as given in the *Bhagavad Gita*. He makes the bodies of his difficult pupils return to a normal shape, size and state by applying the processes of involution.

It is this precision and sense of balance which makes the teaching of Acharya Iyengar unique. These two qualities—precision and balance—lead to total awareness by the pupils of their most intimate possession, their own bodies. He instils in his pupils a part of his own confidence in himself *(sraddha)*. He charges into them a part of his own enthusiasm and courage *(virya)*. He makes his pupils perform asanas like a military drill, till every aspect of the asana is burned into their memory *(smrti)*. He makes his pupils so absorbed in asanas and pranayama that they forget themselves and they become one with the asanas and their breath *(samadhi)*. The result is not mere knowledge *(jnana),* but illumination *(prajna)*. He who gives light unto others, himself gets illumined.

Acharya Iyengar evolved as a Yoga teacher over a long era of time. His was a classic instance of victory over toil, tears and sweat. In the *Prana Upanisad* there is a

298

phrase which is consistently repeated: *Sa tapo tapyata*—
"He practised austerities ardently." This phrase would
most aptly describe Acharya Iyengar. Though he is a most
vigorous teacher, he is a most devoted pupil. There is
always a fresh approach, always fresh experimentation,
always new techniques, new tools, new gadgets, till it
seems that he is spontaneously inspired to meet a challenge as yet unencountered. His learning and his teaching
flow like a perennial river. There is no stagnation, no
decay, but continuous growth. His first book, *Light on
Yoga,* which is regarded as a Bible of yogasanas and a
classic source book on the subject, may now be regarded as
a bit obsolete by reason of newer nuances of the human
anatomy discovered by him. The same might be said
about *Light on Pranayama,* which is a much tougher
book to read and digest. A fresh book on the Yoga Sutras
of Patanjali is now being prepared. The process of learning and teaching will grow in ever widening circles. This
is what makes Yoga total education, and Acharya Iyengar
a teacher of universality.

Let us salute the Master who, like Brahma, the creator, creates a sense of total awareness; who, like Visnu,
the preserver, helps to maintain physical, mental, moral
and spiritual health and equilibrium; and who, like Siva,
the destroyer, destroys the ignorance of his pupils and the
sense of their own self-importance.

POT-POURRI

Iyengar does mayurasana on Diana Clifton's back.

B.K.S. IYENGAR COMES TO THE UNITED STATES

by Mary Palmer

W E IN ANN ARBOR, MICHIGAN, have often considered it our good fortune to have had a teacher who very early in our Yoga experiences introduced us to what she considered to be the finest text on Yoga. Through her encouragement we slowly learned the importance she attached to *Light on Yoga*—a book in which she found a system at work. When she went to live in another city, she left us without a teacher. But *Light on Yoga* remained with us, and for a while it became our only teacher. Perhaps we sensed that "It was better to follow a good book than a poor teacher." As a group, then, and perhaps without knowing it, we were testing it—our Guru—as we met together weekly to do postures and to study the text.

It can also be said that it was this book that has led many of us to travel across the world to find the man who was guiding our practice by way of photograph and page. We found this man in his home, teaching not only his devoted Pune pupils but students like ourselves from many other countries of the world. The man in the photographs was teaching and touching with the force and love of a Master. This experience brought encouragement in Yoga from a most exacting source. Mr. Iyengar made his indelible stamp. Our bodies were responding with meaning. The discovery was thrilling.

It was inevitable that we could not miss the opportunity for further classes with Mr. Iyengar. In England in 1970—and again in 1971—Mr. Iyengar's superb teaching left us with the feeling that there was no end to what might be called his virtuosity. There was a cue for each of us. We from Michigan now began urging him to come to our country. At the Ann Arbor "Y" we had been using his teaching methods, and here his work was best known. We invited him to come. He understood our need, and he came.

The Ann Arbor "Y" teachers and staff then set up a schedule for his classes and lecture-demonstrations not only in Ann Arbor but other cities, including the United Nations in New York. Two visits to this midwestern university city have brought together Yoga teachers and students from every part of the United States to study with him. We like to think of Ann Arbor as being his home in the U.S.

Students feeling the impact of his presence and teaching have tried to express what he has meant to them:

"I am only a beginner. He knows so much. How does he bring himself to my level?"

"After being in one of his classes, I will never go back to my old imprecise practice."

"His method has completely changed my approach to the postures. When he asked us, 'Where does the body end and the mind begin?', Yoga began to have some meaning for me."

304

"He continually demanded more than I felt there was to give, and there seemed to be more to give."

"He came to us as a Master teacher. We found him to be one."

From a teacher: "I feel that now I am just beginning to understand what Yoga is."

"He seems to roam through the class as a free spirit—creating unity."

"Every class was a period of discovery and new awareness." "In his own teaching and practice he has set the highest example for us to follow."

"The precision with which he performed the asanas and the discipline of the body and mind which was projected to the audience in his lecture-demonstration gave those who were skeptical of the value of Yoga a completely fresh understanding."

"He has given me the hope and means to refine my body as he had refined his—to house the spirit."

The eyes are the windows of the brain and the nerves are
the windows of the soul.

THE LION AND THE LAMB

by Elizabeth Kent

ONE MONDAY MORNING in May in Berkeley, California, a group of people gathered together to begin a week-long Yoga workshop with B.K.S. Iyengar. There were 100 or so people present for each session, most dressed as participants in leotards and shorts, the rest of us standing or sitting around the edge of the room observing.

Mr. Iyengar stood in front of the class with his hands on his hips, wearing form-fitting maroon trunks. Around his neck were the *Brahmopavita* threads which are given to young members of the Brahman community when they are initiated into prayers and mantras. A red line, a religious mark, runs from his hairline to the bridge of his nose. He is not much changed from the pictures in *Light on Yoga;* he is shorter than I expected, the hair is grayer, the waist a little thicker, perhaps. But the strong, angular face, the bushy eyebrows, the expanded pranayama chest and the long flexible legs are all familiar sights to those of us who have read and studied his book.

"Let me see now," he begins with a smile, his hands on his hips, "Which of you are old strings and which of you are new strings?" From a show of hands he divides the class into two groups: new students (those new to the

307

Iyengar method) on one side of the room, and old students on the other side. Then he begins the process of placing each body precisely where he wants it. "You stand here," he orders, jerking someone into place. "No, not there. I said here." One by one, he goes down each line pulling, pushing and jerking bodies around, putting them in place like pawns on a chessboard. His manner is brusque and definite. Like a tough army sergeant or a very strict Zen Master, he knows exactly what he wants and no one dares contradict him.

With everyone in place he strides about the room, hands on hips, adjusting someone here, correcting someone there and barking out a continuous flow of mind-boggling instructions. "This should never be stretched!" he roars. "How to teach you if you can't understand what I say!" I sat in a corner watching him, my feminist sensibilities awakening. I thought, "I have never seen such a blatant display of male arrogance and egotism." But I took consolation in the fact that he treated men and women alike. His voice is loud and powerful, easily heard, but not so easily understood when he gets excited and the words roll together in a staccato-like thunder.

"Bring the feet together," he orders, as everyone takes the standing pose *Tadasana*. "When you bring the feet together you have to feel the life flowing at the bottom of the feet. . . the inner knees and the outer knees should be felt. See whether they are running parallel to each other or not. The length of the inner right leg and the length of the inner left leg should run parallel to each other. The median plane of the right leg and the median plane of the left leg should face each other. You have to revolve the skin from the back to the front in order to bring the center of the legs to face each other. The right leg challenges the left. The left leg challenges the right."

And all the while he's slapping, poking and adjusting bodies as he strides about the room.

Rumors of Mr. Iyengar's "fierce" teaching style have been filtering around for years. Still, one is unprepared for the shock of seeing people being struck, kicked, pulled by the hair, lifted by the seat of the pants, yelled at, mocked and humiliated. Recalling the bars on the windows of the tiny stone room where she first met Iyengar, Rama Jyoti Vernon said jokingly, "I suspected they were there to keep the students from escaping." But Mr. Iyengar's students do not want to escape; in fact, they were all paying good money for the opportunity to be pulled and pushed about by his quick but sure hands—and feet. One is struck by the intelligence in Mr. Iyengar's feet—and he uses them like another pair of hands.

When I thought about it later, I realized that in all of the kicking and poking he did that morning, I could remember seeing only one person wince with pain. A few looked surprised, but no one looked hurt. On the contrary, some found relief. Jan Carpenter, a Yoga teacher from Berkeley came to class with acute pains in her right shoulder, pains so severe that at the beginning of the workshop she could not raise her arm more than thirty degrees. What exactly was wrong with the shoulder was not clear: "Some doctors tell me it's a virus infection; others say acute tendonitis. Who knows?" asked Jan. Still, it had been deteriorating rapidly for the past year and she had stopped doing Yoga because of the increasing pain. "If I had continued, my arm would be hanging at my side by now," she said.

Mr. Iyengar worked with her frequently during the week, adjusting her shoulders in the postures, and putting her through a series of shoulder stretches in which her arms were extended backwards, out over her head from a forward bend, then weighted down with a heavy pipe which she held in her hands. She was helped into headstands and shoulderstands, and held there. In short, she was encouraged to use the shoulder in specific ways. By the middle of the week the movement of her arm had inceased dramatically. Then near the end of the week, Mr. Iyengar made another adjustment and opened the shoulder even further; by Friday Jan was able to fully extend her arm. "It really is remarkable," she said and disclosed that she had had an astrological chart cast some time prior to the workshop and had been told that she was to have an extraordinary period between the dates May 11th and May 21st. I didn't know how beneficial Iyengar's method could be when I observed that first Monday morning class. Nor would I have believed it when I participated that afternoon.

"Stretch! Stretch! Stretch!" he yells. You are standing in a pose, stretching, you think, with every fiber in your body when suddenly there is a slap on your shoulder and a harsh voice says, "Move the skin *here!*" You try to think of your skin moving and hope something is happening. Another slap on the back, "You did not move like I tell you. Armpits roll from back to top. Why are you so slow? Am I explaining correctly or incorrectly? Eh?" He stands in front of you, demonstrates, then pushing a seemingly angry face directly in front of yours, he yells, "You understand? You understand?" Bewildered, embarrassed, you shyly answer "Yes." "So see if you can love like that," he says and walks away, smiling his broad, white-toothed smile. "To show compassion," he explains to the class, "you must be merciless. . . unless I shout she will not love." By "love," Iyengar means practice with devotion.

It is the surface contradictions that make the man so difficult, at first, to comprehend. "One minute I hate him and the next minute I love him," reflects a student after the first day. Then, laughing, "I would like to go to India to study, but I don't want to get an ulcer studying Yoga." Another student sees the classroom drama as just that—a drama. "He isn't caught up in it," she says. "It's just a show. If you look, you can see that his eyes are always soft." For myself, I can say that the Iyengar drama gets results. I, who had never been in a headstand longer than 60 seconds, stayed upside down that afternoon for five minutes, waiting for *permission* to come down.

Iyengar, describing himself, says, "I am an old-fashioned teacher. Even if you are good, I say you are not good. For me, if I see there is good, I have to be satisfied within myself, but I will never say it outside. The moment I say it, I close the door to your progress. To be a teacher, you must roar like a lion on the outside and be meek as a lamb on the inside."

However meek he may be on the inside, it does not show in the classroom. In class he is intensely concentrated, thorough in his explanation, and impatient with those who don't push themselves. Outside the classroom the question of ego does not arise; in fact, he appears quiet, almost mild-mannered in comparison to the intense, dramatic personality in the classroom. He is warm and obliging and has immense energy for a multitude of interests. Besides the two, high-powered, three-hour long classes he conducted each day during the workshop, he was also going sailing in the afternoons, visiting prisons to observe Yoga programs, going to the symphony and theater at night and getting up at five every morning to do three hours of Yoga before the nine o'clock classes.

It is this high-powered drive, the urge to do, to perfect, that is felt in the classroom. To perfect ourselves, says Iyengar, we must suffer; we must experience pain and learn how to deal with it. If you have a pain, he says, great; thank God, because you can learn so much from it. Pain teaches us about fear. When we face pain, we face fear, and facing fear leads to freedom.

Facing fear, facing the unknown is a fundamental part of Iyengar's Yoga. To face that fear, says Iyengar, to put yourself into a headstand, for instance, and conquer it, is to expand your freedom in both body and mind. When this happens, the unknown—what it is like to be upside down—becomes the known, and we are no longer afraid; we have penetrated some dark corner of the mind and have uprooted ignorance. To go further, to continue expanding, he says, we must again and again face the unknown and challenge our fears. For Iyengar and his students Yoga provides this continuous challenge. Yoga, as he defines it, is using the body as an instrument to sharpen the brain. "Where does the known end?" he asks, "Where does the unknown begin? Always known and unknown are going together. The known is where the brain goes with ease; here it is not stretched at all. There is no challenge as long as you stay within your limits."

Also basic to the Iyengar method is the belief that we cannot separate mind and body, that we are whole people with the consciousness or intelligence waiting to be awakened in every cell of the body. "How can I do with my body without my consciousness?" he asks. "One intelligence moves the arm, another keeps another part still. There is intelligence in the whole body. The skin is the outer intelligence, the self is the inner intelligence, and there should be tremendous communication between the two." "One should see with a thousand eyes," he says.

He talks a lot about the skin, pointing out movements so subtle, so minute as to be often imperceptible to the average eye. He watches the color of the skin to determine points of pressure; dry skin tells him that too much energy is directed inward; he can tell by touching the skin whether or not the consciousness is awake at that point. In his own practice the control of his skin has become so subtle that he can cause the skin to expand just by breathing. "It isn't necessarily the muscles that are moving;" observed Yoga teacher Felicity Hall, "it is so slow that it's like watching the skin open up." Iyengar can also control the hairs on his legs, causing them to stand up or lie down at will. Studying Yoga with someone whose control over the body is so developed, so refined, can be both fascinating and frustrating. As another teacher, Judith Lasater, put it, "It's like studying art with Michael-angelo, when what you need to know first is how to hold a paintbrush."

What makes studying with Iyengar unique are his powerful, somewhat ferocious teaching style, the use of props such as tables, chairs, walls and broom handles to achieve maximum stretch, the large number of standing poses he has developed and, most important, the particular way in which growth in consciousness is combined with work on the body. In the Wednesday morning class, using the asanas and the concepts of present, past, and future, he explained how consciousness works in movement. In my understanding it goes something like this: As the position of the body changes, the intelligence or consciousness must change to adapt to the movement; motion and consciousness go together. In other words, where the body is, the mind should be also. However, he distinguishes between consciousness and the thinking *process,* saying there is no static brain or consciousness, only a static process of thinking. When the thinking process is static, the mind stays in the security of the known; it rests in the past. This state of mind can be seen in the body that does not seek the unknown in a posture but remains within its limits; the posture is not alive. Or the body may rush into the posture toward the future while the mind is still in the past, and without motion and mind working together—without mindfulness—instability is created. This was demonstrated with a student doing the headstand: "Now, look what happened to the legs," says Iyengar. "The legs went to the future. Before there is stability, the legs went up. So confusion starts. Watch. Before she adjusted the head, the legs went up. The legs move to the future; the head remains in the past, so there is no security."

In Iyengar's Yoga the subtle minute movements—the tightening of the groin, the movement of the skin in the arch of the foot, the lifting of a kneecap—are the essentials of one-pointedness. These are called *actions.* The grosser right-foot-out-left-foot-in movements are called *motions.* Motions get you into a pose; actions refine it. So in a head balance, says Mr. Iyengar, "With forward extention, the action is from the center. The body balances in such a way that if you bring the heel back, the shoulders have to take the weight. . . . And when you stretch the front leg, you should tell the back leg, 'My dear friend, I am stretching here, so be aware. I will not allow you to be just sitting.' And the back leg should say, 'No, I am going to be attentive.' Create action in the back leg and then challenge the front to the back." *Actions,* then are the microscopic movements that begin to awaken consciousness in the body, and awakening consciousness is what the Iyengar method is all about.

Mr. Iyengar doesn't care for the Guru-worship style—people prostrating at his feet and such. "Soul is

314

pure," he says, "and your soul is as pure as mine." One of his students gave him a flower on Friday and said, "I think you are a great Master and I love you." He turned away like a shy little boy, then turned back and said, "Thank you."

And we say, "Thank you, Mr. Iyengar—and may your work prosper."

THE SELF IS IN EVERY CELL

by Mardi Erdman

Mr. IYENGAR was talking to us about posture as mandala—how the form has a center and lines radiate from that center. He moved easily into Trikonasana as if he lived there all the time. I was reminded of the meaning of asana: a dwelling place.

"The way I present myself is a mandala," he told us. "Why all this interest in mandalas to gaze at? Why not work in mandala? Is every cell, every limb in its position? Where is my intelligence? Is it only in a remote corner of my mind, or is it in the cells of my feet, my hands— everywhere? *That* is self-realization. The self is in every cell."

My first asanas under his direction were new experiences for me. His questions probed my tissues. Was my knee flexing in the mandala? What had gone outside the planes of the mandala? Were my fingers stretching equally? Then I was rudely awakened by the sound of a slap and realized that if his word didn't get the body's intelligence awakened, his slap would!

During the first few days I often felt disappointed, disillusioned and scared. I asked myself, as I agonized in

Parsvottanasana, why I had come. Why did I do Yoga? What did I need to learn? I kept thinking of my friends and teachers who has been here not once, but several times. Did they have some perverted need for punishment? Why would they go through this humiliation and very difficult work?

In class we found ourselves angered and bewildered by his arrogance and ferocity, but in awe of his artistry in teaching, his use of aids and metaphors to open our joints and minds, and his incedible mastery of the asanas and pranayama. He insisted on discrimination and integrity. Every word must have the power of clarity. To teachers he said, "Don't watch the eyes of your students as you say, 'Bend your knee.' Watch every knee and see *how* it bends." He held us accountable for what we said. Once, while a student was doing *Parsvakonasana,* he said, "Does the knee hit the arm?" "I think so." came the reply. He roared back, "You *think* so!? Either you know or you don't know. There is no *think* so!" It reminded me of Yoda's words in "The Empire Strikes Back:" "Do, or do not. There is no try." Another time, after a demonstration and a question a student mumbled, "Then it doesn't matter." He pounced. An off-hand remark became a valuable lesson in meaning what you say. "That's not Yoga, 'It doesn't matter.' It *matters!*" And in the flame of his eyes I understood the integrity of life, thought, work and action.

After a particularly rough workout in *Sarvangasana,* Mr. Iyengar said to us, as we surrendered to *Savasana,* "That innocent mind you have just experienced is the divine mind. That is what I have given you a glimpse of—spiritual silence! Now you can go home."

Would I go back? You bet! Today, if I could. Mr. Iyengar teaches the essence of Yoga. He was not always fair—neither is life. He often changed his mind. He baffled us, disturbed us, angered us, and levelled us. But as our bodies became light and obedient, our spirits became buoyant and free. He is one of those great teachers who call us to be our best selves. He corrects, rather than protects. And under his persistent guidance, we learn the meaning of Yoga.

Excerpted from "The Self is in Every Cell" by Mardi Erdman. Reprinted with permission from *Yoga Journal*, January/February 1984. Copyright © 1984 *Yoga Journal*.

The way I present myself is a mandala. Why all this interest in mandalas to gaze at? Why not work in mandala? Is every cell, every limb in its position? Where is my intelligence? Is it only in a remote corner of my mind, or is it in the cells of my feet, my hands—everywhere? That is self-realization. The self in every cell.

IYENGAR
—A RETROSPECTIVE

Compiled by Bill Graham.

The following are excerpts from interviews originally published in the newsletter of the *Victoria Yoga Centre,* British Columbia, Canada, where some of Mr. Iyengar's American and Canadian students talked about their teacher.

Ramanand Patel
In a 1981 interview in Victoria, Ramanand was asked if he had found that a person's way of teaching could be more powerful than the specific technique taught.

I'm very convinced that the words spoken to me by Mr. Iyengar make a greater difference than exactly the same words coming from some other person.

I'll give you a very simple example of a student who is a very, very good student, who came to me and said, "I have a problem in my hips during forward bends." Now, her forward bends were very, very good, better than mine. I looked and realised what she was doing. I said, "You are not turning your knees properly. Do it this way;" but she kept doing it, and kept complaining of the problem, never turning as much as she should. I kept saying, "this is

321

where your problem is," but she was looking for a much deeper answer to explain why that problem was there.

We were both in a class with Mr. Iyengar later. She bent down, got the same pain, reacted to that and told Mr. Iyengar, "It hurts." He came and put his foot on it, and she said, "God, the pain is gone!" All he did with his foot was turn the knee the way I was trying to tell her all the time.

In a sense, she must have seen my posture and, although she regarded me as her teacher, she must have felt in her own mind that her posture was better than mine. Hence, if I was saying something very simple to her, that was not going to appeal to her. Yet, that very simple thing coming from Mr. Iyengar immediately made sense to her and her pain was gone.

In March 1982, Ramanand again spoke of Mr. Iyengar's excellence as a teacher:

I think the one thing that really stands out in my mind is the very first time I attended what was considered a teacher's training group or class in Brighton in England. My teacher who introduced me to Mr. Iyengar was Helena Thomas. This was the first time I'd met Mr. Iyengar. We were all standing in Tadasana. He walked around and came to me. No one had told him anything about my shoulder, and if you looked at it, you could not immediately say that there was anything wrong with the shoulder. He was the first person, of all the people, all the experts that I had seen, who immediately asked what was wrong with my shoulder. That obviously had a very strong impact on me that I never forgot. The man has x-ray eyes. Very often he corrects you in a sense that may appear callous or careless or haphazard. Within that haphazard movement on the surface lies a tremendous amount of care and exactness that I haven't seen anywhere else. Not just in Yoga but in life in general.

After a class that was supposed to last three hours but had actually lasted four, when everybody was pretty tired and wet, he put me in the shoulderstand. Then he put his toe under my cervical spine and lifted it from the floor. It not only takes a lot of strength in the toes to do that but it gave me an experience like an opening of the posture that I had never before experienced in any posture. He smiled and said, "That's what you should get with every posture." It convinced me, if I needed convincing by then, that the man knew what he was talking about.

Maureen Carruthers
In an interview published in March 1982, Maureen spoke about Iyengar the teacher:

He is a genius. I know people in dance and great conductors are very eccentric. I would say Mr. Iyengar's eccentric side comes out, and you go deeper than that to understand him. You also see his impatience and the frustration, I would say more frustration than impatience, at us being blind.

I can remember Mr. Iyengar saying to Bruce (Carruthers), "You see, you see, nobody sees these things, nobody sees what I am doing." From the deepest part of himself he wants to share this work. He is very brave. Warriors are very brave. He is that kind of man. He takes the warrior stance.

This is his way of working and it is not for everybody. If you decide that's the way you can learn, Mr. Iyengar is a good teacher. I don't think it's the only way. It comes from his essence and he must use it. What comes from my essence, I must use. To keep working as a teacher is to keep knowing what's true in me. I think that's how it comes for Mr. Iyengar.

Shirley Daventry French
In a 1982 interview, Shirley was asked if she had felt prepared for her first trip to study with Mr. Iyengar:

In a sense you can never be prepared to study with Mr. Iyengar, because he will always take you to that edge and beyond. He will demand as much as you're capable of giving at any time. Really, you do the best you can in preparation and go with sincerity. I think that's the at I was ready in the sense that my previous work had prepared me psychologically, but my body—I could see how much more there was to do and how far ahead he was of the place I was working. I would come out of the classes sometimes and think, "What did I understand?" It was overwhelming. There was so much detail, so much refinement and so much depth. And then the physical endurance: just staying with it—working, working, in the heat, to the ends of your endurance. But there was a trust that some of it would be going in—I had to trust that process.

During the course I would have moments when I would be very excited. I would think: I just can't wait until I go back and try and pass some of this on to other people. Then when I did get back to Canada, I thought: how can I teach? I don't know anything. This man is a genius. He's so far ahead of anything I've ever experienced; how could I possibly teach? There was a period of real insecurity. Fortunately it was Christmas, and there weren't any classes. When the time came to begin teaching, I felt very strange before the first class, very unsure about what I was going to do and how any of it was going to come out. Then I began to notice that some of it was beginning to come out, in my words, my interpretation from my own experience. So that trust was rewarded.

We worked in the morning for two or three hours—it would depend. He would suddenly say at some point, "Enough for today" and walk out, and the class was over. I don't know why, and he didn't explain why. Probably he just sensed that people were fatigued, and there was no point in carrying on, because "intensive" is the right word to describe the course. We've joked that when people say they've "studied intensively" with Mr. Iyengar, the word "intensive" is superfluous, because there's no other way!

Later in the same interview, Shirley told of an experience she had while in Pune in 1979:

In the afternoon practice sessions, one of the most interesting things for me, was that sometimes I would come and be doing various poses when I would suddenly notice that Mr. Iyengar had been there all the time doing his own practice—yet I hadn't noticed him at all. It was strange. In the morning classes when he was teaching, he was everywhere in the room. He would be teaching in one corner; you would be in another corner, and he would see you, know exactly what you were doing and sometimes come bounding over. But this man—whose presence was everywhere, whom you wouldn't possibly ignore when he was teaching—when he was doing his own practice was almost invisible. At these times his practice was so internalized, you would not think of intruding once you did notice that he was there. You would know if he was open to being asked anything or if he was just working at his own practice. It was very interesting, because Patanjali in the last section of his Yoga Sutras talks about the fruits of the practice of Yoga, and one of them is the ability to become invisible. When I read that, I thought that it meant something like the film *The Invisible Man* (laughs), and perhaps it does too, but then in India I began to think about this in different terms. To all intents and purposes, Mr. Iyengar was invisible, yet he was very much there—his body was there. So that's another way of looking at that.

—and after studying with Mr. Iyengar a second time:

How do I feel? The answer is "sober."

There was no "blinding flash on the road to Damascus"—no dramatic breakthrough—only a reaffirmation that Yoga is hard work, constant practice, vigilance and (paradoxically) surrender; that on this path you need courage, endurance and the willingness to get on with the work without looking for instant reward. That is not to say that there were not moments of revelation when ignorance was replaced by understanding, but for the present, these are bits and pieces of an experience that is correctly called "intense."

Real break-throughs come as a result of sustained practice. Mr. Iyengar has worked for nearly fifty years refining his art and, not surprisingly, has harsh words for those of us in the West who call ourselves experts after a year or two, a few months or even a few weeks. That is why I chose the word "sober." To work with the Master is humbling; it is also an awakening.

326

From previous experience I knew how demanding a teacher he is—but I had forgotten just *how* hard his classes are. I knew what a fine teacher he is—but I had forgotten *how* good and the extent of his genius. Experiences fade in memory. So perhaps after all there was a flash in the presence of the Master as he illuminated the depth of my ignorance.

Carole Miller
February 1983—on her first class with the Master

On November 15th with great anticipation we arrived at the Institute at Pune. The class began at 9:00 am. At 9:03 we were filled with electrifiying attention. Mr. Iyengar had begun in a way that most Westerners were not accustomed to. With great shouts he was certainly letting us know what obedience meant. The first class was three hours long. Experiencing the unlimited way in which we could work our bodies and the degree of concentration with which we worked amazed me. We were totally immersed. I likened the experience to giving birth for the first time. No one can really be "prepared!"

For me, that was one of the most difficult days of the Intensive. During the course, Mr. Iyengar never let up in his demands of us, and we never stopped trying. Each time he shouted, it was as if we were being charged with a renewed energy allowing us to go to new places. We worked very basic asanas and he reminded us of a sense of humility both in his language and his eye.

The work with Mr. Iyengar was intense. He demanded concentration and obedience. Without this ability to surrender on the part of the student, true learning cannot take place. He was most critical when he sensed resistance or inattention. When this occurred, his temper was at its fiercest. He showed a sense of humour and compassion, however, when we were able to work with awareness and began to have a glimmer of understanding. It was then that we heard the greatly appreciated words, "Not bad." We would laugh along with him and his assistants. A feeling of warmth filled us.

Ingelise Nherlan Segato
From an interview published in April 1982

I went to India to study with Mr. Iyengar in 1976 and again in 1979. Those two experiences were like night and day, and the third time will probably be different again.

I think he is such a typical example of a true Guru, because wherever you are at, you take from him. He is so complete; but that doesn't mean perfect; he is human too, and I'm sure he has his faults. He doesn't grab hold of you and say, "This is how you should do it. This is what you must do in your character." He just leaves you to learn. His presence is simply there for you to learn from, so whatever you need, you can take it from him, because he is just there being himself all the time.

At the end of this interview, Ingelise told a story about an encounter she had with Mr. Iyengar during her first trip to India which became a very important incident in her life.

The first time I was in India, during my last two weeks at that time, Mr. Iyengar and I were just beginning to come together, and he was beginning to appreciate my work there. I was learning; I accepted his teaching, and I was learning a new me. It was time to go home, and we came to Bombay. At the beginning of the class I didn't want to intrude particularly; I was ready to take his Bombay class, but I didn't know if I was allowed to do that, so I just sat quietly and waited, and he started the class. Then he came up and stood towering over me and looked down with his famous grin and his twinkly eyes and sort of hit me gently across the arm and said, "Are you going to sit there or are you going to do?" I sat there and said, "Well, I don't know; what should I do?" He looked at me with so much compassion—I'll never in my life forget it—and there was an urge in his voice, like please hear what I'm saying, and he said, "Do, do, do!" and since then I have been doing, doing, doing, and when I don't "do" I hear his voice, because it was just love, "Please do."

He said "Do, do, do!" and since then I have been doing,
doing, doing, and when I don't, I hear his voice,
because it was just love, **"please** do."

Ingalese Segato

A GATHERING
IN SAN FRANCISCO

—The First International
Iyengar Yoga Convention
by Manouso Manos

IN THE FALL OF 1984 more than eight hundred Yoga practitioners from around the world came to San Francisco, California to attend the First International Iyengar Yoga Convention. For ten days they immersed themselves in the art and science of Yoga, exchanging ideas, sharing practices, and honoring Yogacharya B.K.S. Iyengar and his work.

The idea of a convention had been tossed around the Iyengar Yoga community for a number of years. Some people sought the opportunity to be around many different practitioners of the yogic arts; others were more interested in concentrated study with some of the best teachers in the subject. All seemed to be in agreement that the opportunity to study with B.K.S. Iyengar was something not be missed. When we received the news that Mr. Iyengar himself would attend, there was an air of excitement. Long-time students who had been fortunate enough to study with him in person eagerly anticipated a reunion

331

with "Guruji," while others looked forward to seeing and studying with him for the first time. For a small percentage of those who attended the convention it was their first exposure to Iyengar Yoga, but for the majority it was an opportunity to deepen their understanding of Mr. Iyengar's work and refine previously gained yogic skills.

Mr. Iyengar had not been in the United States since 1976, and the North American Yoga community was ready for his return. Interest in Yoga had increased on all of Mr. Iyengar's previous visits; each time more and more people had clamoured to study with him. Everywhere that this Guru has gone in recent years has had a "full house," and this convention was no exception. There was a waiting list of almost two hundred people attracted by the possibility of working with and being around this great man.

In addition to the chance to meet Mr. Iyengar, participants were offered a selection of classes with advanced teachers of Iyengar Yoga from around the world. Mr. Iyengar brought with him some of his most experienced Indian teachers, all long-time pupils who had studied with him on a regular basis for many years. The International Faculty also included world-renowned teachers from Europe and South Africa, with outstanding personal reputations. Senior teachers of Iyengar Yoga from the United States and Canada formed a North American Faculty which also included many teachers of international repute. Such a gathering of experience and talent was unique. Many of these teachers command a large personal following and their pupils expressed excitement at the possibility of taking classes with their favorite teacher and learning from Mr. Iyengar as well.

Those who attended the convention came to pay homage to a man whose personal integrity and dedication to his art inspires and encourages others to become refined in their own practice of Yoga. Mr. Iyengar has not created a group of clones or bunch of sheep, but has nurtured the yogic ideal of self-examination and self-growth in all his pupils. Teachers trained by him are encouraged to develop their individual talents and use them to create a love of Yoga and to nurture the soul of each practitioner. This convention allowed free expression and sprouting of the many individual branches of this great yogic tree.

Participants began each morning with a two hour asana class; in the afternoon they were offered either pranayama or another asana class. The evening offerings ranged from questions and answers with Mr. Iyengar to a medical panel where the yogic practices and their therapeutic value were discussed by a group of physicians who are students of Mr. Iyengar. One evening there was a display of Yoga dance and Indian dancing. Mr. Iyengar's days were spent rotating from class to class to help in instruction. Both pupils and teachers were challenged and helped by the possibility of this man observing their work. There were nearly two hundred and eighty classes at the convention, and Mr. Iyengar participated in more than eighty of these.

The climax of the ten days came when Mr. Iyengar took the stage for a lecture-demonstration before an audience of two thousand people. To listen to a man who has practiced Yoga for over fifty years is a rare treat. To match one's own inhalation or exhalation against one who has done pranayama (the science of breath) for as long as B.K.S. Iyengar is to be humbled. To watch a man in his mid-sixties move with such grace and agility is an inspiration.

The feedback after the convention was extremely positive. A questionnaire was sent out a few months after the event, and when asked what the best part of the convention was, the overwhelming response was the opportunity to study with B.K.S. Iyengar. He was the reason for considering this venture in the first place, and the major force in its being such a successful gathering.

Mr. Iyengar had been promised the profits from the lecture-demonstration in advance of the actual convention. Upon his departure from the United States he asked that this money be used to help the local Yoga community strengthen and grow. His generosity has made the San Francisco Iyengar Yoga Institute one of the world's best places to explore the subject of Yoga.

Looking back at those ten days in 1984, I realize what a remarkable man Shri B.K.S. Iyengar really is. It was his work, energy and enthusiasm that brought this diverse group of individuals together in the spirit of Yoga. Those who have been touched by him will never forget him, and will be influenced and inspired by this contact for many years to come.

B.K.S. IYENGAR...
HIMSELF

by Bill Graham

I REALLY DIDN'T KNOW what I was getting into when I volunteered to report on B.K.S. Iyengar's visit to Victoria. I thought at the time that it was going to be a fairly normal sort of event to describe. I would take pictures of the three morning asana classes at the "Y," and try to build up a general set of impressions of Iyengar the man and the teacher as he checked the quality of Yoga teaching done in his name. In effect, that is what I did.

I did not, however, come prepared to experience the whirlwind that is Mr. Iyengar. This whirlwind quality is giving me problems now, as I try to describe that very busy day.

First some background. For the last six or eight months a flurry of activity had been building in preparation for his visit. First there was information about the International Iyengar Yoga Convention in San Francisco. Then rumours that Mr. Iyengar would use his North American visit to travel and see whether or not teachers using his name were honestly working in a way he approved of. The rumours became plans. Iyengar himself would be first in Vancouver. . . then perhaps. . . then definitely in Victoria. It was some time before the details of dates, times, possibilities could be settled, but preparation began. Teachers began to work together and individually to refine their skills in case they were the one checked by the Master. Committees formed, fund raising events were planned and executed. The result was an emotional rollercoaster of a summer for many of our most active members. The fund raising dance had to be cancelled, probably because we scheduled it too close to the summer break. Not enough people were willing to commit themselves to buying a ticket in advance to warrant all the preparation that would be required. Then there were doubts about all of our preparation. Did our group have enough energy to make this event a success? The activity continued through the summer, with large groups of people involving themselves in planning for the asana classes at the "Y," for the dinner and celebration in honour of Mr. Iyengar, for billeting all of our visitors, providing transportation, making sure that everyone was well cared for.

Finally, and almost by surprise, the visit was upon us. Because most things had been done in advance there was a slight lull as many of our members went to the Conference in San Francisco. Then, all at once it was September 6th.

Down at the "Y," there were lists of which students were to be in what room, everyone classified by level. Which teachers were to be where? After a flurry of confusion, classes began. Mr. Iyengar was not there yet, nor any of the others staying at the French home, but the students were waiting. I stayed in the hall, preparing to use extra cameras I had borrowed, and generally tying up odds and ends.

336

When Mr. Iyengar finally arrived, it was incredible. He is a vortex of energy. Perhaps he was irritated at having been late, or perhaps he always moves at that speed, but he was *ready to go.*

The next three hours were extraordinary. I followed from class to class watching, taking photographs, and staying out of the way.

Frankly, I am at a loss to describe what happened. First of all, I think it is unfair for a non-participant to attempt to present what passed between Mr. Iyengar and his teachers. Immediately on entering the first room he began to offer suggestions, to criticise, to question. To one on the outside, some of these comments seemed to come from nowhere. He did not seem to have the time to judge what ought to be said. Still, I have talked with many of the teachers with whom he worked, and they agree that what he said to them was apt, and what was needed—though perhaps not what was wanted.

The students in the sessions were very interesting to observe, too. Reactions were very mixed. Some were shocked and confused. Mr. Iyengar's piercing vision brought many suggestions and questions about their ways of working. His assumptions sometimes missed the mark, but most often were dead on. Some students were protective of their teachers. These are our teachers, and they are good teachers. This criticism was too harsh, or too strange. There was some indignation and much surprise. There was also a very highly charged atmosphere, and some very serious work.

Iyengar moved through the three rooms which held the classes. With each teacher he was different. Those moving with him were privileged to see many different men in one. In some cases he was the lion which is so often reported on. With other teachers he was the mentor, gently but firmly guiding toward deeper understanding. With others we saw an impishness, and a playfulness which surprised me. In all circumstances we saw love. Iyengar has the most incisive vision that I have ever witnessed. He sees things beyond all of us. He sees them quickly. Above all, he really cares. His approach to several students, from the most senior to relatively junior, was to take them back from levels to which they aspired, suggesting ways of using furniture and props to release tight areas, to ease pain, to get the full benefit of their asanas. Often his suggestion was harder work. He pointed out how we are afraid to work hard enough to pass through our limitations and pain into a true understanding of Yoga.

For the last hour of the session, all three groups joined in the gym for one huge class. Mr. Iyengar himself taught. "You are lucky I am teaching," he said. "I am breaking my promise." We *were* lucky. I certainly ached to join in the class. It was very, very difficult to stay on the sidelines. But, from the sidelines, I witnessed the most remarkable Yoga class I have ever seen. The group moved from the most complete concentration to chaos, as everyone crowded around to watch a point demonstrated, and then back into utter one-pointedness as Iyengar led them through a series of standing poses. These seventy-five people truly were lucky. We may never have an opportunity like that in Victoria again.

Then it was over.

Teachers and special guests had been invited to a luncheon at Shambhala House. Swami Sivananda Radha had travelled from Yasodhara Ashram for the occasion, and the two of them clearly enjoyed meeting again.

338

Felicity Hall and Donald Moyer had also come to join us there. After the intensity of the morning classes, it was a great pleasure to relax and talk with friends, for many the first opportunity since summer.

In the evening there was the Celebration and Dinner for Mr. Iyengar at the Crystal Gardens. The setting was beautiful, and the event moved with hardly a hitch. An hour-long reception provided over 150 guests with an opportunity to meet Mr. Iyengar and those travelling with him. The dinner was followed by a series of brief speeches. Yoga Centre President, Shirley Daventry French, introduced the head table guests and the people involved in preparing for and carrying through the day's activities. Victoria Mayor Peter Pollen extended an official welcome to Mr. Iyengar and his party from the city. Derek French welcomed Swami Radha and Mr. Iyengar.

Then Swami Radha offered an appreciation of Mr. Iyengar and his work. She described how she had come to visit Mr. Iyengar during her last trip to India. Speaking of Guruji Iyengar, she said "On a personal level I have not met anybody of a combination that is so unique—generosity, kindness, and also the very fierce and demanding teacher that I have seen when watching him in the class; who knows precisely what he is doing to not only a millimeter but a fraction, and to penetrate most of the things that we hear pass by. (Others) don't have enough power. There's not enough behind it that will catch and really penetrate to a level of conviction that will change our lives; and this is what it is necessary to do. Our lives have to be changed; we have to ask the question over and over again 'what do we live for,' and all you here, who have much more, and much longer contact with Mr.

Iyengar: don't listen only with your ears—listen with your intuition. You might never hear so much compassion again."

Mr. Iyengar responded with thanks for the honour shown him, and for his teachers, who carry the message of Yoga. Referring to the dinner we had just consumed, he said, "As you all know I will not speak much about Yoga, because if I speak on Yoga the food which you have eaten where the blood is concentrating—the moment I speak the blood will rush to the brain and you will get indigestion. . . so I try to control myself so that you will feel bodily healthy and mentally peaceful so that the day may go very well tomorrow."

His message was brief: "One reason why you should do Yoga is that, as with a country that is weak the aggressor annexes that nation, so with the body. Diseases are outside of our skin, and we do not know the time that they might enter. If we are slightly careless about keeping the body healthy, the disease which is waiting outside the skin finds its dwelling place and brings unhappiness and disturbs our balance of mind, our balance of thinking. Then emotional upheavals come, and intellectual clarity fades.

"So I request you all to see that the diseases do not penetrate this body so that we can carry the message of health not only in this generation but also in the coming generations. Unless and until we take the responsibility of today, the future will not be bright at all. So please, continue your practice for the sake of the coming generation, so that (they) may have a tremendous intellectual stability, intellectual clarity, emotional stability, physical health and happy minds. I request this and take leave of you. God bless you all!"

And so ended the visit. Volunteers transported members of Mr. Iyengar's party who had been billeted around the city to the airport for an 8 am flight on to Edmonton.

We can already see, however, that the visit will go on for some time. As the fall session of Yoga classes began at the Victoria "Y," Mr. Iyengar was present. In my regular class things have changed. We are taking new directions, and making new approaches, based on what Mr. Iyengar offered during his short stay. I have heard that not only my present teacher has been affected in this way. I know from experience that this change will go on, and it will be some time before the full benefit of this brief encounter is realized.

This article was first published in the *Victoria Yoga Centre newsletter,* October 1984 on the occasion of Mr. Iyengar's first visit to Canada.

Freedom is precision and Yoga takes me to that.

PORTRAIT OF B.K.S. IYENGAR

by Karin Stephan

OFTEN REFERRED TO as both the lion and the lamb, Iyengar is at once a severe task master in class (whose precision and pedagogical techniques have caused people to refer to him as the Martha Graham of Yoga), and a charming, humorous, and playful personality outside of class. At sixty-four he has an energy and magnetism which few men can match. Above all, he is totally and unconditionally himself at all times—probably one of the main reasons he is so loved by those who know him.

I first met Iyengar in Pune in the summer of 1970. I had gone there with no expectations, but had simply heard his name while I was studying Yoga in Mysore earlier that year. As with the meeting of any remarkable human being, it was a seemingly insignificant incident which nonetheless left an indelible impression. We had been asked to do the shoulderstand, and as I was attempting to put myself into the posture, Iyengar came over to me, folded my legs into a lotus position, then bent them over first to the right side of my head so that the knees touched the floor and then over to the left in the same manner. He grunted sternly, "Ah, tell me now, has any other Yoga teacher made you work like this?" There was obviously a challenge in his voice and I responded meekly but truthfully, "No Sir, not at all." As I tried to undo the knot he had put me in, I wondered exactly what I was doing there. But after class, when I went out into the sticky night air of Pune, I was overcome with a sense of elation. I had received a big challenge, one I was determined to meet.

The next time I encountered Iyengar was in London in 1972. He was giving a seminar there and I rejoiced when I heard he would be in Europe as I was living in Paris at the time. This second time the challenges were even greater, the sense of excitement and newness even more enhanced than that first class in Pune. That moment had established something for me in my mind forever. I kept thinking about a quote I had read in one of Carlos Castaneda's books about what a true warrior was. Don Juan was chiding Castaneda for something: "I once told you that the freedom of a warrior here is either to act impeccably or act like a nincompoop. Impeccability is indeed the only act which is free and thus the true measure of a warrior's spirit." It was this word "impeccability"—without flaw or fault—which kept ringing in my ears as I would think of working with Iyengar. Impeccability and freedom, freedom through impeccability. I learned, during subsequent years of study with him that this, coupled with the initial sense of challenge I had received in the summer of 1970, were the hallmarks of his teaching.

My last encounter came this past January when I went to study with him at his Institute in Pune. There was a group of over forty students, mostly from the

United States but some from Holland, England, and South Africa.

I had been to the Institute four years previously but had forgotten the long arduous flight from Boston to London, to New Delhi, to Bombay, to Pune. Fortunately, upon arrival I found a comfortable hotel to stay in overnight to prepare myself for again studying with Iyengar.

The next morning, as I climbed into the rickshaw to go across town, the sun hitting my eyes from the early morning traffic, I was overcome once again with a quiet peace and joy that I would soon be working again under the sharp eye of my teacher. I had forgotten the distance from the hotel to the Institute and was so nervous about getting there in time that I almost failed to see the irridescent beauty of the blue-grey swampy waters beneath the bridge we were crossing over or the sparkling colors of the saris in the early morning sun.

Nevertheless, we pulled up in front of the Institute in ample time and I noticed outside the gates the familiar sight of the scooters belonging to his students, mostly Indians but also some foreigners, from the seven o'clock class. As I walked towards the building which rose up into a pyramid at the top, I had time to catch a glimpse of the lush flowers and perfectly trimmed garden lining the path to the entrance way. Very shortly the students from the early morning class descended the stairs, and though there were some familiar faces amongst the group, there was little time to chat. Upstairs the students mingled or began to warm up, careful to avoid any complicated postures for fear of Iyengar's reprimands about "showing off."

The clock struck the hour, which brought a hush in the room as people found positions on the floor for

345

themselves. Iyengar appeared, dressed in white cotton Indian shirt and dhoti with his bright colored Yoga shorts underneath. On his forehead was the familiar descending red line going from the root of his hair to the middle of his eyebrows. His hair, which was a silver grey, had grown somewhat longer since I last saw him, and perhaps he had put on a little weight. Except for that, the same energy was there, the same expansive smile, the same sonorous quality in his voice, the same sternness—all was intact, and even though he was sixty-four, he appeared as alive, as vital, as full of fire as ever.

After catching the eye of all of us, he started in immediately, even before the minute hand had gone beyond the hour of nine: "All right, everybody take their place." Coming around to each of us, he placed us in a particular position in the room which we would maintain throughout the seminar.

"What's happening in your right foot? What's happening in your left? Your right thigh, left thigh, spine, right side of the back, left side of the back?" he challenged us. We immediately became totally aware of our bodies, descending our awareness to each and every part, each and every cell. The posture was *tadasana,* which means mountain, and it is the very first posture he teaches. "How can you learn to stand on your head if you can't even stand on your feet?" he chided us. For Iyengar, a student must know how to do the simplest posture with the greatest amount of awareness and intelligence before he or she can execute complicated asanas. It is like working on the limbs of the tree without having strengthened the trunk.

Some of us were secretly awaiting the more difficult postures, the ones which make us "work," but it was not up to us. Gradually we became aware that Iyengar fully intended to bring us back to zero again before he went on, to help us understand the essence of the pose and not the pose itself.

As the days passed, the group continued to grow together, sharing each other's victories and each other's setbacks. We knew we had not come to be flattered because, according to Iyengar, once he flatters a student, that student will no longer work to the maximum. We realized as well that we had not come for new techniques either, but rather, to receive the flower of Iyengar's forty-seven years of experience as a teacher in India, Europe, Africa and North America. We had come to learn, moreover, what it means to experience that which Iyengar tells us over and over again, that "Yoga is precision in action", that only through precise action does freedom flow throughout the body.

"Stephan," he once yelled at me from the other side of the room, as I was doing a sitting pose with my back to him, "I can tell from the dullness of your hair that your posture is dull!" "Keep the candles of your cells on fire," he cried out at another time as we moved into a difficult balancing posture. As we tried to execute the poses with the greatest amount of awareness, we would feel the energy of his voice running throughout the veins and arteries of our bodies to our brains and then back to our toes again.

Taking a class with Iyengar, one sometimes gets the impression that he literally has eyes in the back of his head. When questioned on this he answered, "When I'm teaching, I have to watch hundreds of times those bodies and in that observation of one minute, I may be seeing twenty or thirty times what you may never see. So my

347

eyes, in a split second, are moving everywhere." At a later time he commented, "You see, it's like fire. Fire has no limit, does it? It just lightens everywhere. So when I'm teaching, I'm nothing but fire."

Anyone who has had the opportunity to study with Iyengar is aware of this Iyengar energy. There is an almost electrifying atmosphere in the classroom which lasts from beginning to end. It keeps students so tuned to the moment that though the mind may wander from time to time, caught by the piercing cry of the chick pea vendor in the street or the sight of the brilliant red flowers on the trees outside the classroom, the energy itself brings one constantly back to the present. In fact, as one senior pupil of Iyengar's, Angela Farmer, commented, this can act as something of a drawback. "He has a special kind of energy and part of the response is to that energy and not to his instructions," she said.

Though many students come for help with mental problems as well as physical difficulties, Iyengar feels that the most important thing is to work first with the body. In fact, at different times, he has referred to himself as a gardener: "As the gardener gives tremendous attention to the tree, how to clean it, how to keep it healthy, what to do, what not to do, where to look, and as he removes the weeds so that the plant may not be destroyed, so each individual is a gardener in this divine body."

This perception of matter as being also divine has its roots in the Indian philosophy of Vishnuism which Iyengar follows. "In the philosophy of Vishnuism, nature and spirit both are eternal. Nature changes, but the spirit does not change." "Whereas some think," he continues, "that the world is illusion or 'maya' and that all things which exist are 'maya', you should not be attracted to that illusion. So naturally, if everything is illusion, even to realize the soul becomes an illusion. But the Vishnuite says, 'no, both are eternal, but transformation takes place, and though matter is eternal, it is also changeable—changeable, but not an illusion.'"

It is out of this philosophy of the concrete that Iyengar has set himself the task of understanding how Yoga asanas are able to work as a therapy as well as a spiritual discipline. Hence, over the past several years, he has developed not only the art of teaching and practising the asanas, but also the science of applying them to difficult nervous system, circulatory system, or spinal problems. For the past five or six years he has held weekly medical classes at his institute, classes which are attended not only by people who need help, but by many of his student teachers as well.

Iyengar can often spot a student's physical weakness as soon as he or she walks into the room, but some of the problems are more apparent than others. Students have come to him with a wide range of difficulties, including muscular dystrophy, acute arthritis, stroke, cancer, slipped disc, hernia, migraine headache and insomnia. In each case, the therapeutic method he employs is unique. He makes use of ropes, benches, bolsters, (thick, heavy pillows), bandages which he ties around the eyes to create an immediate sense of relaxation, weights, and chairs. Every "patient" works on a series of exercises which he or she has been taught, often being helped into the postures by Iyengar and his assistants. Iyengar prefers to use the props to support the students so that they can work independently. He feels that it is essential for students to develop their own will for the healing process to take place.

The asanas interact on the body producing multiple effects on various parts. Mary Schatz, M.D., a pathologist from Tennessee who is writing a book on Iyengar's medical work, has codified and documented his work over the past four years, showing how Yoga affects simultaneously the relaxation response, the parasympathetic and sympathetic nervous systems, as well as respiration and circulation. Iyengar himself believes that the circulatory and respiratory systems are the "gates of our existence. If these two gates are not kept very well, the rest of the system will never function at all. Through these systems we develop tremendous vital energy, which is absorbed into the blood stream. We 'irrigate' different areas of the body with various postures and we have to observe which posture is going to act on that area. So the yogi says, 'Unfocus the blood in one area and bring it to another area, then the organ is supplied sufficiently and improves from the disease.'"

Iyengar feels that the most important quality of any teacher, especially when working with sick people, is to learn "how to put your body into their body and bring it to the place where you yourself are." For him it is absolutely essential to break down the barrier between the teacher and the student. "The most essential quality for a teacher is to be sincere and to treat the body of whomever you are teaching as if it were your own body. Then only does the oneness between the teacher and the taught come," he says.

Iyengar admits that he has no system when it comes to his medical cases. He works more by a sense of empathy and a direct, intuitive perception of what must be done from moment to moment. That is why it is difficult to imitate his work in this area and most teachers who go to study with him, although they may observe and sometimes help in the medical classes, will concentrate on healthy students back home.

In the normal classroom situation, among students training to become Yoga teachers, Iyengar becomes not only the true pedagogue but the true artist as well. Working simultaneously with a detailed analysis of the body and poetic imagery to help understand the movement, he takes the students from one posture to the next with a myriad of details to help them understand how to execute the pose.

Some people in fact have often wondered what the Iyengar technique really means. Is it any different from standard Hatha Yoga? The difference has been in the interpretation of how to execute the postures, not the postures themselves. With Iyengar's flair for precision, a sense of perfection in each movement, an undaunted awareness of every cell and muscle of the body as you flow through the postures, and a meticulousness in observation which he instills in each and every teacher, there has necessarily developed a certain approach which distinguishes itself from others. As Iyengar comments, "Yoga belongs to a civilization which is 3,000 years old. It cannot be my Yoga or somebody else's Yoga, but as everything has to have a common brand, my Yoga has a brand."

Iyengar will reprove students very quickly if he senses that they have been practicing or working mechanically. "Do not perform the asanas mechanically," he says, "with the mind wandering elsewhere. Perform them with total movement and involvement. Penetrate the intelligence from one end of the body to the other—vertically, horizontally, circumferentially, as well as crosswise. This will bring uniformity and harmony to the body."

351

Although some students tend to get caught up in the specific details, Iyengar eschews this gravitation toward the specific without grasping the whole. More and more he encourages his students to learn how to observe, not so much what to observe. He himself is constantly changing and the details that he gives for a posture one year may be totally changed the following year. "As a teacher, knowing that the student cannot catch everything from one angle, I show the same point in hundreds of ways. Some students cannot follow it exactly as you are doing it, so you have to change. If you go from top to bottom, you go from bottom to top."

As Angela Farmer, who has been working with Iyengar over the past twenty years puts it, "There is nothing new in Iyengar except that he is always new." Since her initial contact with him in London in the early sixties his methods have evolved considerably over the years: "Before it was difficult to catch what he was doing," she comments. "He taught the postures very rapidly and it was sort of like Lord Shiva's dance. Although *he* was under control, his students would go and try to teach like him. Now he's been refining a method which is very safe and can be given out step by step to large numbers of people. His own work has reached such a level that he's got to give it out in a very organized way."

Fun loving and curious about almost everything, when Iyengar travelled to the various countries to teach, he spent his leisure time going to museums, concerts, meeting heads of state, or just sipping a coffee with some of his students. He is simple, authentic and warm, and believes that it is very important to be part of life, not just some yogi meditating in the Himalayas.

The day I was to leave Pune for Bombay, I had to see Iyengar on some urgent business regarding his daughter, Geeta's book on Yoga for women, which I am trying to get published in the U.S. I had come to say goodbye as well, but had not realized when I asked his son, Prashant if I could see his father that Iyengar was resting. I said that I would return later, but no sooner did I begin to put my shoes on to leave than he appeared at the door. Dressed in his white cotton dhoti, slightly rumpled from the nap, he came out to the garden and sat next to me on the bench. After discussing the business matter, I proceeded to thank him for the challenging remarks he had made to me during the seminar, remarks that didn't at first make me feel exactly proud of myself. I told him that upon reflection, I was able to understand what he meant and that it had changed, once again, my relationship with my Yoga practice. He looked at me with a mysterious smile, one which combined that of a knowing father with that of a stern task master, and said to me, "Just make sure your practice is continuous and constant, and everything will go well for you in life. All problems can be overcome, even the most difficult ones." And then folding his hands on his chest in the gesture of *namaste,* he bade me farewell. Hopping the rickshaw from the Institute to the airport I was no longer nervous about getting somewhere on time. I, like he, knew exactly why I had come.

The
FRUITS

WHO IS A TRULY HEALTHY MAN

compiled by Sam Motivala

A PERSON WHO HAS his physical, mental and spiritual personalities well under control and is trying to integrate the energies of his body and mind to fuse with the total energy of the universe—he is a man people can approach with their troubles—physical, mental and spiritual. Such were the *rishis* of old, living in the absolute present, without any regrets for their past nor any anxieties for the future.

In our modern day society without penchant for specialisation, the rishis slowly gave way to the doctors of today who cater to the physical problems of the society, the psychoanalysts who specialise in mental problems and the priests and philosophers who help to sort out the spiritual problems.

Inter-communication and integration of the above three is not there. Each one specialises in his own discipline to the exclusion of the other fields. This lack of cohesiveness is the root problem of today.

Rarely does one come across a person who is able to help in all the above three fields and is able to integrate the personality of the individual. One such man is Guruji, Shri B.K.S. Iyengar.

To integrate the physical, mental and spiritual personalities of an individual is YOGA and is brought about magnificently by Iyengar.

Illness is an enemy which attacks a weakened person. Yoga helps in combating it, by expelling the toxins of the body and creating internal resistance against diseases. Yoga is not only a preventive but also a very powerful and potent curative system, which successfully deals with the organic as well as psychosomatic diseases. Though it is not only a preventive, but also a curative science, people usually take to Yoga as a curative system when their health is shattered due to physical and emotional stress and strain. The most common ailments for which people join Yoga classes are arthritis, asthma, breathlessness, diabetes, hypertension, slipped disc, spondylosis and frequent colds. In this chapter some of Iyengar's pupils enumerate for the layman the cures brought about in them by the practice of Yoga under him.

YOGA THERAPEUTICS

by Geeta Iyengar

Treatment of diseases by means
of asanas and pranayama

N ature's abundance enabled man to enjoy an easy
life and he forgot the virtues of life. He became infirm and
weak and death faced him sooner than he anticipated. He
was compelled to retrace his steps in order to regain
longevity, firmness, vigour and strength. So man had to
discipline his body and mind to be free from misery,
sorrow and fatality. The body was the primary means of
all his achievements. He had to cultivate awareness in and
around him, to ward off sources of discontentment, sorrow and misery and to ensure freedom from illness of the
body and mind.

In course of time, man was caught up in the pursuit
of pleasure *(bhoga)*. His pleasures increased. He gave up
his disciplines in preference to fulfilment of pleasures
which transformed his physical and mental being. Medical systems grew rapidly for rejuvenation of vigour and
vitality.

In spite of the stupendous advancement in medicine,
there are a number of ailments that do not respond to

modern medical treatment. As a last resort sufferers started turning towards Yoga therapeutics. The doctors as well as those who suffered saw the progress Yoga had made. Thus Yoga became popular, not because of its inherent spiritual values, but as a remedy for illnesses. It gained further momentum as technically advanced countries of the West preferred natural methods of cure, rather than drugs. Thanks to the West, India started to realise the value of Yoga and began to respect it and follow its precepts. Yet, the West has more practitioners today than we have in India.

Yoga is a discipline, regulating one's body and mind to reach the Supreme, step by step. No one can by-pass any one step in his zeal to learn meditation. Theoretical study will not make one perfect. One has to practise and experience for himself. Good health is man's primary need.

From his teens, my father, B.K.S. Iyengar, started teaching Yoga as a health promoting avocation. He had to experiment by trial and error to achieve harmony between theory and practice. Those experiments prompted him to utilise new ideas for clinical purposes, when pupils came to him with their troubles. The curative effects brought about in those who had suffered made my father's system popular, and people came in large numbers to ask for his help for relief from their suffering.

My father had necessarily to study anatomy, physiology and psychology before he could commence his treatment. When I was young, I had suffered from nephritis. My condition deteriorated and doctors in Pune had given up hopes of my recovery. Various types of treatment had failed. As a last resort I started Yoga and it yielded astonishing results. I recovered fully. I became my father's pupil and devoted myself to serve the cause of Yoga.

My father's knowledge of Yoga and his studies in anatomy, physiology, psychology and paediatrics enabled him to understand the troubles of his patients which they themselves could seldom explain. His first touch would be on the appropriate place where pain or discomfort was felt. That created confidence in the mind of the patient, as he pinpointed the source of pain and focussed his attention on that. He proposed remedies to obtain a radical cure. His dexterity lay in his fingers. He adjusted the bodies of the patients in particular postures. By such adjustments, the patients' limbs, joints and organs which had been malfunctioning, non-functioning, deformed, or in pain were restored to their normal functioning. My father's keen insight and years of experience helped him to decide the methods to be adopted for each patient. The treatment continued until such time that he was satisfied that the patient could look after himself and follow his directions. He tested the range of movements of the limbs and joints. For example, patients with knee injuries or broken femurs cannot bend or sit on floors. My father does not allow the patients to be satisfied with a minimum range of movements. He gives them confidence to put in their maximum efforts and had made them sit even in *Padmasana.*

My father does not teach *sat-kriyas,* the six-fold cleansing processes explained in traditional Yoga texts for *antara suddhi* (internal cleansing of the organs). He subscribes to the view that these kriyas were not intended for all, but they were to be prescribed for those who have excess of fat *(medas)* and phlegm *(slesma).*He believes that antara suddhi could be obtained by asanas and pranayama without ill-effect on the patients.

Asanas and pranayama bring about chemical changes from within the body of the patient, due to proper circulation of blood and regulation of hormone balances. Examples of father's methods of treatment may be given. There is a *kriya* called *neti* for removing sinus congestion by insertion of a tube or a thread through nasal passages. The sinus congestion could be removed by performing asanas like *Halasana* and *Setubandha Sarvangasana*. *Dhouti* is another kriya where a piece of cloth is introduced into the esophagus for removing phlegm. Instead of performing dhouti, one can perform *Supta Virasana, Sirsasana, Navasana, Dvipada Viparita Dandasana, Jathara Parivartanasa* or *Sarvangasana*. One cannot overlook the risk involved in performance of kriyas. In neti or dhouti, the tube, thread or cloth may not be clean. The thread may break or a piece of it may remain inside. Due to gulping of cloth the patient may develop a stooping back and drooping shoulders, which may hinder correct breathing. My father's method of treatment is to see how the chest of the patient could be opened so as to make abnormal breathing normal and smooth and to see that blood circulates freely. By observing the position of the patient's chest, he is able to locate the blockage and provide means of removing it. If *sutra-neti* (neti with a thread) or *jala-neti* (neti with water) are considered good for clearing the nose or sinus, why not adopt the safer alternative method of pranayama and cleanse the nasal passages and sinuses by *prana-neti?* Many pupils come to my father for guidance as incorrect practice of kriyas or asanas had adverse effects on them. These adverse effects were removed by correct practices shown to them.

The asanas prescribed vary from person to person according to their constitution, just as physical frames, mental attitudes and states of the body vary at different times. For instance, in treatment of patients of asthma, asanas may differ when spasms are present and when spasms are absent. In his book, *Light on Yoga*, my father has dealt with the curative effects of asanas and their physical and spiritual influences on the body and mind. He has been able to discern polarities in practices. There are positive effects by practising asanas correctly, and adverse effects by their wrong practices.

My father does not normally stipulate restriction on the diet, yet he forbids certain ingredients which might aggravate the ailment. He tells all not to eat in the absence of salivation when food is served.

His creativity is noteworthy. He lays emphasis on standing poses. But old and infirm patients are made to perform asanas like *Trikonasana* and *Parsvakonasana* in lying down positions to create movements in legs. He has made women in advanced stages of pregnancy perform specific asanas after noting their responses and putting them in comfortable positions. These eventually help them to have easy deliveries. Disabled persons like amputees and persons fitted with artificial limbs have also been helped by my father. There was a middle aged man who used to practise head balance regularly, who lost an arm as a result of a war injury. He greatly desired to revert to head balance, but could not find anyone to guide him. He approached my father who gave the matter his attention. He brought a wooden brick, placed it vertically on the floor and rested the amputated arm correctly on it, placed the normal hand behind the man's head and made him do the head balance for five minutes at a stretch. Having found a way, the man happily continues his balance practice regularly.

Pranayama is difficult for people who do not have physical or nervous stability. Therefore, my father never advises treatment by pranayama until the patient has built up sufficient stamina by performing asanas. In order to cultivate the body and the mind, he has adopted a method by which pranayama can be practised in supine position in *Savasana* rather than in a sitting position. The brain and nerves relax while one is lying down, whereas they tend to be taut while one is sitting. My father has devised special aids like odd-shaped stools and benches, planks, bricks, pillows, blankets, mats and ropes. He uses these accessories taking into account the patient's age, stiffness and responsiveness to the complaint. He thinks that old age is no excuse for giving up Yoga. He got his inspiration while thinking of Bhisma lying on his bed of arrows in the *Mahabharata* war.

Men and women lacking a firm foundation on the physical or mental plane should not plunge into spirituality without proper guidance. There are only a few teachers who can teach and initiate one into spiritual discipline, after correctly judging the physical, mental and moral stage of development of the pupil. The steps of spiritual ascendency are not uniform. Many people are misguided through the advertising media in trying to acquire spiritual awareness, and as a result they suffer from nervous breakdown, loss of will power, confusion, mental derangement, dullness, inactivity and frustration. They abandon their education, jobs and family responsibilities. Their approach to life becomes negative and they become a burden to themselves and to society. Some of them become aggressive and uncontrollable and become a curse to themselves and their loved ones. In such psychosomatic cases, it needs great effort to bring them back to normal life.

Many people with psychosomatic troubles are ill-advised to do asanas slowly without strain or exertion. Such slow movements exhaust patients before they reach the final positions. Savasana, pranayama or meditation do not help such persons, as they do not have confidence in themselves and are afraid to close their eyes due to blankness, fear, confusion and feelings of insecurity. Hence, slow, medium and fast movements have to be varied, depending on their physical fitness and mental calibre. Several such persons approached my father, who infused courage into them by introducing a change in the duration and frequency of performance of asanas. He brought back their confidence by his dynamic way of doing asanas like *Viparita Dandasana, Viparita Chakrasana, Halasana* and *Paschimottansanana* cycle in quick succession. These poses stimulate and intensify circulation and feed the brain. By this their dejection disappears and they learn to think and act positively. Only when such a change is noticed, Savasana and pranayama are taught to them to help them to regain confidence.

It is not my intention to elaborate on the history of the treatment undertaken, but to enlighten the reader about the extent of Yoga therapy. It is a presentation of the ancient art, science and philosophy of Yoga to suit modern conditions and bring about positive results. Since Yoga therapy began to throw its light on the life of man, the contempt with which it was once looked upon has turned to admiration. Will it not be wise to take Yoga to higher altitudes of research rather than leave it where it now stands? In its hidden recesses, Yoga has vast scope to work its wonders in man's physical, mental, intellectual, moral and spiritual life.

Use caution and be bold.

MY CURE

by Freny Motivala

M Y TROUBLE STARTED way back in the year 1958 when I was twenty-eight years old. I had a fall and consequently injured my spine. This led to arthritic changes in the 10th and 11th dorsal vertebrae with disc degeneration.

All possible remedies were tried and the best of orthopaedic surgeons were consulted. They only prescribed drugs, which would numb the pain for some time, after which it would return with renewed vigour. I was asked never to do any forward bending movements or I'd be a cripple for the rest of my life. Lifting of any object, heavy or otherwise, was an agony and so was taboo. Pain of this nature acted as a warning that all was not well with my body. Anxiety warned me that all was not well in my mind. I was greatly disturbed, as the main obstacle in the relief of pain and tension was my belief that I could do nothing about it save taking increasing doses of sedatives, tranquilizers and pain-killing drugs for the rest of my life.

Caught up in this vicious circle I suffered for four years. Realising that I was not living a normal and purposeful life, I longed for a way out. By that time, there was no strength left in my spine due to disuse of the muscles, and even simple movements of walking briskly and sitting up at a stretch were painful.

Once again we consulted the doctors and the suggestion given for a permanent cure was an operation for spinal fusion of the tenth and eleventh discs. It was at this time that my father, who was staying in Pune, insisted that I should try Yoga with B.K.S. Iyengar and I took it as a last resort. My husband Sam also joined me to give me courage.

To be very honest, in the beginning I had grave doubts about all that Yoga was capable of achieving, but gradually perservering with leech-like tenacity and with the able guidance of Guruji all my apprehensions were set at rest. It took me two years to be completely cured. Today, though I am sixteen years older, I feel much younger and I have more stamina and internal strength than ever before. My back trouble has become a thing of the past, and now I have to make a conscious effort to remember what that pain was like.

For twelve years I have been conducting classes in Yoga six times a week along with my family at Dadar. I am able to bend and stretch in all directions with effortless ease. My whole family still attends Iyengar's class in Bombay and derives the full benefit of his masterly teaching.

Thanks to our dear Guruji, who helped me to snap out of all ruts and self-delusions and led me to a better, healthier and happier life.

MY FIGHT AGAINST ARTHRITIS

by Smt. Pushpa Gurumani

I FIRST CONTRACTED ARTHRITIS one November evening in 1976 with a dull pain in my left shoulder joint which steadily started getting worse, and within a few weeks I was finding it difficult to get up from the bed. I was nineteen years old and had been married just a year back. When pain killers did not bring relief, my husband took me to a physician who said I had arthralgia. My sedimentation rate—the speed with which the red blood cells settle in a test tube—was considerably more than normal and my haemogram showed me to be marginally anaemic. I was prescribed salycylic acid tablets and antacids along with corticosteroids. There was some relief for some time but the familiar pattern of pain returned with a vengeance. The medicines were having adverse side effects on me—hyperacidity and fluid retention—and the doctor referred me to a homeopath, who was able to keep my condition in check for sometime but later the pains got worse.

On referring to an ayurvedic physician I was told my condition, known as *amavata* was brought about by poor digestion—the waste materials tended to accumulate within my body and when these got deposited round my joints, they became inflamed and caused my pain. It was the ayurvedic physician who recommended Yoga for me.

At this time I had been asked to keep myself immobile due to pains brought about by little physical activity. Things were at their worst when I came to see Mr. B.K.S. Iyengar in September 1977. Right from the start, Guruji encouraged me to lead a normal life and warned me that it was going to be a long, painful battle. His treatment put the problem of dealing with the disease where it belonged; with the patient. Far from being passive observers we were now actively fighting the disease with Guruji's help. Guruji assessed my case with clinical precision. On my first meeting with him, after the meeting was over he gave me a slap on the back right where it hurts most and then he burst into that full-throated laughter of his. It hurt me immensely then, but now, looking back, I am glad he did that because after that I knew that no exercise of his would hurt me more than that slap.

This is the way it is in his classes. I work more because I don't want him to come and slap me. He has thus put a target for me to strive for. My hip that troubled me most was the centre of concentration of Guruji. I got no pity from him. My self-pity was replaced by self-confidence as I did more and more asanas in each session. My old cheerfulness and optimism returned. Every day without fail I spend about ninety minutes on my Yoga asanas, and twice a week I attend Guruji's classes at the RAMAMANI IYENGAR YOGA INSTITUTE. I do not claim to have conquered the disease but at least now I am half way to recovery.

YOGA AND I

by Dr. A.S. Batliwala, M.B.B.S.

For years together I had been suffering from myocardial ischaemia (poor circulation of the blood in the muscle wall of the heart) and hypertension (high blood pressure) and constant anginal pains on exertion—since my first cardiac episode in 1961—and now over again, a similar problem but with milder intensity, cropped up in April 1977. I was again flat on my back for a couple of weeks under medical treatment.

It was then that my friends Freny and Sam Motivala prevailed upon me to give a sincere and conscientious trial to Yoga, which they assured me would ease my tension, which was the basic and root cause of my suffering from hypertension and pain.

Daily *Savasana* for fifteen to twenty minutes under supervision of the two Iyengar Yoga teachers for nearly a fortnight brought about comfort and ease in my breathing. My threshold for fatigue, anginal pain and for becoming breathless on climbing staircases was much higher. Above all I felt improvement in my hypertension.

Within a couple of months there was no need for me to take daily anti-hypertensive drugs, on which I literally used to live. The most important fact that I noticed was that my diastolic blood pressure (the lower reading of blood pressure, which indicates the condition and tone of one's heart musculature), which for years had never been under 110, had started registering for the first time the low reading of 90.

After this I expressed a desire to Freny and Sam to attend B.K.S. Iyengar's class in Bombay. Guruji took a special care and interest in my case and put me through the various asanas gradually. He started making me do the headstand. As a medical man I would have never attempted it, knowing the conditions of my heart and high blood pressure. Under his guidance, however, not once did I feel any ill effects. What was most astonishing was that in a routine check-up I found that a miracle had happened.

My E.C.G. showed a change, which I would never have believed from any other patient of mine. The "T" waves in "V5" and "V6" leads, which had for years remained persistently inverted, were suddenly upright and normal.

I mention this as a great, fitting and right tribute to Yoga and the great exponent of the art, B.K.S. Iyengar, who showed me a new approach to living—free from pain and free from drugs.

DOUBLE CURE

by Smt. Mary Sethna

ONE DAY ON WAKING UP after a good night's rest, I found that I could not open my mouth. On looking into the mirror my face appeared to be lopsided, sagging toward the left. I was unable to swallow any liquids; and me an elocution teacher! I could not close my left eye and had to wear a mask over it to sleep. There was no movement whatsoever on my left cheek—not even the slightest twitch. I was suffering from facial paralysis.

I consulted Iyengar, my Yoga teacher, and he promptly advised me to rest completely for a week. After that, when I went to him, he started me off on certain exercises which I performed daily without fail. Gradually the eyelid descended a bit, but when I could raise my upper cheek I almost danced with joy. After about two months all was well with me and I was able to resume my vocation. Even today, years after my attack, in the standing poses Iyengar insists on my extending the eyelids to gaze in various directions, to strengthen the muscles there.

Once again after a couple of years, on getting up in the morning I found my left shoulder frozen stiff. I could only move my left arm about six inches away from my thigh—upwards. Sideways or back movements were impossible. The slightest jerk provoked electric shocks, which on occasions were unbearable. I could wear only such clothes as buttoned up in front. Unfortunately for me, Guruji was abroad and would return only after two months. Having complete faith only in him, I just waited without consulting any doctor or any one. This I realised later was my mistake—the calcification had increased.

When he saw my condition he was furious that I had neither done anything about it nor contacted any of his teacher-pupils. For three years since then I used to quiver every time he approached me in the Yoga class and gave my arm the necessary painful stretches. The pulling and twisting of my arm being extremely painful I resisted, instead of relaxing. In retrospect now I realise that he was being cruel to be kind. I have never experienced such excruciating pains—not even when my daughter was born. Every day, after I had reached the maximum limits of voluntary movement, I would ask the person helping me to extend it further. In all sincerity I thank Guruji from the bottom of my heart for his shock treatment. Now I am completely cured.

So mine has been a case of a double blessing from the Master.

BAMBOO SPINE

by Pervez Irani

I CAME TO SEE GURUJI in the class at Bombay in May 1975. He looked me up and down and said, "You seem to be one who will be able to bear the pain. In the initial stages it will be very severe, but after about six months if you continue the exercises that I will make you do in the class, then you will be able to get some relief. But it all depends on how much effort you are willing to put in, because yours is a wasting disease and you have to fight it all the way—maybe almost throughout your life." I had no choice but to agree.

Let me trace my disease and its history. I was thirteen years old when the first symptoms started. Pain was shooting up from the coccyx region towards the upper spine and moving all along the rib cage at the sides. Little by little my movements of the hip joints and the back became restricted. Because of the pain and in consultation with the doctors, at first I was advised to rest. After a couple of months the doctors recommended some exercises and I took up exercise with weights. I feel that this was a folly since it tended to bring the spaces of the spine's vertebral column closer together, and mine became a muscular body with deformed bones. After a couple of years my legs from the hip downwards to the ankles started paining me and movement in the pelvic region was completely frozen. Doctors recommended traction and physiotherapy which gave me marginal relief for some time, but the pain returned with a vengeance, my chest started sinking in and the dorsal region of my back started rounding. Added to this, as a result of a scooter accident and a later fall, both my shoulder joints were getting dislocated.

At this time I was continuously on drugs which would give me spasmodic relief from excruciating pains, but no permanent cure. By the time I was about twenty years old, walking was painful; I could not even stand for a long time and had to sit or lie down. I could only walk short distances with intermittent rest. I was mobile only because of my scooter. I could afford to get any drug recommended by the doctors since we have a family chemist shop, and I had access to some of the best drugs available in the profession. The result of this was that I started taking drugs a little indiscriminately to relieve the pains. By this time I was thirty years old and married, with two children. When I used to take my children to school the other children would look at me as if I was a freak, since my stoop at this stage was like that of an old person of fifty or sixty years. I could not take part in any social activity and was ashamed to see my friends. I had become withdrawn and irritable. Now I had reached such a stage that I could not even lie down flat on my back, but was like a seesaw with my coccyx and hip area as the centre. The doctors announced at this stage that my disease, which has been diagnosed as *Ankylosing Spondylitis* (bamboo spine) was not responding to medication and there was nothing more they could do about it. It seems that this disease is a genetic one and affects any family member, especially the males. My father had it in mild form and has passed it on to me. I have also been responsible in passing it on to my son who is about five years old. I have already admitted him under an Iyengar Yoga teacher for doing the asanas.

The first few times when Iyengar worked on me it was sheer torture. Sometimes I felt that I just could not take it any more, but when I saw the effort on his face and the sweat on his body while he was helping me in the poses, I just clenched my teeth and held on. Thank God I did; otherwise I would still be the same person that I was before I met him. Due to the weight lifting my body had become very muscular and stiff and sometimes even Iyengar had to take the help of one or two senior pupils in the class to work on me. After the first two months, my greatest relief and joy was that my pains eased off; they disappeared completely after about eight months of Yoga. At this stage I developed faith in Guruji's teachings and started wholeheartedly co-operating with him by doing the exercises every day without fail.

Guruji also advised me that since once a week was not considered sufficient I should go to Freny and Sam Motivala, his pupils, who were teaching in my vicinity. This teaching and help of two classes brought about better results. After Guruji's class on Saturday afternoon I would be completely stiff till Monday, but doing the exercises on my own every day brought about better mobility. Again midweek on Wednesday, I would attend the class at Dadar, and this also helped me to face Saturday classes with confidence.

My brother, who is an amateur photographer, took a photo of me in September 1975. This was my first picture that I had allowed to be taken in seven years. The curvature of my dorsal spine and the stiffness in the coccyx can be very easily noticed. In the other one the stretch in the back thighs and the improvement in the dorsal region is especially noticeable. Since the last photograph was taken I have still improved.

After about a year the area around my coccyx region which had been one solid fused mass became a little mobile. I could bend forward a little, the pain was completely gone and, what was most important, I was now completely off any drugs. My outlook on life also changed. From a shy, withdrawn person, I was becoming cheerful and was able to face life squarely. My wife and children, realising the benefit that Yoga has bestowed on me, have started doing it. Even my mother, who is about sixty years old, and who was first quite sceptical about the whole thing, has taken to Yoga. So today we are a family of three generations all bound with a single thread of Yoga.

I thank the Almighty for blessing me with a Guru like Shri B.K.S. Iyengar and on this auspicious occasion I convey to him the heartfelt thanks of my family and myself.

CURES GALORE

by Dhan Palkhivala

I WAS A BUNDLE OF AILMENTS when I started Yoga with Mr. B.K.S. Iyengar. Determinedly, but almost imperceptibly, he rid me of them. Today they are things of the forgotten past, and I dig deep into my memory for them.

Myxoedema (non-functioning of the thyroid), rheumatism, asthma and migraine were my legacies. Dysentery, malaria and jaundice were self-acquisitions. Attempted medical remedies sometimes added their own problems, leaving my physique weak as wool. Dysmenorrhoea (unbearably severe cramps in the lower abdomen for three days every month) once drove me to a gynaecologist. He was of the opinion the pain-killers could be my only resort, and that the prolapse of the uterus would never permit me to bear a child. He asked me to try Yoga. I did—with Iyengar—in 1957. Within weeks the pain in the joints and in the back lessened; the cramps in the abdomen were bearable; the body resistance increased. Life seemed different.

Spurred by such fast results, I twice over-stepped the limits. Once I did *Kapotasana* after Guruji had asked me to stop. The next day I was glued to bed. Pills and injections were of no avail. Another time by overdoing *Hala-*

sana I developed hiatus hernia which caused pain in the chest and made me breathless. On both occasions, I came out of the ordeal by doing asanas the special way as directed by Guruji.

When I decided to have a baby, contrary to the medical opinion, I conceived at once. This time I consulted another gynaecologist who also showed surprise. He warned me that considering the position of the uterus there was every likelihood of a miscarriage and strictly forbade me Yoga. Guruji said that Yoga was the only guarantee against miscarriage. "Do as I tell you to do and the uterus will get back to the correct position in the fifth month." Things happened exactly as he had said. Throughout the remaining months, I worked hard under his supervision doing *Sirsasana, Sarvangasana* and various other asanas including *Yoganidrasanana* at times. How prophetic were his words and how sure his technique, I realised fully only when the second pregnancy resulted in a miscarriage. At that time he was absent from India; and I was not to practise asanas except under his supervision. On two later occasions when I conceived, Guruji was in India and supervised my asanas. Each time I had a normal delivery.

In 1967 I had kidney trouble. Pain had to be relieved by intravenous injections. X-rays showed no stone and urine reports were clear. In one of the classes Guruji took pranayama. Upright sitting for forty-five minutes in pranayama apparently worked wonders, and immediately after the class I passed a stone. Guruji then explained to me how the pranayama activates the kidneys.

In 1968 I was to be operated on for appendectomy, hernioplasty (repair of the hernia wall), hysterectomy (removal of the uterus), repair of the bladder and perineorraphy (repair of the muscles around the perineum). When, during the preparation ether was applied to my body, asthma flared up, and the operation had to be postponed. Asanas and pranayama once again did their work, and within a forthnight the operation could be performed. Continuous pranayama even in bed kept me free of asthma and brought about a quick recovery.

I was not spared dislocation of shoulders which sometimes comes with strenuous teaching of Yoga. At one stage, calcification near the shoulder blade was also suspected. Both these were very painful and disabling, but with the practice of asanas according to Guruji's method, they disappeared.

What more? During the first pregnancy the dislocation of the sacroiliac joints. Oil injections in the joints were ineffective—standing poses cured the pain. Twisting of the tailbone during the second delivery, helped by standing poses and finally cured by the third delivery. Continuous breathlessness compelling constant gasping—cured only by pranayama. Cramps in the feet and in the calves at night causing abrupt unimaginable pain—cured by *Virasana*. Frightening flashes before the eyes—cured by doing *Sirsasana* and *Sarvangasana* with eyes covered as directed by Guruji.

The last in the line so far has been spondylitis. No collar, no traction. Only asanas—including, surprisingly, *Sirsasana* in the manner suggested by Guruji. Needless to say, it is cured.

I had a hard time recollecting the ailments I had suffered. I may have missed quite a few. Today, thanks to Yoga I have left them all behind. Even migraine, a frequent invader for three decades which, according to a neuro-surgeon, would have brought in its wake epileptic fits, bowed out at last, conceding victory to pranayama.

My husband suffered excruciating pain in the abdomen and could not sit with it even for half an hour at a stretch. The best of physicians and surgeons were consulted but to no avail. He started Yoga, as a last resort, with Guruji, and now he can hardly recollect the type of pain he had suffered.

One who has suffered much, has come out of the suffering and has seen others come out of the suffering too, is hard put to find an ailment, physical or mental, which the discipline of asanas and the vastness of pranayama cannot conquer.

THE LURE OF YOGA

by Mary Palmer

My problems and how Yoga has helped me

WHAT IS THERE IN THE SUBJECT that first attracts one? What is there inherent in it that slowly begins wedding object with subject? What is there in it that reveals glimpses of its vastness wherein lie untold answers? Unresolved questions and needs prompted me to take the first step. Physical disturbances of unknown origin, general depression, energy loss, trauma in aching knees, chronic sinusitis, and a general hopelessness in the efficacy of prescribed treatment demanded that something be done.

The prescribed treatment came after exhaustive tests and x-rays. In conference with a physician I was told: "You know, you are getting older. You are not as young as you once were. Take aspirin if you need it." In answer to my question concerning the value of some kind of exercise the answer came: "Try it if you want to." There was no encouragement or assurance that it might be of help.

Fortunately, this was not my last contact with professional medical help. A wise, older physician advised: "We do not know all the answers. I think you can find them for yourself." This prompted the search.

It began slowly, alone, a wondering: what is Yoga? Will it help aching knees which were slowly inhibiting normal walking and climbing stairs? I listened to my husband relate a fascinating story about his Indian friend, a fellow student at the University of Michigan, who practised Yoga. This yogi had an inner knowledge of his own strength, breath, and certain cleansing techniques. The seed was planted. I wondered. With a friend, Priscilla Neel, I enrolled in a Yoga class at the Ann Arbor "Y." It was in 1967. A gifted young woman who had just returned from a Peace Corps. assignment in India taught the class. She guided us for two years in the practice of the asanas as she knew them and the philosophy as she understood it. Before she left to live in another city she admonished: "You must teach Yoga. Use this book, *Light on Yoga,* by B.K.S. Iyengar." For a while, Priscilla and I taught together, side by side, as both of us felt we didn't know enough to teach alone. Fifteen years later we still like to teach together.

A trip to India lay ahead. In 1969, with my husband on sabbatical leave from the University, we went to Pune to contact Mr. Iyengar. Mr. Yehudi Menuhin, without hesitation, had encouraged me to do so.

Perhaps my great timidity in the presence of Mr. Iyengar was a blessing. I didn't have to tell him my problems. He knew immediately and responded: "For you, I'll do what I can."

For ten days this great man was my teacher.

I learned to know the Iyengar family. Dear Geeta was there to teach me when Mr. Iyengar went to Bombay. Gracious Mrs. Iyengar was present. Added were my new friends from Holland, Australia, France, Japan. All of us lived and practised together. We were to meet later in England when Mr. Iyengar would be teaching there.

It was obvious to me that a slow immersion in the teaching of this Master was taking place within me. Other systems were by-passed. An appreciation began deepening as Mr. Iyengar tested and interpreted for us the Yoga of Patanjali.

My own practice was producing changes. Just as my early problems of rigidity had appeared slowly, so relief came slowly. A sense of well-being gradually replaced depression. Reflection on the means by which the changes came about has led me to the conclusion that, although there were certain postures which were more intriguing than others and thereby held my interest in practice, the impact came from the practice of the full range of postures as taught by Mr. Iyengar. The interplay of the various asanas was fascinating in the results they produced—not only in my own body—but in the great number of students who have participated in the Ann Arbor "Y" program.

It also became obvious to me that experience and training was needed to deal with special problems and specific needs. Observing Mr. Iyengar using the postures therapeutically in innumerable variations deepened my understanding of the sense of purpose in his life. So skillful, so creative is he in each instance, with his attention riveted to his charge. The awakening in his students that "one must be able to stand alone and meet with equilibrium what life brings" is a reminder that this man has filled the lives of his students with profound thought— many of which have been drawn together in *Sparks of Divinity.*

Over and over again in the classes one meets students who want to proceed too fast, skipping the demands and disciplines of the asanas to leap prematurely into faulty and frustrating practice of pranayama. Now the subject has been given the attention of this Master. With the publishing of *Light on Pranayama*, his students have, as an example, his practice of the art.

During the span of years I have devoted to Yoga, my husband and I have together made a garden. For a time the plan of the garden was not defined. We started developing a path to lead through the garden. It was then my interest in gardening blossomed. The path became the way to experience the garden. My chosen path in Yoga is with my teacher leading and sometimes by my side, strengthening and guiding so that some day I may walk alone—with the spirit.

The lure demands from one the highest potential. At the same time it reveals one's weaknesses. The moment of truth cannot be experienced without the constant play of these opposing forces. As in Arjuna's dilemma—without the play there would be no replay.

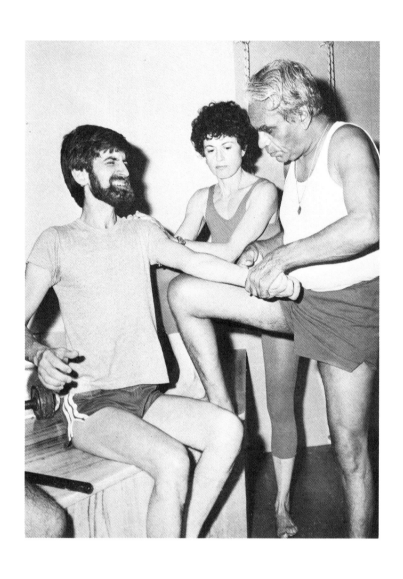

Curing to be kind—releasing the arm from the grip of calcification.

ROBERT'S STORY

by Marian Garfinkel

WHEN MR. IYENGAR conducts hatha Yoga classes, it is usual for "problem cases" to request his personal help. I have seen people assisted who were considered intractable by physicians, or who had so many restrictions placed upon them that they were disheartened and had little will to continue living. Mr. Iyengar's unique ability to penetrate the nature of physical conditions, and to follow through with constructive and restorative therapy is well known. This article will give testimony about a personal and amazing story—the story of Robert, whose mobility and responsiveness to life was radically influenced by B.K.S. Iyengar.

When Robert was fourteen, he had an unfortunate accident. He was severely injured by a flying golf ball that hit him on the head. He survived two major brain operations, but the left side of his body remained partially paralyzed, and he lost the use of his left arm and hand. Two years after his accident, Robert suffered his first epileptic seizure, for which he subsequently took daily medication. Teams of doctors and therapists treated him over a period of fifteen years. With hard work and determination, he managed to finish college and was able to assume a responsible position in a family business, and lead a reasonably normal life.

However, calcium deposits formed in various joints on the afflicted left side of his body, particularly in the shoulder, elbow and wrist. What little mobility he had in his arm began to decrease. And chronic use of drugs produced undesirable side effects such as irascibility, depression, anxiety, confusion, and nausea. He depended on the drugs to prevent epileptic seizures and resigned himself to a lifetime of restricted activity with major personality changes.

While touring the U.S.A. in May of 1976, Mr. Iyengar gave a demonstration and lecture at Haverford College, Philadelphia. It was at this time that he worked with Robert in our presence. By manually controlling various parts of his body, Mr. Iyengar had Robert holding objects that he had not been able to hold in his hand for fifteen years. Among those of us who watched this therapeutic session was Ron Chalfont, an Iyengar-trained Yoga instructor and chiropractor from Ann Arbor, Michigan. Later, Robert went to Michigan several times for further work with Ron, where he learned various asanas and strengthened his body. Ron tried to continue what Mr. Iyengar had begun with Robert. Finally when Robert returned home, the two of us began to work on a daily practice schedule.

Light on Yoga, written by Mr. Iyengar, was our guiding light, along with photographs of Iyengar as he had worked with Robert in various postures. During this time Robert began to feel better about himself and reduced his medication by half. (Although he hadn't had an epileptic seizure for nearly ten years, Robert was still advised to continue his medication as a preventive.)

Before we left for India, Robert had a brain scan which indicated that the blood supply to the brain had increased, and that the brain waves were stable for the first time in years. Robert's doctor was more than pleased and agreed that the daily Yoga practice was helpful. We stressed that it was not Yoga, but Mr. Iyengar's particular approach and knowledge of the subject, and his particular program for Robert which improved his condition.

At the end of June 1977, Robert and I left for India to work with Mr. Iyengar at his Institute in Pune. Day after day, Mr. Iyengar personally supervised Robert's therapy and rehabilitation. He supported both Robert's body and mind. Through the force of his personality and determination, Mr. Iyengar was able to encourage Robert to face the physical pain he had to work through in bringing back to life limbs frozen by many years of inactivity.

Throughout these sessions Iyengar's eyes were sparkling, like a thousand light bulbs exploding in all directions. In a flash he would focus first on one part of Robert's body and then on another. At the wall he had Robert doing headstand and shoulderstand, and on the ropes and benches, somersaults and stretches to flush his brain when Robert felt dull. As he worked with Robert, he devised mechanical aids which solved particular problems as they developed. Iyengar treated whatever reactive symptoms appeared. We were there for nearly two months of daily work.

During the first week of July, Robert progressed enough to stop his medication completely. It was on July 4th, coincidentally enough, that Mr. Iyengar proclaimed the liberation, "Today you are free; you need have no fear." What a special day that was. It was difficult for Robert to withdraw, but with the Master's encouragement, there was no turning back. Many times Iyengar demanded that Robert face excruciating pain, in order to loosen the calcium deposits so that he would feel new mobility in his limbs. I remember Iyengar's voice bellowing, "Don't say 'I *tried* to push.' Say,' I **pushed!**'" He re-educated Robert and showed him that he had two hands and two arms. One day Robert announced, "You are right, Mr. Iyengar. It *is* easier to button my jeans with two hands. It's hard for me to remember that I can use my left hand."

By the time we left India, in August 1977, Robert's arm was straight rather than permanently crooked, and his fingers had opened and become strong enough to hold a cricket ball firmly in his hand. The calcium deposits were gone. (Mr. Iyengar had broken the adhesions manually.) The flow of blood to the brain had been increased and Robert showed healthy colour. A new incentive for life and work had developed as his mobility returned.

Today Robert feels vitality in a body that he had once thought imprisoned him. He continues his Yoga practice and hopes to return to India one day for further assistance. To quote Robert: "The feeling of having life in various parts of my body that I thought were dead is very difficult to explain. I can't. Only *I* know. And I'm extremely grateful to Mr. Iyengar for a second chance to live."

Caring for Robert during our trip to India required my providing him with emotional support and physical care, as well as fulfilling many social needs. But in India Robert's sixteen years of emotional, physical, and social restriction began to end. Sharing his experience—seeing a disruption of his habitual pattern of living, with which I was familiar, was an adventure and a great revelation.

Being in the presence of Mr. Iyengar and watching him work on Robert, and taking his classes, was an intense learning—one which I am still assimilating. I, too, am grateful to B.K.S. Iyengar for the enrichment and change in my own life.

Reprinted, with permission, from *Yoga Journal,* September/October 1978. Copyright © 1978 *Yoga Journal.*

YOGA FOR WOMEN

by Geeta Iyengar

ALL MEN ARE CREATED EQUAL, so runs the adage, but most males prefer to believe themselves more "equal" than women.

Certain spheres of human activity are felt to be exclusively male, and the unwary female who ventures into such fields is regarded with attitudes that range from tolerant amusement to cynical scepticism. For a long time, especially in India, the field of personal development—whether intellectual or physical—was barred to women. Gradually, however, these barriers are breaking down and it is with relief that one notes the entrance of women into the educational fields.

Although India is the classical land of Yoga, a belief seems to have gained ground that Yoga is not for women. Women, it is argued, do not have the requisite stamina for it. They are occupied with hundreds of household chores, they even breathe differently!

Imagine a woman standing on her head with her two-year old child pulling at her hair! Women were supposed to leave this field of spiritual and physical development strictly to the superior male.

Historically, however, Yoga has had a number of women adherents in the past. In fact the first disciple of Lord Siva in this sacred art was his wife Parvati. The sage Yajnavalkya instructed his wife Maitreyi in vedic times in Yoga.

The great epic *Ramayama* tells us that when Rama was banished by his father at the instance of Kaikeyi, his step-mother, he asked his own mother Kausalya for her blessing before going into exile, and she did so after becoming tranquil in mind through Yoga. As is natural for a mother on such occasions, she was emotionally upset and refused to bless him till she had calmed herself with the practice of asanas and pranayama. Then she blessed him with a pure mind and a pure heart.

Yogic exercises in particular are not only very helpful to women but also extremely convenient. Whereas the normal run of games and exercises develop only certain parts of the body, yogic exercises develop all parts and at the same time have a definite effect on the mind, emotions and inner self.

Again, not every woman can go to the club or sports ground to exercise her body. She is very often kept at home either by social convention or household work, especially by small children.

Indian women feel shy to exercise themselves in public. Yoga is a convenient form of exercise for women because it requires only a small even surface, fresh air and a blanket, which every house will certainly have.

Yoga exercises are useful to women and seem also specially invented for their use. The female body is more supple, soft and tender than that of the male due to the presence of different hormones.

396

Menstruation, pregnancy, childbirth and lactation all influence her bodily development in the line of softness and passivity. But this pliability and suppleness have also their reverse mental side.

Women are by nature more pliant, more submissive and more passive than men. This can tend very often to mental depression and emotional disturbances. Woman has been characterised as the weaker sex throughout the ages and social convention has forced on her an inferior role to that of man. Women may therefore suffer from inferiority complexes.

On the physical side the female body inclines very rapidly to obesity, fat deposits accumulate around the waist and abdomen especially after childbirth. Difficulties in the menstrual cycle such as overflow or irregularity in the flow are also experienced by a number of women, which leaves them nervous and irritable. Pregnancy and childbirth are for many a trying period, both for physical reasons as well as because of old wives' tales about the difficulties of childbirth.

Most women also experience mental and emotional crises at the time of menopause, while the building of varicose veins seems to be almost a normal occurrence in females. Constipation also is another plague of women.

All these physical, emotional and mental disorders can be rectified by making use of a gift given by nature to woman—her flexibility of body—through yogic exercises.

Yogic asanas make the body not only supple but strong, strengthen the nerves and ligaments, purify the blood and skin, tone up the internal organs and give general health, agility, balance, endurance and vitality. Mentally and emotionally yogic exercises—asanas and pranayama—improve mental equilibrium, calm emotional disturbances and give an even and balanced personality.

Although Yoga can be begun at any age, the best period for women to begin its practice is at the start of menstruation in puberty. Physical and emotional development at puberty, as well as purification of the blood, are aided by the correct performance of yogic exercises at that period. Balance is given to the growing girl both in her deportment and in her physical appearance and the stress and strain of puberty is minimised.

In general women should avoid the practice of asanas especially the inverted poses like *Sirsasana* (Headstand), *Sarvangasana* (Shoulderstand) during the menstrual period for about three or four days. *Pranayama* breathing exercises) and *Savasana* (relaxation) should be kept up.

Relief can be got from pain in the back and abdomen during menstruation with the help of *Uttanasana, Paschimottanasana, Baddhakonasana* and *Upavistakonasana.*

During pregnancy the asanas listed below in the daily practice can be done regularly for the first three months. *Baddhakonasana* and *Upavistakonasana* should be done throughout the period of pregnancy.

It will interest readers to know that exercises mentioned in Dr. Dick Read's book *Childbirth without Fear* are very similar to these two exercises. The practice of Pranayama and Savasana (relaxation) should be kept up as they are great helps during delivery.

Other rules apply both to men and women, such as performing the exercise on an empty stomach (for example four hours should elapse after a heavy meal, two hours after a light one made up of, let us say, biscuits and tea), eating half an hour after exercising, not bathing immediately before and after exercise.

While any time is suitable, provided the stomach is empty, the early morning hours are more suitable for the practice of pranayama (breathing techniques) while late afternoon or early evening would be good for doing asanas. Some women are afraid that the practice of Yoga will turn them into muscular amazons without any feminine grace or charm. Yogic exercises, however, develop more the nerves, ligaments and internal organs. They help the blood circulation, give inner poise and outward body balance and strengthen each part so that the figure is properly proportioned. They enhance feminine beauty, not diminish it.

Due to increased blood circulation, the skin is no longer dry and rough, but soft and velvety. The voice becomes more melodious and pleasing. The eyes get an added sparkle, breath is purified and sweetened. The entire personality has added grace, charm and a deeper spiritual presence.

The woman who practises Yoga does not need cosmetics, stays, excessive scent and other things to enhance her beauty. As the Bible says, "her beauty is from within"—something that cannot be rubbed off with soap and warm water.

Women are often heard to remark that ceasing practice will mean that excessive fat layers will develop on them. This again is not true. Yogic exercises are organic also and not simply muscular and no fat deposits result from stopping them.

However, once the inner yogic fire has been kindled, very few are willing to give up exercises which they know to be not only beneficial and soothing but also very pleasant to perform.

I give below a series of exercises to be performed daily. The exercises are not difficult to perform and will give the harassed housewife much mental and physical relief amidst daily chores.

1. *Sirsasana*—Pure blood supply to brain cells: Relieves colds, coughs, and palpitation.
2. *Sarvangasana*—Healthy blood supply to neck and chest: Relieves breathlessness, asthma, throat ailments, nervous breakdown, insomnia, and has soothing effect on nerves.
3. *Halasana*—Relieves high blood pressure, backache, arthritis, and lumbago.
4. *Paschimottanasana*—Tones up the abdominal organs and takes off their sluggishness, improves digestion, tones the kidneys and rejuvenates the whole spine.
5. *Upavistakonasana*—Regulates menstrual flow, stimulates ovaries, prevents hernia, relieves sciatic pain.
6. *Baddhakonasana*—Checks irregular menstrual periods, tones kidneys and urinary bladder, relieves pain during delivery.
7. *Ardhamatsyendrasana*—Relieves backache, hip pain, sluggishness of liver and spleen, tones intestines.
8. *Adhomukha-svanasana*—Relieves backache, sluggishness of liver and tones intestines.

YOGA AND AYURVEDA

by Geeta S. Iyengar

THE FOUR VEDAS—*Rig Veda, Yajur Veda, Sama Veda* and *Atharva Veda*—are the course of all spiritual knowledge. Yoga and Ayurveda both stem from the Vedas and aim at the betterment of man. *Ayu* means life, and *veda* means knowledge (knowledge of life), and Yoga is the knowledge of the known, knowable and knowing.

The four aims of man are to lead a religious life *(dharma)* to earn a livelihood *(artha)*, to culture oneself *(kama)*, and finally to reach emancipation. These aims are dealt with successively at a philosophical level in the four chapters of the *Yoga-sutras* of Patanjali. Ayurveda *(Charak-samhita)* claims to give health and well-being as a whole in order to achieve these aims.

Both the sciences adopt the premises of evolutionary theory accepted by Samkhya. According to Samkhya, the entire cosmos consists of two primary entities: *purusha,* the life principle, and *prakriti,* nature. Both Yoga and Ayurveda add to this a third entity, *Ishwara,* the Universal Soul.

Nature in its unmanifested original state is called *mula-prakriti* and it possesses three inherent qualities *(gunas)* of illumination *(sattva)*, energy *(rajas)* and inertia *(tamas)*. In mula-prakriti these qualities remain in a state of equilibrium *(samyavastha);* hence nature is dormant, inactive and stagnant. When purusha, the life-principle, comes in contact with nature, this equilibrium is disturbed, the gunas start moving and vibrating, and nature comes out of its dormant state. Here begins the evolutionary process.

Nature's first evolute is *avyakta* (unevolved matter), or *alinga* (undifferentiated matter). From this evolves *mahat* or *buddhi* (cosmic intelligence) which is full of sattva-guna. From buddhi with predominating rajas (energy principle), *ahamkar* (the ego principle) evolves. This is known as *tejas ahamkara.*In Ayurveda it is called *agni* (fire). Any disturbance, lack or excess is a cause of disease. Then ahamkara, together with the gunas in different combinations, forms itself into the subtle elements (smell, taste, colour, touch and sound) and the five corresponding gross elements (earth, water, fire, air, ether). This is called *bhutadi ahamkara.*

The ahamkara further evolves as *vaikarik* (modifying) ahamkara into the *panch-jnanendriyas,* the five organs of perception, and the *panch-karmendriyas,* the five organs of action. Lastly comes the eleventh organ, *manas,* the mind.

Sushruta, while defining disease and health, says that the inequilibrated state of ingredients is a "disease-state" and the equilibrated state is an "at-ease state." So also, in Yoga, the equilibrated state of qualities is the "original state" and the inequilibrated state is an "artificial state."

It is necessary to know the *triguna* concept, which is pivotal in Yoga, and the *tridosha* concept, which is pivotal in Ayurveda.

On a material, physical or biological plane, sattva becomes the essence of intelligence *(prakasha),* rajas is energy or motion *(kriya),* and tamas is inertia or mass *(sthiti).* On a psychological plane, sattva is placidity *(shanta),* rajas is turbulence, pain and delusion respectively. Purusha adopts prakriti for illuminating, activating and restraining itself. On the other side, the trigunas with their nature of evolution and involution are meant for experience and emancipation.

The trigunas co-exist, act together, support and suppress each other and produce evolutes together. They act, react, interact, unite, separate and reunite. They are imperishable, indestructible, infinite and independent. When in equilibrium, they are quiescent. In contact with purusha they get violated, vibrated and unbalanced. At this stage purusha is called *jivatma.* They exist in various porportions, forming diversity among human beings. In any pattern the preponderant guna becomes manifest and the other two are latent. In active, dynamic life, rajas is dominant and overcomes the resistance of tamas. When sattva is preponderant, rajas is transformed and volitional consciousness is accompanied by the resistance of tamas. Tamas helps to hold the illumination of sattva, remaining dormant so that sattva dominates.

The aim of Yoga is to bring back the trigunas to equilibrium, and the aim of Ayurveda is to bring back the tridoshas to equilibrium.

The doshas are humours called *vata, pitta* and *kapha* (air, fire and water). They are made of the five gross elements and they sustain the body metabolism. They are the three constituent complexes in the physiological system.

The first evolute of the five elements is ether, which is all-pervasive. The last evolute is earth, which is gross and inert. Both have no movement and are incapable of moving on their own. The middle three elements— water, fire and air—are in motion. Air has motion and velocity. Fire has heat and light. Water brings cohesion by mixing the inner particles of the body. These three elements are dynamic, possess and cause movement, and act as a fuel of the body. It is because of them that the body acts, works and functions. When the dynamism of these elements fails or is obstructed, disorder sets in and the body suffers.

Vata causes all movement, voluntary and involuntary sensations, consciousness and moods. Pitta produces heat and transforms food nutrients through the digestive system into cells and tissues. Kapha provides the ingredients to build up the body from the body. It breaks down cells, builds up new cells and protects them from destruction or excessive vata and pitta.

In this way the tridoshas build up and sustain the body and dispose of its waste matter. They maintain metabolic equilibrium.

Together with the doshas, the body is made up of seven constituents *(saptadhatu)* and three impurities *(trimala)*. The seven constituents of the body are chyle, blood, flesh, fat, bones, marrow and semen. The entire anatomical and physiological body is composed of these seven items.

The impurities *(mala)* are harmful if not excreted. Their retention and excessive excretion also cause disease. They are faeces, urine, sweat, menstrual blood and mother's milk.

Thus these are the three fundamentals of the body and its mechanism.

There is yet another vital ingredient, and that is *ojas,* vitality or essence. Ojas is the collected essence of the seven constituents and the seat of it is the heart. If ojas vanishes the humours lose their equilibrium. A person of ojas is not vulnerable to disease, due to its intensity and vitality.

The sphere of treatment of Yoga differs from Ayurveda. Health according to Yoga is (1) the removal of disease from body and mind, (2) the removal of sorrows, and (3) the control over the movements of consciousness. Beyond health, Yoga aims at stability of mind and identity with the soul *(svaruppavastha).*

Ayurveda deals with a specific form of evolution *(vishesha parva),* which is called *vikkriti.* Ayurveda aims to bring equilibrium in the tridoshas.

Ayurveda tries to arrest disease *(roganirodh)* and Yoga tries to arrest the mental modifications *(vrittinirodh).*

The trigunas and tridoshas are all-pervasive and there is no situation where one or the other is absent. Likewise, there is no such thing as perfect balance in the doshas or gunas. The whole of humanity is under the influence of triguna and tridosha. Only in a state of beatitude does a yogi bring equilibrium in the gunas (samyavastha). He becomes a *gunatita* or *sattvatita.*

Fluctuations in the balance of doshas cause disease. These fluctuations are caused by varying patterns of food, sleep, moods, behaviour, environmental factors and character.

The trigunas also vary in the chitta of all human beings, causing different types of mentality, tempera-

405

ment, intellect, morality and so on (cf. *Bhagavad Gita* ch. 17). Yoga categorises citta on five planes:—

(1.) *Kshipta*—wandering (predominance of rajoguna)

(2.) *Mudha*—forgetful; excess of inertia (predominance of tamas)

(3.) *Vikshipta*—occasionally steady (predominance of rajas and sattva)

(4.) *Ekagra*—one-pointed (predominance of sattva)

(5.) *Niruddha*—modification in a restrained state (sattvatita)

Both Yoga and Ayurveda are *chikitsa shastras,* therapeutic sciences, and man is a *chikitsya purusha,* a treatable being. Yoga treats chitta (intellect, ego, mind and citta) and Ayurveda treats the body and the phase of mind which is in contact with the body.

Both Ayurveda and Yoga lay stress on code of conduct and personal hygiene. Ayurveda calls it *sad vritta* and Yoga calls it *yama-niyama,* but there is a vast difference in their aim. Ayurveda aims at health and Yoga aims at self-realisation.

Yama is non-violence, truthfulness, non-stealing, chastity and freedom from greed, and niyama is cleanliness, delight, religious fervour, study of self and surrender of oneself to the supreme Self.

Charaka gives four steps to maintain health :

1. Food, sleep and control over the mind. These are the three pillars on which health is based *(upastambha).*
2. Daily and seasonal disciplined routine to maintain health.
3. The impulses are to be controlled and discarded.
4. Avoidance of intrinsic and extrinsic diseases.

Let us go through each and compare them with yogic life :

406

1. The first step consists of the three pillars (upastambha) on which health is based: *ahara*—food; *nidra*—sleep; and *brahmacharya*—control over the mind. Due to *avidya,* ignorance, these pillars are constantly shaken as a result of wrong habits and behaviour, misuse, wrong judgements, and so on.

   a) *Ahara*—food: It should be wholesome, nourishing, fresh, clean, sanctified and easy to digest and metabolise. It should be able to maintain agni (heat) in the body. Also, it should be suitable according to season.

   There are three seasons. Doshas are accumulated in one season, provoked in the next and pacified in the third. There is an accumulation of pitta in the rainy season, kapha in autumn and vata in spring. Food taken in a season should be such as will not accumulate a dosha further.

   According to Charaka, many serious diseases arise from irregular food habits. Food should be beneficial, taken according to proper measure, at a proper time and with proper rituals (cooking, processing, sanctifying by offering to the Lord, etc.). Secondly, one should keep the senses under control. Then one is free from diseases.

   Patanjali wants aspirants to observe *shauch,* internal and external cleanliness which includes the cleanliness and restraining of food intake.

   b) *Nidra*—sleep: This is the second pillar. One should not have *tamonidra,* heavy dull sleep. Sleep should be natural, not induced, and it should be free from dreams. Vagbhatta says that happiness and misery, strength or weakness, knowledge or ignorance, and

407

ultimately life or death, depend on sleep.

Patanjali demands sattvic sleep—pure, genuine and virtuous—from the sadhaka.

c) Brahmacharya—celibacy: This is the third pillar. It is mainly control over sensual pleasures, not merely control over sexual pleasures. This is pratyahara which is explained in Yoga. It is a greatly desired principle and yet at the same time it is often avoided on grounds of convenience. This should not be so.

The Ayurvedacharyas have warned married people not to indulge in sexual intercourse at the wrong time and in wrong seasons. On festival days, inauspicious days and during the menstrual period intercourse is to be avoided.

There are three stages of brahmacharya:
 (i) physical—celibacy regulated family life;
 (ii) mental balance of mind against indulgence; and,
 (iii) spiritual—purity of mind to acquire true knowledge of *Brahman, Ishvara.* Yoga demands this celibacy.

The yogi has to continuously correct and establish life on these three pillars in order to maintain physical and mental health.

2. The second step to maintain health is to keep *dinacharya* and *ritucharya.* This is keeping a daily and seasonal routine to maintain health. Going against discipline invites disease. This is based on Patanjali's niyama.

Discretion should be maintained at all levels concerning health. That is in food, sleep, bath, evacuation, cleaning the teeth, gargling, washing the eyes, mouth, face, feet and hands, wearing clean and suitable clothes according to the season, exercise, sexual intercourse, worshipping the Lord, and so on.

Life should be well organised, well disciplined. If life is undisciplined, without heeding the above facts, life becomes miserable.

3. The third step to maintain health is *dharaniya* and *adharaniya vegas*. There are impulses which have to be controlled and heeded, and others to be discarded. Charaka explains which physical and mental urges and impulses have to be controlled and which discarded.

Calls of nature have to be attended to—it is a duty. Urges such as the passing of wind through the mouth or anus, stool, urine, semen; acts of sneezing, throwing out phlegm, blowing mucous, coughing, yawning, vomitting, weeping—all these should not be stopped but should be carried out naturally.

However, anger, greed, desire, grief, jealousy, violence, cruelty, stealing, rape, boasting, harsh talk—these should be checked, avoided and eradicated, otherwise they cause disease. The yamas have to be followed to cleanse the citta so that it does not get soiled by these mental disturbances.

Good and proper habits should be developed. One should not indulge in worldly life and invite disease. Indulgence causes vitiated doshas.

4. The fourth step to maintain health is to avoid intrinsic and extrinsic disease.

Intrinsic diseases are mainly due to the inherent character of the doshas to get vitiated into abnormal conditions.

409

The causes of extrinsic diseases are twofold. The first is *asatmyendriartha samyoga*. This is contact of the senses with objects of the senses which may be defective, excessive or perverted. It is misuse, non-use or overuse of the *indriyas*. If there is no control, then the utilisation power of the indriyas will suffer.

The second cause is *prajnaparadham*. This is *viparyaya vritti*, faulty understanding or a defect of the intellect (buddhi dosha). To avoid this, Ayurveda recommends following dharma, virtuous living, doing right karma. Body *(kaya)*, mind *(manas)* and speech *(vach)*, these three should be disciplined. Yoga recommends the development of embellishing, purifying mental modifications which lead towards self-realisation.

The third cause is *parinama*, change. This is concerned with time, *kala*. There are three seasons of the year: rainy, autumn and spring. The tridoshas show their predominance by effect. One should understand the time of accumulation *(sanchaya)*, provocation *(prakopa)*, and pacification *(shaman)*. The three doshas change a lifestyle according to predominance as previously explained.

Here it becomes clear how Ashtanga Yoga can be used as a curative measure for disease. All the four steps above draw attention to the practice of Yoga. The individual disciplines of niyama and the control over the mind given in yama as moral and ethical bindings, are the path of prevention and cure. Asana, pranayama and pratyahara help to keep the tridosha under control. Dharana, dhyana and samadhi help to keep the mind, ego and intellect under control.

Now let us see how asan-pranayam work on the human being as a line of treatment.

410

Yoga and Ayurveda accept two ways of treatment: *shodhan vidhi* and *shaman vidhi*. Shodhan vidhi is a purification of the body by eliminating the morbid humours, constituents and impurities through emesis *(vaman)*, purgation *(virechana)*, enemation *(bhasti)*, nose and eyes cleansing *(shirovirechana)* and blood-letting *(raktamakshan)*. This last method being drastic, Charaka warns that it should be administered very carefully. If it is over-used it can cause considerable damage and injury to the body.

The *shat-kriya* for body cleansing, explained in the *Hatha Yoga Pradipika* is akin to the shodhan vidhi of Ayurveda. These kriyas are *dhauti, basti, neti, trataka, nauli and kapalbhati*. Swatmaram introduces these kriyas only to those who have excessive fat and phlegm, and not to all (*Hatha Yoga Pradipika* II.37). Hence, Charaka and Swatmaram both specify shodhan vidhi to be used in exceptional cases.

Shaman vidhi is a pacification method meant to pacify, soothe, alleviate and settle the vitiated doshas. It includes fasting, dieting, controlling the intake of liquid, exercise, sun-bath, fresh air, and correcting the digestion and metabolism. The two methods—purification and pacification—use medicines which purify and pacify respectively.

Though the asan-pranayam therapy falls mainly under the method of pacification, there cannot be a rigid demarcation. Pharmacology is a branch of medical science which deals with medical substance. The drug acts on the body and the body reacts to the drug and the disease is eradicated. The drug is a chemical substance and the body functions due to biochemical changes—reactions. That is how chemistry goes with chemistry.

411

Now asan-pranayam is not an object. Then how does it work as a medicine?

Charaka says that all the matter available from the plant and animal kingdoms and in organic and inorganic substances has some medicinal value or other, since matter is nothing but the combination of five elements. He also says that there is nothing in this world which is unfit to be used as a medicine if it is used rationally and for a definite purpose.

The organic body-machine functions on the bio-chemicals which exist in the humours, constituents and excreta. The five elements which make the chemical universe outside exist as a mini-universe in the body too. Though not consisting of matter, asan-pranayam are performed by the body-matter. Again, consciousness is involved in yogic practice to bring the expected change in the biochemical substance of the body, through proper blood circulation and metabolism. That is how the limbs of Yoga work as medicine. The body enlivens asana and asana enlivens the body. The body vitalises pranayama and pranayama vitalises the body. Primarily, it is the application of intelligence in the utilisation of the body-mind substance, while performing asan-pranayam to bring the effective change. The asan-pranayam is performed by a living biological person who animates the chemical body by infilling the bioenergy in it. He does not borrow the substance from outside, but brings about the required effect through physio-chemical and bio-chemical changes in the organs, hormones, blood content and chemical substances, etc.

This composite and complex body-machine works on the movements of vital energy—the five pranas *(prana, apana, vyana, udana, samana);* the five pittas

412

(pachak, ranjak, sadhak, bhrajak, alochak); and the five kaphas *(bodhak, avalambak, kledak, samsleshmak, tarpak).* These elementary principles, which are virtually material entities, regulate the system.

The five pranas exist in the skin, bone, ears, thighs, waist and large intestines. Their physiological function is to create inspiration, expiration, movement and energisation.

They equilibrate the seven constituents and evacuate the excretory channels. The five pittas exist in the stomach, small intestines, lymphatic and blood vessels, eyes, skin, liver, spleen and pancreas. The physiological function of pitta is to have proper digestion, to maintain the body heat, to preserve the eyesight, and to add lustre to the body. Pitta keeps mental equanimity and sharpens the intelligence. The five kaphas exist in the chest, throat, head, oesophagus, joints, stomach, lymph, fat, nose and tongue. Physiologically they preserve normal moisture, stability in joints, firmness of body, strength, endurance, courage, manhood and proportionate weight.

The asan-pranayam method works on these three humours. It helps them to function and corrects any faulty or deranged actions and imbalances. Apart from this, the asan-pranayam mechanism works on the other evolutes: intellect, ego and the five subtle elements.

Medicine works on the body because it has a specific taste *(rasa)*, quality *(guna)*, potency *(veerya)*, effect *(vipaka)* and capacity *(prabhava)*. Similarly, an asana has a perfect shape or correct formation *(rasa)*, peculiar quality *(guna)*, definite potency and intensity *(veerya)*, final resultant effect *(vipaka)* and specific nurturing capacity *(prabhava)*. In fact, the number with an asterisk after the name of each asana in *Light on Yoga* is indicative of these

413

five aspects which point out the quality, potentiality, intensity, effectuality, substantiality and relishability. The grouping of asanas is done on this basis alone. One cannot expect quick relief with yogic treatment since the body has to undergo the change as an effect of the asan-pranayam mechanism. However, the asanas can be grouped into two categories. The asanas in all bring a slow, mild and gradual result, but some asanas bring a quick, intense and immediate result.

Asan-pranayam is administered according to the root cause of the diagnosed disease, though the visible and peripheral symptoms are not neglected since these symptoms require an immediate pacification. The order and sequence of asan-pranayam on every disease is charted out on the basis of anatomical structure, physiological functioning, progressive intensity, purifying and pacifying capacity, and the stage of the disease, the age of the patient as well as the basic constitution of the patient. The length of time for staying in the pose is also decided considering the above factors.

Asan-pranayam increases immunity and resistance to disease as well as reducing the severity of disease. Not only that, a practitioner of Yoga reveals the hidden cause of inevitable disease stored for the future.

Again, the asan-pranayam is categorised according to its strength-giving capacity. Some asanas have the tendency to create heat, hunger, thirst, digestion, circulation, etc. which help to reduce vata and kapha. Others have the tendency to create a cooling, soothing and nourishing sensation. They cause the condensation of tissues and control excessive secretion in glands and organs. These asanas regulate the pitta and blood by modifying the intensity of circulation. For example, forward extension cools the kidneys, heart, brain, reproductive system, endocrine system, etc., but makes the digestive system hot. That is how forward bendings quieten the brain and increase the appetite. Again, the same asana creates heat at one place and cools the body at another. For example, *Viparita Dandasana* creates heat around the chest area and cools the abdomen. Therefore the same asana is a medicine for colds, coughs, etc. and for diarrhoea too. On the other hand two asanas of opposite potency and tendency work on the same disease for multiple reasons. For example, *Viparita Dandasana* and *Paschimottanasana* are both beneficial for kidney problems, but the former circulates the blood in and around the kidneys and flushes them, while the latter controls the circulation, cools and pacifies the kidneys. The former activates the adrenals and the latter pacifies them.

The shat kriyas are not utilised in Guruji Iyengar's method, hence he is criticised. Let me clear it here. In our method *trataka, nauli* and *kapalbhati* are included, and *dhauti, neti* and *basti* are excluded. The statements of Charaka and Swatmaram are already given above. It is clearly stated that the shodhan vidhi should be used with discretion. However, Iyengar's method is enriched with varieties of asanas and pranayama. The Yoga text says that the number of asanas is as many as the living beings in this universe. Each asana has a therapeutic value, as well as a yogic and spiritual value; they have the capacity to bring about change in an aspirant at physical, mental and spiritual levels. The same holds true for pranayama. These varieties of asan-pranayam are used as curative and preventative measures. The shat-kriyas cleanse the nose, oesophagus, stomach and intestines outwardly, whereas the asanas penetrate deeper than them, bringing a radical change in the functioning itself. For example, the lateral twists of the spine, *Urdhva Padmasana, Parshvapindasana, Halasana,* etc., work as basti (cleansing the intestines). The inverted asanas, kapalbhati, bhastrika, digital pranyama work as neti, sutra neti etc. The backward extensions work as dhauti. There are many asanas which bring similar effects to the kriyas, but are more internal and permanently effective, as they radically change the body function without creating any harmful side-effects.

Medicines, due to their specific qualities, work on the body in a specific way. They work as tonics, nourishing the body. They cleanse, induce perspiration and produce moisture. They stimulate, arrest, condense the body activities and eradicate disease. The asanas also consist of actions such as scraping, rubbing, rinsing, squeezing, massaging, freezing, drying, cleansing, condensing, pacifying, activising, stimulating, supporting, soothing, causing perspiration, producing moisture, solidifying, liquidifying, attenuating, penetrating, narrowing, spreading, fixing, knotting, warming, cooling etc. The asan-pranayam is sensitively grafted on the body. The movements consists of contortion, contraction, expansion, extension, circumduction and abduction. Again there is vertical, horizontal, circular, spiral and circumferential movement. The asana penetrates the depth, width and length of the physiological body depthwise. The asana reaches into the body, penetrating it from all dimensions.

The practitioner of asanas has to undergo three stages while performing the asana, namely:

(1.) beginning of the asana to reach the asana *(arambha);*

(2.) remaining in the asana *(sthiti);* and

(3.) concluding the asana to regain the normal position of the body *(visarjan).*

416

All these three steps have a therapeutic value and psychological effect. Each stage of asana and pranayama, whether intermediate or final, can yield something as a therapy. While doing asana, each action and movement by the body, and the stability and establishment of the body in the asana, is significant and important. The vital breath is circulated and perambulated through the system by the proper inhalation-exhalation-retention mechanism, and by proper activisation and relaxation.

Therefore, the asan-pranayam method works as a curative and preventative measure.

Using props such as chairs, tables, bricks, stools, benches and the wall while doing asanas are also beneficial and effective. The suffering patient does the asana correctly without feeling any exertion. The body is exactly grafted onto the props. The limited capacities, age, the nature of disease, negative approach, inner refusal, disabilities, inabilities, pains, weaknesses, fear and lack of will-power restrict and restrain the patient from doing asanas. Here the props help. They create confidence, lessen the pain, support the body and avoid faulty movements.

The asanas are performed in different ways to bring the expected and required effect. One has to know where the impetus should be and where the gravitational centre should be. One should know where, when and how the energy should be diffused, infused and instilled. Using props results towards this fructification though the major role is played by the teacher and the patient need not worry about it.

This is how the asan-pranayam method has become applicable as a therapy in a multi-channelled and a multi-dimensional way due to its multi-potentiality.

The goal of Yoga is to free (liberate) the purusha (soul) from the entanglement of prakriti. Prakriti does not abandon the purusha until it is cleansed, cleaned and purified. Yoga is a method to purify prakriti. In this process of purification, health comes as a by-product and side-effect, and the disease, which is like a parasite, is removed. The aspirant conquers these small peaks while reaching the highest peak—like Everest—*kaivalya* or final emancipation.

The
ESSENCES

A MUSICAL LIGHT
ON "LIGHT ON YOGA"

by Peter Leek

MUSIC, ONE MIGHT SAY, brought Yoga to Europe. For it was at the invitation of Yehudi Menuhin that B.K.S. Iyengar travelled to Europe in 1954 and gave his first Yoga demonstrations in Switzerland and France. Menuhin had been introduced to Iyengar by Pandit Nehru when, during a concert tour of India, the violinist was struck by a muscular pain which literally threatened his musical career. Thanks to Iyengar's instruction, Menuhin recovered—and today, twenty years later, he still uses Yoga to relax before concerts and solo recitals.

Music also supplied the background for the birth of the Iyengar organisation in Britain. Iyengar's first classes in London (attended by a dozen or so people, among them Clifford Curzon, the pianist, and his wife) were arranged by Angela Marris, membership secretary of the Asian Music Circle. Angela quickly became one of Iyengar's most devoted admirers—soon joined by Beatrice Harthan, whom she had met through the Asian Music Circle. Together they set about organising regular classes with Iyengar-trained teachers, and their enthusiasm and energy, plus the efforts of pupils, teachers and well-wishers too numerous to mention, rapidly made Iyengar's name known to a wider public and eventually led to the appointment of Iyengar-trained teachers for the first Yoga classes provided by the Inner London Education Authority.

It was music too that helped bring about the publication of *Light on Yoga*. In the summer of 1964 Iyengar came over at Yehudi Menuhin's request to the Gstaad Music Festival. During the Festival Iyengar presented Beatrice Harthan with the first two chapters, in long hand, of his *Yoga Dipika*. These she faithfully typed out on a rickety typewriter at her chalet, then took them back to England in her suitcase. A few days later Gerald Yorke, adviser to Allen & Unwin on Yoga as well as oriental religions and mysticism, offered Beatrice a lift in his car to the Buddhist Society summer school. Knowing her wide circle of acquaintances and even broader range of interests, Yorke mentioned somewhat casually that he was looking for an authoritative and comprehensive book on Yoga. "Look no further," came the reply, "I have the first two chapters in my bag!" A brief glance was enough to tell Yorke that this was indeed the book he was after. He at once wrote to Iyengar for the rest of the manuscript—and when he showed it to Philip Unwin he had no doubt that this was a book that Allen & Unwin simply had to publish.

Quite a few months later, Iyengar having put the finishing touches to the manuscript and after the long task of cross-referencing and proof-reading, *Light on Yoga* saw the light of day. It was at once recognised in Wilfred Clarke's words, as "the Yoga Bible" and was hailed by *Yoga and Health* as a book that no enthusiast or

424

teacher could afford to be without, and by *The Times of India* as the finest manual on the subject.

Since then the British edition alone has sold over 100,000 copies, while separate editions have been published in France, Germany, Italy and Spain. In India it has been translated into Hindi, Kannada and Marathi—and at this moment a Japanese translation is in preparation and a new Unwin Paper back edition with a new cover design.[1]

No article about *Light on Yoga* would be complete without a word about its author. Philip Unwin affectionately recalls how at their first encounter he was struck by Iyengar's commanding presence and enormous vitality. Also, that in no time at all he suddenly found himself performing headstands on the office carpet! For my own part, I have known Iyengar for ten years or more and can truly say not only that it has been a very great pleasure and privilege to work with him, but also that today at sixty he radiates that same wonderful aura of grace and energy which I too noticed when I first met him in Philip Unwin's office a decade ago.

1. By December 1985 the British Edition of *Light on Yoga* had sold 116,00 copies and the American edition 140,000. Since 1978, *Light on Yoga* has been published in Danish and Gujarati, and the *Concise Light on Yoga* in Portugese. *Light on Pranayama* is available in English, French, German, Italian, Japanese, Hindi and Marathi. B.K.S. Iyengar's latest book, *The Art of Yoga*, published in English, will soon be available in French and Japanese.

HOW "LIGHT ON YOGA" WAS WRITTEN

by B.I. Taraporewala

ON RECEIVING A COPY of *Light on Yoga,* R. Ramanna, head of the Bhabha Atomic Research Centre of the Government of India, wrote to B.K.S. Iyengar: "You did me great honour by presenting me a copy of your book on Yoga, which I find very useful and is probably the most comprehensive book on the subject by a man who has spent a lifetime on studying its values. I am most grateful to you for the honoured present."

Another reviewer went on to state: "It is rare for a book to become a classic almost at its inception. This work is in that privileged category. Iyengar himself is almost a legend in his own lifetime. . . . Definitely the best book there is on Hatha Yoga."

What the reviewer did not know was how the book was written and how it saw the light of day. Twenty-five years of *tapas* and unrivalled experience were there before a single page of it was written. There were also the skills and experiences of others who helped in seeing the project through. The book took five years to write and edit. Like a giant tree of the forest the book grew slowly. Its roots were deep, penetrating to the very source of life.

One Saturday in December 1956 there came into Iyengar's life a man who was to become his friend and associate in bringing out the book *Light on Yoga.* The place where they met was "Hasman," a cultural centre of the Bhulabhai Memorial Institute at Bombay. There flourished the arts—music, dance, painting and sculpture. To this was added the mother of all arts—Yoga—taught by Iyengar on the terrace during weekends.

Iyengar looked up from his teaching to see a tall, bespectacled, greying man with a Groucho Marx moustache. I was that man and I introduced myself and said that my wife and I wished to take Yoga lessons. Iyengar said that we could start the following week. That was the uneventful start of a life-long friendship.

One Saturday afternoon in 1960, Smt. Mehra Melegaumwala, an old friend of Iyengar, came beaming to the Bombay Yoga class and told him that one of the leading publishers of Bombay had shown an interest in bringing out a publication on Yoga-asanas for the international market. As I was Iyengar's pupil from 1956, I phoned the publisher. I took an appointment and wrote to Iyengar to bring his albums of photographs of asanas. The publisher saw the photographs and liked them, and after some discussion, it was decided that some text had to be written to show the technique of performing the asana by describing the intermediate stages whereby one reached the final pose. It was decided that I should write in the first instance about three basic standing poses. The scheme evolved was this: First, the name of the asana was explained and a brief note given about the personality or legend connected with the name. Next, the technique was described in numbered paragraphs step by step in a language as simple as possible. Last, the benefits of the asana were stated.

I had been reporting legal decisions of the High Court for newspapers for some years. I had the benefit of being trained by Iyengar in performing asanas. My training in legal-journalism helped me in writing about things in a manner so that an average reader could grasp what had been written. Iyengar and I wanted to do a book which would become in course of time a source-book. We felt that we should prepare a textbook, simple to read and understand, liberally illustrated to show the stages and not likely to go out of date.

Our proposed deal with the Bombay publisher, however, did not materialise. It was a disappointment which eventually turned out to be a blessing. In the meantime, Iyengar had his photographs taken by Welling Studios at Pune, showing how to do the asanas, stage by stage. It was gruelling work to pose under the hot studio lights and do several retakes if the result was not up to the mark.

Every few weeks, Iyengar would come to Bombay with handwritten notes. These were made during his limited spare time or during his train journeys to and from Bombay. He had given me books from his own library. These were source books like the *Hatha Yoga Pradipika,* the *Gheranda Samhita,* the *Siva Samhita,* translations of the *Gita* and the *Upanishads,* standard books on Indian philosophy and on Patanjali's *Yoga Sutras.* I had also books from my own library. The book which was indispensable was *Apte's Sanskrit-English Dictionary.* I had my notes of discourses on the *Yoga Sutras* given by a learned Pandit.

Every Saturday evening after the asana sessions, Iyengar, a friend or two, my wife and I would proceed to the flat of Smt. Martha Wartenburger, one of Iyengar's oldest pupils, with our papers and files. There, after refreshments and cups of strong coffee prepared in the continental style, we would read the typescript prepared by me. Often the expressions used in a paragraph or two would stump us and there would follow discussions about the selection of the proper word. Martha would pour out cups of coffee and tell me that I should yield to the words selected by Iyengar, for after all it was his book and not mine, and I would hold on to the view that the word did not correctly reflect what was in Iyengar's mind when he put it on paper.

It appeared that while our negotiations with the Bombay publishers were proceeding, unknown to any of us, our good fairy had not forgotten us. In 1962, Iyengar's pupil, Mrs. Beatrice Harthan of London, showed his photographs and typescript to Mr. Gerald Yorke, who showed keen interest in the proposed book. Yorke, literary adviser to several leading English publishers, was in search of new works to take the place of books on Yoga by Theos Bernard. Yorke has unrivalled and unique experience in selection of books, and his judgment in selection was, and is, highly respected. His command over the English language and his ability to condense and clarify are uncanny, and with a few excisions and revisions, he can improve what one has written so that the writer's work is improved immeasurably. Yorke had seen Iyengar at work, made extensive enquiries and satisfied himself about the potentials of the proposed book. When Iyengar had gone to England in 1963, he met Yorke through Beatrice Harthan. Yorke told Iyengar that he had seen the typescript and he felt that Iyengar was a teacher, but not a writer. Yorke felt that the typescript would need extensive revision and editing. The proposed book had an introduction which was too long and required pruning and polishing. He persuaded Messrs. George Allen and

430

Unwin to publish *Light on Yoga*. The ultimate success of the book is in no small measure due to the efforts of Yorke.

During the summer vacation of the High Court in May and June 1961, I had gone to Iyengar's house at Pune. His children had gone to Bangalore, and he and his wife Ramamani entertained me and feasted me royally on South Indian dishes. I had come to work with him on the chapter on pranayama, literally to be pumped out of Iyengar by a fortnight's cross-examination. The writing of this chapter reminded me of the legend of *Veda-Vyasa* and Ganapati collaborating on the writing of the *Mahabharata,* where Ganapati refused to pen a word he could not understand.

While the writing, revison, editing and photography in connection with the book were progressing, Iyengar was busy preparing the Appendices. These dealt with a three hundred weeks' course on asanas and pranayama, and also the curative poses for various ailments. Every page of *Light on Yoga* was written and revised at least four times. Fourteen versions were done of the translation of Sankaracharya's *Atma Satakam,* which appears at the end of the introduction. It was a search for simplicity and perfection which characterised the publication of the book.

What are the causes for the success of the book? First and foremost was the dedicated work of Iyengar in perfecting the asana techniques. Next was his unmatched teaching experience with a variety of human bodies—several of them stiff, ailing and deformed, to provide relief for them. Another factor was the photography by Welling Studios, highlighting the salient features of each asana. Added to this was the highly skilful editing by

Yorke and our fortune in getting world-famous publishers like Messrs. George Allen and Unwin. Within a dozen years the book has sold over a hundred thousand copies. It has been translated into Spanish, Italian, German, French, Danish and Japanese. In India the book has been published in Kannada, Hindi, Gujarati and Marathi.

When Prime Minister of India, Moraji Desai, himself an ardent practitioner of Yoga, received a copy of *Light on Yoga,* he wrote: "When Yoga is being distorted and commercialised, it is good to have some standard work to remind its students of its higher purpose in regard to the wealth of the body, mind and soul of man."

The book has been accepted as a standard work on the subject of Yoga. Wilfred Clark, President of the British Wheel of Yoga referred to the book as being a "Bible of Yoga."

LIGHT ON PRANAYAMA

A book review by the late Swami Venkatesananda

Y OGACHARYA B.K.S. IYENGAR'S TEACHING rests on these four Pillars (Ps)—Practicability, Precision, Purity and Perfection. Nothing is left to the student's imagination or misunderstanding. Nothing is taken for granted. Iyengar explains every step precisely and painstakingly. Example, "Pare the nails so that they do not hurt the delicate nasal skin while doing digital pranayama."

In his *Light on Yoga* which deals exhaustively with Yoga asanas, he introduced us to the subject of pranayama. Now, in his *Light on Pranayama* he takes us through the labyrinth of this fascinating inner world of the life-force. He literally grabs us by the arm—as he demands that we should "grab the diaphragm!"—and takes us step by clear step from wherever we may be to where he wishes us to be—healthy, holy and harmonized humans, capable of living wisely in today's world.

Iyengar emphasizes the urgency of the need to practice pranayama: "Owing to the development of technology, modern life has become endlessly competitive, resulting in increased strain on both men and women. It is difficult to maintain a balanced life. Anxieties and diseases affecting the nervous and circulatory systems have multiplied. In despair, people become addicted to psyche-delic drugs, smoking and drinking or indiscriminate sex to find relief. These activities allow one to forget oneself temporarily, but the causes remain unsolved and the dis-eases return. Only pranayama gives real relief from these problems." Very true.

That pranayama is not merely inhaling and exhaling becomes obvious very soon as Iyengar explains the signif-icance of prana and what pranayama really means. There is no vagueness even in areas where vagueness is gener-ally encountered—in theoretical explanation. Iyengar is firmly rooted in tradition and scriptural authority; but these do not tie him down or hinder his exploration.

One of the most extraordinary features of this book is the wealth of anatomical and physiological information it gives us. These are carefully and exactly correlated to the spirit of pranayama. Extraordinarily beautiful illus-trations clarify the theory. The numerous photographs (of Iyengar himself) provide the clearest instruction pos-sible in practice.

The benefits are succinctly described and the words of caution are judiciously introduced where an overenthu-siastic or non-vigilant student might err. Iyengar also points out what to look for and where. As with the instructions in Yoga asanas, in describing the various pranayama techniques, Iyengar emphasizes the mobility of the skin as a criterion for the correctness or incorrect-ness of the practice. This is something unique, which I have not come across in the teaching of anyone else. Example: "Each pore of the skin of the trunk should act as the eye of intelligence *(jnana chaksu)* for absorbing prana." Fantastic.

Doubtless this beautifully produced volume will become the spiritual text for Yoga teachers and serious yoga students all over the world, as a companion to the author's *Light on Yoga*.[1]

1. *Light on Pranayama* is available in English, French, Italian, German, Japanese, Hindi and Marathi.

He is a very warm-hearted and friendly person, but when it comes to his art, he is exacting, tenacious, and as fanatical as any artist must be.

Menuhin

IYENGAR—THE ARTIST

by B.I. Taraporewala

B.K.S. IYENGAR HAS PRESENTED *yogasanas* in four continents as an artist, through the media of lecture-demonstrations, television, videotapes and films. He has appeared before distinguished audiences in various cities and countries of the world like New York, Washington, London, Paris, Geneva, Berne, Zurich, Munich, Brussels, the Vatican, Rome, Venice, Nairobi, Swaziland, Lesotho, Colombo and Mauritius. He has also given demonstrations of his art in New Delhi, Bombay, Pune, Hyderabad and other cities of India.

His demonstrations of this pure and unique art are always as unique as they are enlightening. While demonstrating his art, he intersperses his asanas with a running commentary. It is stunning to see him maintain the most exacting postures with astounding ease and effortless grace. His asanas are of unforgettable precision, beauty and poise signifying the majesty, speed and power of creatures of the wild and also the serenity of sages. The fluid yet dynamic movements of his body keep the audience spellbound, for they are seeing superb sculptured forms of the human anatomy come alive. The silence of the audience is a tangible thing—a mere whisper could shatter it!

As a cultural ambassador abroad, Iyengar created an excellent impression both by his performance and by his exquisite urbanity. It made Indian ambassadors proud of their country and their fellow citizens. The foreign audiences told them, after witnessing his lecture-demonstrations, that they had never dreamed that such skill was possible. They were struck by his complete mastery over the art which kept them fully absorbed.

Iyengar's approach to Yoga is not merely physical. Apa P. Pant, former High Commissioner for India to U.K., said: "Yoga is to join the limited to the unlimited, the finite to the infinite. The human consciousness when it is circumscribed and limited is full of contradictions, confusion and sorrow. To release human consciousness from this confinement is the task of Yoga. No one can do it better than Mr. Iyengar."

He has used his supreme art in the service of humanity for collecting large sums of money—both in India and abroad—for education, health, medical relief, flood relief and other charitable causes.

He appeared in a forty-five minute television film, which formed a part of the Culture of the World series, and was screened at the Olympic Games held in Munich in 1972.

He was probably the first man to give a lecture-demonstration of the ancient Indian yogasanas at the United Nations Organisation.

He has appeared in several B.B.C. Television programmes, including a half hour interview entitled *Menuhin and his Guru*. The B.B.C. went on to describe him as the "Michaelangelo of Yoga."

In 1976, the Ann Arbor "Y" of Michigan made a videotape recording of an hour-long demonstration given by him, entitled, *The Ultimate Truth*. The Associate Director of Ann Arbor "Y", Thomas P. Huntzicker, said that the videotape was "an excellent programme without parallel in its field."

In 1977, an impressionistic film on Iyengar and his Institute entitled *Samadhi,* was produced by the Film and Television Institute of India. It won for its director, John Shankaramangalam, a national award for the best experimental film. It is a creative documentary with high artistic merit. Mr. L.K. Advani, Minister for Information and Broadcasting, Government of India, felt sure that through the documentary *Samadhi* the message of Yoga would be disseminated widely for the benefit of the people in India as well as abroad.

After watching a demonstration of Iyengar's art at the National Defence Academy, Pune, in 1957, Nikita Krushchev, Premier of Russia, expressed satisfaction that he had seen something of the truly India ethos, something which no other country could match in the sphere of harmonious development of both mind and body.

One of Iyengar's performances at Brighton prompted Therese, a French artiste, to write: "How greatly I admired and enjoyed the performance of the great sage. What was particularly fascinating was the simplicity and truly spiritual integrity of the man. He left in one's mind an unforgettable impression. His movements and postures were sheer music to the spirit and the eye. So much effort concealed under such utter serenity. He was the true symbol, in all he said and did, of *La largesse de l'Orient*—of which our poor Western world is in such dire need."

439

The *Yoga and Health* magazine of London wrote about his work: "Because Iyengar is so patently 'King of the asanas,' people are apt not to realise how closely spiritual is his real message and intent."

Penderell Reed of Manchester said that after watching a B.B.C. Television programme of a demonstration by Iyengar, a new dimension of Yoga was opened up for her and she realised that she had been on the periphery of something very profound

It was a rare experience for Dr. Perin Cabinetmaker to watch a performance given by Iyengar, where each pose appeared to be a statue of chiselled perfection. She felt that it was not Iyengar's body doing an asana, but some hidden power deep within him expressing itself through his body.

Yehudi Menuhin called Iyengar, "the superb exponent of one of India's most prized arts—that of Hatha Yoga." In the course of a lesson Menuhin had with him, Iyengar had compared the human body to a musical instrument. The head of the instrument was like our brain, its stem like our spine, its knobs like our vertebrae and its strings like our nerves. As the instrument produces rhythm with the help of its head, stem, knobs and strings, the human body can also produce rhythm by the proper exercise of our brain, spine, vertebrae and nerves. Our human body must function smoothly like a well-tuned musical instrument. Then there will be harmony in life.

Menuhin also wrote: "A painter needs his brushes and paints, a musician needs his instrument, but Mr. Iyengar needs only his body for his art. . . . He is as dedicated to his work as any artist, but his is an art which has been reduced to its simplest form, because it requires no instrument at all except this finest and most complex instrument of all—the body. There is no formal choreography, no script, no rules laid down for form, but all the rules of the choreographer, of the artist and the writer are inherent in the body itself. To perfect this art, however, requires a lifetime of patient and persistent effort, always trying to perfect this instrument, the body.

"He is a very warm-hearted and friendly person, but when it comes to his art, he is exacting, tenacious, and as fanatical as any artist must be."

Writing about a lecture-demonstration given by Iyengar in London, Bharati Kansara referred to him as a "divine gymnast" who moulded his body into asanas with such ease that it seemed as if he were moulding plasticine. She wrote: "With his thinly clad body alone, while performing intricate yogic asanas or postures he shows us a perfect control of mind over body, an amazing harmony and grace of movement that springs from a true fusion of physical, mental and spiritual planes. . . . He talked gaily, expounding yogic philosophy and relating mythological stories connected with each asana, while balancing cross-legged on his hands or some other unlikely part of his anatomy, as if it was an easy-chair. His teaching, so lucid and profound, is interspersed with a constant stream of witticisms."

In May 1976, Iyengar gave a lecture-demonstration at Haverford College, Pennsylvania. In the audience were Robert Engman, a famous American sculptor, Alan L. Fishman, a leading American architect, George Rockberg, a composer, and E. Simons, a photographer.

After the performance Engman wrote to Iyengar: "It was absolutely the most incredible and most moving physical and mental expression I've ever witnessed in my life, barring none. I've never seen anyone master his mind and body with complete control the way you did. And it was backed by a wealth of wisdom and gentleness and concern for life that I myself have sought for."

Engman, Chairman of the Graduate Department of Fine Arts at the University of Pennsylvania, was so impressed by the virtuoso performance, that he himself made a fifteen-foot sculpture and called it "After Iyengar." The statue is now installed in the University campus.

Fishman, in a letter to Iyengar, said: "I was especially impressed with the artistic form of your demonstration. The form and movements exhibited in your Yoga touched my architectural sensitivities. I consider your Yoga to be a true form of art and you an artist of great talent.

"I found a common relationship in your approach to Yoga and in my approach to architectural design. In both forms of art, physical movement and form are meaningfully communicated to the observer and user (in your case participants, I suppose) in such a way that the mind and spirit become intimately involved with the physical experience."

Rochberg, who is Composer-in-Residence, University of Pennsylvania, wrote some months later to Iyengar as follows: "Ever since seeing your incredible demonstration of Yoga this past May at Haverford College, I have wanted to write you to express my sincere admiration for your remarkable achievement in the art of integrating the physical body and the spirit into a living unity of human expression.

"I remember listening intently to your discussion of what Yoga is and couldn't help 'translating' everything you said into my own way of thinking about music and

442

what music represents, an emanation of the spiritual world projected on the screen of human physical reality and realization. In my mind Yoga and music join together in the intensity of life-discipline and life experience—the two interpenetrating each other to create living forms of art, whether of the physical body or the soul.

"Yours is a rare achievement, and it would give me the greatest pleasure some day to have the opportunity to witness your art again and be able to exchange views on Yoga and music."

According to Simons, Iyengar was to Yoga what Renoir was to painting, Rodin was to sculpture and Steichen was to photography—all Masters in their respective arts.

Photographing the Haverford College demonstration was an experience for Simons that "only comes but rarely in one's life, that is, seeing an artist of the highest calibre create the approach, technique and form in his or her art that only a Master can."

Donald Moyer came twice from the United States of America to the Institute at Pune to attend seminars conducted by Iyengar. In an article describing his experience Moyer said, "Mr. Iyengar is one of the great creative artists of our time and his finest classes are sublime poems that only happen once. To me he is comparable to another hot-tempered Sagittarian mystic, William Blake. Iyengar, like Blake... has tutored himself by the intensity of his inner vision. When I look at the flame-like movement of Blake's drawings, I sense his spiritual kinship with Iyengar. For both of them, the body is an ever-changing, ever-flickering radiance."

"With relentless single-mindedness, Iyengar is ever in pursuit of perfection in his art. He has a creative faculty which makes Yoga an ever-evolving method for taking man higher and higher in the region of consciousness. Yoga is a science and art of conscious human evolution which has great future, and his contribution to the development is substantial," said R.R. Diwakar, Chairman, Gandhi Peace Foundation.

Refinement of technique is the art *(kala)* of Yoga. As Iyengar's technique became finer and more polished, the sheer artistry of the human form broke through. The art transformed the science *(sastra)* into a higher form of religion *(dharma),* the culture of the Self.

Writing about the work of Iyengar, Father Anthony Lobo, an old pupil of his, observed: "He has made Yoga scientific, not by installing a huge laboratory filled with glittering gauges, but by showing that for the scientific study of the self, the most sensitive gauge is the human consciousness created in every nerve end. He has made it an art, not only by the wizardry of his own postures, but by creating techniques to develop the beauty of the human form and human consciousness. He has finally moved to the ultimate by showing the unity of life and death in the witnessing state of pure innocence. This is his achievement."

THE YOGA INSTITUTE
by Madhu Tijoriwala

IN HIS MESSAGE on the occasion of the opening of the Ramamani Iyengar Memorial Yoga Institute, Guruji's old and grateful disciple Yehudi Menuhin, world famous violinist, wrote: "Having planted the seed of Yoga all over the world, Mr. Iyengar has brought his great art and knowledge back to his own native country and home in the shape of this fine institute. My Yoga Guru, Mr. B.K.S. Iyengar, has contributed more than his share to the spread of this human awareness which is Yoga. I hope the Yoga Institute, in its attractive new building, will uphold Mr. Iyengar's life work and become a place of pilgrimage and dedication as indeed in his own life."

Born in 1918 during the world influenza epidemic, Guruji survived to remain a sickly child with thin arms and legs, a protruding stomach and a top-heavy head. No one could guide him to health. His condition deteriorated and suspected tuberculosis of the lungs brought him almost to the point of death.

Ekalavya of *Mahabharata* was a brilliant student. No Guru would teach him archery as he was a Sudra belonging to a low caste. He made a statue of Drona, Guru of the Pandavas and Kauravas, and practised archery before the

445

statue. He became a skilled archer only by his devotion and sincere practice. Guruji was taught a little of Yoga by his brother-in-law whom he accepted as his Guru. After coming to Pune when Guruji was barely eighteen years old, he had to practise by himself like Ekalavya with devotion without any further help from his Guru to pursue the subject. He had to face untold hardships and had to correct himself by his own power of discrimination.

Through trials and tribulations, he has risen to become a world-famous Yoga practitioner and teacher. From the days of his struggle he has risen to acquire name, fame and prosperity throughout the world.

Many institutes came up in several parts of the world named after Guruji and which carried out the propagation of Iyengar teaching techniques. However, until 1973, no institute was established in India.

A piece of land at Hare Krishna Mandir Road in Pune was purchased and transferred to Guruji, Geeta and Prashant. Shrimati Ramamani, the beloved wife of Guruji, performed the Bhoomi Puja on January 25th, 1973, three days before her death. She was loved by all those who came in contact with the Iyengar family. Her death was a great blow to all who knew her.

As a personal testimonial and token of the esteem and regard for Guruji, Ramamani, Geeta and Prashant, and to perpetuate the memory of Ramamani, pupils, friends and well-wishers conceived the idea of presenting to the Iyengar family a Yoga Institute where Yoga could be taught.

In order to effectively carry out their wishes, a committee of eight members by the name of "The Ramamani Iyengar Memorial Yoga Institute Committee" was

446

formed. The committee issued an appeal to friends and admirers in and outside India, to contribute their mite for getting the Institute built and make a gift of it to Guruji, Geeta and Prashant, who have devoted their lives to Yoga.

The Institute was built and formally handed over on December 14th, 1974, which was the birthday of Guruji. The members of the committee recorded that as a testimonial and mark of personal affection and regard that their pupils, friends and admirers had for Guruji, Geeta and Prashant, the Yoga Institute named as the RAMAMANI IYENGAR MEMORIAL YOGA INSTITUTE was handed over to them. The committee was confident that the Institute would serve its purpose of propagation of Yoga, and people from all parts of the world would come to the Institute and acquire benefit under the able guidance of the three teachers. It was felt that they would play an important role in the propagation of Yoga for many years under the Divine Light.

On January 19th, 1975, the Ramamani Iyengar Memorial Yoga Institute was inaugurated by Ayurveda Chakravarti, Vaidya Ratna, Pandit Shiv Sharma. Pupils from all parts of the world came to Pune and participated in the function, which was a great success.

The members of the committee had to experience several problems during the time of the construction of the Institute. Cement was in short supply and efforts had to be made in Bombay for the steady supply of cement. They had to request those in charge of supervision of the construction work to see to it that the building was completed in time for the opening function. The work had progressed slowly in the beginning, but was speeded up as the deadline approached. With concerted efforts made

447

Puja at the inauguration of the Institute,
January 19, 1975.

in every direction by all concerned, the inaugural function was held on time as scheduled.

The day previous to the inaugural date will never be forgotten by those who were at the Institute. All building tools, materials, scaffolding and other articles had to be removed. The tiles had to be polished by machines. The hall had to be washed and decorated. The pupils who had come from various parts of the world came to the help of the committee. Several of them rolled up their sleeves and took buckets of water with swabs and broomstick in their hands. The result was that after four to five hours of tedious, hard work, the Institute looked spick-and-span for the inauguration the next day. The work of cleaning and decoration was done with love and affection.

The Institute has a unique architectural design resembling a semicircular-shaped pyramid. It consists of a ground floor with a foyer and four residential rooms for pupils, the main hall on the first floor for practice of pranayama and a basement housing the library. The three-tier building (ground, first and second floors) represents *bahiranga* (external), *antaranga* (internal) and *antaratma* (the innermost) *sadhana* (practice) of Yoga.

The height of the building, the steps, the main column, the eight beams, the eight outside columns and the space between each column can be explained in yogic and spiritual terms.

The idol of Sage Patanjali, author of the *Yoga Sutras,* is installed at the entrance of the main hall, so that the seeker may pay his respects to the sage and get his blessings.

The idol of Lord Hanuman, son of Vayu (Lord of Wind) was installed later at the apex of the building, facing North. Lord Hanuman is the embodiment of

449

strength and stability, intellect and courage, celibacy and humility. He is the master of pranayama, and the hall for practice of pranayama is appropriately located under his feet.

A visit to the Institute is a rewarding experience even to a person not practising Yoga. The bust of Ramamani, the mother of the Institute, gives the visitor an affectionate and cordial welcome. As one enters the gates of the Institute one is surrounded by a lovely garden, full of green plants, roses and other beautiful and fragrant flowers. Whatever is grown in the garden comes up speedily and gracefully for it is planted and cared for with love and affection by the Iyengar family. One enters the Institute building barefoot as one enters a temple. A second welcome is extended by the spirit of Ramamani, which is behind the Institute. Her serene portrait facing the visitors showers love on them and the family alike.

There is also a beautiful coloured portrait of Guruji facing the front entrance of the Institute. This entrance generally remains closed but is opened on important occasions. Whichever way one enters one finds a welcome either by the Mother of the Institute or by the Father.

As one climbs up to the first floor to the main hall one finds beautiful photographs and paintings of Guruji with some of the important people of the world. The bust of Guruji done by the late Elisabeth, Queen Mother of Belgium, adorns the staircase.

As one enters the main hall one is wonderstruck at the sight of hundreds of photographs of asana poses of Guruji fixed high up round the walls of the hall. What a sight for the gods to see! The immaculately clean hall exudes peace and tranquillity. The atmosphere is surcharged with spirituality.

However, it is a different story when the Yoga class is in session. One then sees the Master in full form along with Geeta and Prashant moving round the hall helping the pupils. One hears his commanding voice rising above all others guiding the pupils. There are ropes, wooden planks, wooden bricks, mats, cushions and benches, stools, chairs and other gadgets being used by pupils or kept ready for their use.

When one goes up to the pranayama hall, the serene atmosphere pervading there is never disturbed. Those who come to this hall for pranayama practice do not indulge in talking. They walk softly and the teachers give their instructions in a soft voice.

Thereafter one climbs up the stairway to the top where Lord Hanuman presides. After praying one's obeisance to Lord Hanuman one looks round to find green trees and vegetation all around. There is a beautiful public garden in the vicinity and also farm lands. At a distance one sees hills and houses. At sunrise and sunset the colours in the sky change and a wide variety of birds fly past the Institute.

What was the condition of the Institute when on December 14th, 1974, it was formally handed over to Guruji, Geeta and Prashant, and on January 19th, 1975 when the inaugural function took place? What was handed over were the bare walls of the Institute without any furniture or articles. The building was only white-washed for the time being. With the first monsoon the latent defects in the building became patent. There was profuse leakage from the roof to the halls, ground floor and the basement. The basement was flooded with water from heavy downpours. The water from the basement had to be manually removed. Cracks developed in the

Geeta, Iyengar and Prashant

walls and bathroom tiles began to come out. There were arguments with those who supervised the construction of the Institute. However, with the Master's eye to perfection and with divine discontent in him all defects were cured and the Institute was oil painted and transformed into a place for the gods to visit.

At the Institute annual functions have taken place. Pupils from India and outside have had their Yoga lessons there under the guidance of the three teachers. Guruji's third daughter, Sunita, was married there.

The history of the Institute will be incomplete without reference to the gardener, Baban, as also to Mohan, who works as a watchman, supervisor and general factotum. There is also an old couple who clean the premises. All are looked after as members of the family and they have become part and parcel of the Institute.

Man-made Institutes are not for ever. Will this Institute survive for a considerable length of time? The Master is sixty years young and there are many more years of his fruitful service in the field of Yoga. Geeta and Prashant are teachers in their own right and young as they are they will carry the torch of Yoga for many more years to come. They will train teachers who will carry on the light of Yoga for the benefit of mankind. The children of Guruji, it is sincerely hoped, will produce many more masters in time to come.

The Ramamani Iyengar Memorial Yoga Institute at Pune is and will remain a place of pilgrimage for all Yoga lovers of the world, and it will continue to spread its light of Yoga for the benefit of mankind.

"May the Institute flourish. May it be a beacon of light to many. May its teachings spread far and wide. May the art of Yoga remain with mankind for ever."

People say I'm an aggressive teacher, but I am an
intensive teacher, not an aggressive one.

IYENGAR—THE TEACHER

by B.I. Taraporewala

IYENGAR IS ONE of the world's inspired teachers, who knows how to bring the best out of his pupils, and who knows how to pass the essence of his knowledge from himself to his pupils.

A Yoga session with Iyengar, whether it be of asanas, or pranayama or meditation, is neither merely body-building, nor an experiment in learning the elasticity of the human body. It is an invitation to an expanded consciousness through becoming totally at one with one's most intimate possession, the body.

In teaching Yoga, Iyengar makes the pupil practise so that he learns to make friends with his body. He explores its potential capacity with the clarity, confidence and courage of Iyengar guiding and sustaining him. A stern discipline pervades Iyengar's nature, which is a little cruel that it may be very kind. "No pains, no gains, no thorns, no roses," he often says, while manipulating stiff joints and attempting to release them from the grip of calcification.

Iyengar does not follow the system of taking a slow easy class of postures held only as long as they are comfortable without strain. To perform an asana in a mechanical, slipshod or unthinking manner is alien to his nature. He exhorts: "Sincerity and stupidity cannot go together." He is relentless and intensive in his teaching, taking his pupils to their limits, both physical and mental. In this respect he resembles Professor Higgins in *My Fair Lady,* teaching Eliza Doolittle how to speak correctly. He expects his pupils to perform asanas with total awareness, total consciousness. The pupils should be ever alert with eyes and ears wide open, ready to put in every drop of their energy while performing the asanas. A pupil from whom nothing is ever demanded which he cannot do, never does all he can. As one of his South African pupils, Joyce Stuart, put it: "For the participants, awareness is given in many and wondrous ways. A sharp blow in exactly the right place at exactly the right time brings with it an unforgettable awareness that cannot be lost. The dead part becomes alive. When the flow is accompanied by a penetrating look from eyes that can at one time be like a laser beam and at another as soft as those of a deer, plus eyebrows that literally talk, then the message becomes complete." It is the electrifying jolt that sends the current of life flowing through the body.

Often, during an asana or pranayama session, Iyengar directs the attention of his pupils towards the beauty or uncomeliness of a posture, in order to point out to them those things he would have them do or avoid. These make deeper impressions on his pupils than do any written or verbal rules or instructions. Iyengar is an excellent mimic, and will give a hilarious imitation of a wrongly done posture, and then also show how not to do it. He will equally give his pupils a pose chiselled to perfection, with all its classical simplicity and beauty. He demands total effort from his pupils, but in return he gives, completely, the benefit of his hard-earned knowledge as well as rich and unrivalled experience.

Iyengar is known for introducing the standing asanas, which he believes lay down a solid, unshakable foundation for building up grace, agility and endurance. He makes his pupils do the standing postures day after day, pointing out the interaction of various parts of the body, how movement of the toes, or nails, or stretch of skin produces different effects and how the posture becomes firm. He maintains that standing poses improperly done drain away energy and make you tired. When they are done accurately, the energy of the body is recycled within the confines of the body itself and refreshes you. He will show you how to refine and improve one's postures, and how to use the wall, or a window ledge to practice the asana, till one can become independent. He will guide the pupil through various paths and make him reflect upon them repeatedly, till they grow into such a system that they remain the pupil's permanent possession.

Iyengar has used his own body as his laboratory to gain uncanny knowledge of the human anatomy. He was his own guinea pig. He saw much, suffered much and studied much. These were the three pillars of his learning. He is still the biggest student in his classes, never ashamed of learning more. If a student becomes proud of his accomplishment, he is quickly trimmed to size and made to realise his great ignorance. The hapless student feels loss of face; but it is a lesson in humility which he will not easily forget. If he swallows his pride, he will learn much that he will never learn anywhere else. This is the way the *Guru* purges the *chela*, for to be proud of learning is the greatest ignorance. Iyengar is of the view that our knowledge is little compared with what we have yet to learn.

The more Iyengar practised what he knew, the more he knew what to practise. He studied asanas and pranayama systematically and pragmatically. He performed them again and again, in all their varying nuances, till they gave him strength and nourishment. He studied them closely, thoughtfully, analyzing every subject as he went along, and laid it up carefully and safely in his memory. It is only by this mode that his knowledge became at the same time extensive, accurate and useful.

As the body stretches, it overcomes the obstacles in its way. The passage is often painful in the beginning. One learns to make friends with one's body and make the limbs do things and assume shapes and forms which one has in mind. Beginners in Yoga asanas and pranayama always let their brain and mind dictate to their bodies. After a few months of training with Iyengar, the pupils discover what he often tells them, that the body has it own intelligence apart from the brain and that the body can also dictate its own terms to the brain and mind, which is the centre of emotions. One has to learn to savour the pain, for pain is an excellent teacher. It teaches one to refine one's poses. One starts to learn new things about one's own body. Gradually the limbs learn to function as one would like them to function. This experience is indelible. One learns to take the rough with the smooth and the coarse with the subtle. One gradually sheds fear and learns better orientation. In head-balance, beginners feel very insecure. They do not know which is their left side and which is their right, or what is up or down. Like heroines in melodramas they piteously wail: "Do not leave me or I'll fall and break my neck!" Iyengar does not believe in training a race of men who will be incapable of doing anything which is disagreeable to them.

While Iyengar is meticulous and insists on accuracy of postures, he can be gentle with those whose muscles are not yet strong enough to attain this. One of his pupils, Doyse Royce, seventy-eight years of age, wrote: "I remember trying hard to achieve a certain posture and failing. Instead, I lost my balance and collapsed in humiliation on the mat. I rose, ready to weep, prepared for the blast. Instead, my teacher said comfortingly, 'Do not be disappointed, you made a good try.' Turning to the others he added, 'That was the correct way to fall.' Instantly the sting of failure was withdrawn. I had done something correctly after all, I had fallen correctly. This was one of the ways in which he captured the hearts of his pupils. We feared him, obeyed him implicitly, trusted him utterly and loved him for his human understanding." As the schoolmaster is, so will be the school.

It is the compassion and the ability to descend to the level of the student's capacity and instruct him little by little and to guide him that makes Iyengar an outstanding teacher. Having known gruelling poverty himself, he has never turned away a pupil who could not afford to pay his tuition fees. He only wants from such pupils the ardent desire to learn and has taught many pupils free of charge.

Iyengar believes that learning must be won by study. He has perfect knowledge of his art, but he does not deliver it all at once to his pupils from the very outset, for they would not be able to take it all in. At the same time he raises each pupil in his class to his or her maximum level. The secret of education, said Emerson, lies in respecting the pupil. It is reverence toward others that is wanting in

459

Classes at the Institute.
Yes, by demanding so much of us, you are challenging us
to be our very best, which doesn't happen very often in
one's lifetime. *Karen Stephan*

those who advocate machine-made cast iron systems. Reverence requires imagination, friendliness and warmth; it requires most imagination in respect of those who have least actual achievement or capacity. Iyengar establishes rapport with his pupil by talking to him in his own language giving imagery which the pupil will readily grasp. Rules, though explained in detail, slip out of the memories of most pupils. Iyengar makes his pupils practise as often as the occasion demands it. He will create occasions to make them practise. He will make his pupils practise difficult or tiring poses, like *Surya-Namaskaras* accompanied with vigorous jumpings and balancing poses, when their minds are best disposed and also when they are worst disposed. By the first method, he makes his pupils take great steps forward, by the second method he unravels the knots in their minds. This begets habits in the pupils which, once established, operate by themselves easily and naturally, without the aid of memory.

Iyengar gets and keeps the attention of his pupils and makes them advance as fast as their abilities will carry them. He makes them comprehend the usefulness of what he teaches them. He lets them see by what they have learned that they can now achieve something which they could not do before.

While teaching his pupils the techniques of asanas, Iyengar tells them that poise in the body brings peace and stability in the mind. They have to learn to purge the body before learning to purge the mind. He goads the pupils to perform asanas ethically, and not mechanically. The ethical discipline of the posture is when you extend the body correctly to its maximum capacity.

As life is to be lived dynamically, so also asanas should be performed dynamically. To pupils who can do

461

better and yet perform asanas half-heartedly, he says that if the body can do more and the pupil does not do an asana as it ought to be done, it is immoral practice, for he is cheating himself. When a pupil strains his utmost and groans, Iyengar makes him smile by telling him that the "Ah!" which escaped his lips was not the "Aum" coming from his soul. He exhorts him by saying that today's maximum should be tomorrow's minimum. He demands precision, for according to him, even an asana done wrongly is an obstacle in the progress of Yoga. Often he manipulates a student into a position which that person has never been able to accomplish, simply by one small modification.

The goal of Yoga is the union of the individual soul—the *jivatma*—with the universal soul, the *paramatma*. To achieve this goal, Iyengar believes that training the body and the mind and integrating them leads to the awareness of the soul. Patient attention leads to discovery. The best part of our knowledge teaches us where the known ends and the unknown begins. Where does the body end and the mind begin? Where does the mind end and where does the intellect, the seat of reason begin? Ignorance has no beginning, but it has an end. Knowledge has a beginning, but there is no end to knowledge. The higher one goes, the wider will appear the horizons of knowledge. One must watch, search, and strive always to find and to know. There is divine discontent until the unknown becomes the known. Iyengar's knowledge, like fire, always desires increase. He says: "I am a teacher to those who have not yet opened their eyes, but I am still a learner."

Iyengar used his gifts faithfully and they were enlarged; he practised what he knew and attained to higher knowledge, from worldly knowledge *(avidya)* to spiritual knowledge *(vidya)*. Vidya is that knowledge which liberates. For the quest of the Eternal, for what is true, good and beautiful, the body is the only vehicle given to us. Neglect of the body is a cardinal sin in the code of conduct of Iyengar. He is of the view that proper care of the body ensures stability. The spine brings physical stability, the mind brings mental and emotional stability and the brain brings intellectual stability. The spine is kept healthy by practice of asanas. Emotions are controlled by breath and pranayama. The reason for failure in self-culture is intoxicated intelligence and inflated ego. Intellect is tamed by meditation, by yoking it to the Eternal.

Iyengar kept his eyes on the Eternal and his intellect grew. He never went through any college; instead several educational institutions have been through him. In Great Britain, the Inner London Education Authority, the Greater London Education Authority, the Local Education Authorities and sports Councils of various cities and districts have introduced Yoga courses into their curricula, and teachers trained under systems evolved by Iyengar are imparting training to an ever-growing number of enthusiastic pupils. There are more Yoga practitioners in Great Britain today than anywhere else. The art of Yoga has been recognised as an official option within the Drama Section of the School of English at the University of Exeter, where it is assessed part of the training programme in Dramatic Art. Artists working within the field of Theatre and Dance at the Darlington College of Arts, Devon, have increasingly acknowledged the affinity between their art and the art of Yoga.

Iyengar's system of training in Yoga has been introduced in the United States of America at the Philadelphia

College of Performing Arts and at the American Conservatory Theatre. William Ball, General Director of the American Conservatory Theatre, wrote: "The Department of Education has empowered A.C.T.I. to grant the Master of Fine Arts degree in acting to students who complete the comprehensive three-year course. One of the classes or subjects imparted as part of the Master's program is B.K.S. Iyengar's Yoga, since Yoga is very important and a necessity to our acting students, because it develops a variety of talents and techniques. The Yoga classes help to limber and align the students' body posture as well as relax and balance the students' psycho-spiritual nature in order to produce greater depths of creativity."

Iyengar has taught dancers of Western ballet, like the Joffrey Ballet troup sponsored by Mrs. Harkness, as well as of the Indian classical dance. The Dance borrows heavily from Yoga for final postures as well as movements. Yogic exercises are an asset to a dancer. The perfection of yogic postures results in a relaxed state of body and mind essential to a dancer.

G.S. Pathak, former Vice-President of India, was specially interested in the simple exercises in pranayama which Iyengar showed him. He wrote: "I am convinced that these simple asanas and pranayama exercises if practised as taught by Shri Iyengar will prove immensely useful in generating mental tranquility and physical fitness in the practitioner.

J. Krishnamurti, the renowed philosopher, has been taught Yoga by Iyengar for nearly twenty years. He wrote: "When anybody asked me who was the best teacher, I have always sent them to you."

Iyengar is a walking encyclopaedia of Yoga. He has been responsible for removing the mumbo-jumbo which used to pass off as Yoga and bringing it to the level of a science and an art respected by royalty and commoners alike. Most men use merely one or two faculties with which they are endowed. Iyengar knows how to use the whole of himself. He knows how to make a tool of every faculty, how to open it, how to keep it sharp, and how to apply it all to practical purposes. He teaches his pupils to challenge themselves to break free from their own limitations. Yoga training under him brings to them new awareness and freedom at all levels of their being. He attempts to bring about integration between the body and the mind of the pupil. He seeks perfect alignment of body, mind and spirit. He knows his students inside out; it is this knowledge of the mind combined with the body that makes his teaching more potent in every way. They proceed from ignorance *(ajnana)* to illumination *(prajnana)*.

Quoting from Patanjali's *Yoga Sutras,* Iyengar will tell the pupil that amongst the obstacles in the path of Yoga, the sage enumerated only two which were of a physical nature—sickness *(vyadhi)* and difficulty in breathing *(svasa-prasvasa)*. All other obstacles are psychological in character. While teaching asanas, Iyengar will thump a pupil on the back and shout at him to release his tight shoulders or to expand the ribs. These instructions, apart from having a beneficial effect, have far-reaching psychological effects. They provide release from nervous tension, a boost to confidence and morale, and freedom from fear. The pupils keep working and discovering their whole beings; their real transformations and freedom begin with new flexibility on every level. With the passage of time his pupils become aware of the help—physical, mental and emotional—they receive through his system of Yoga.

Iyengar never tires of telling his students that it is only when we exceed our limitations that the gates of the mind open. To him Yoga is an exact science and an art that demands absolute devotion. He is a great believer in the value of *sadhana*—religious and disciplined practice. The body is the shell of the mind. It is the duty of a *sadhaka* to keep the body and mind clean.

Whilst teaching he becomes a *rajasic* teacher lest his pupils become *tamasic*. In his own practices he is *sattvic*. Every morning he practices pranayama and asanas religiously. These include a hundred and eight *viparitachakrasanas* (backbends) twice a week. Performance of asanas is a means of self-exploration and one has to be ruthlessly honest with one's own performance. He believes what he says: "The day I stop practising, I have lost my purity of heart. You will leave me then, for I shall not be able to help you." Subjective knowledge comes only through correct practice. He says that a learner should always be humble and sattvic in character. Even those who have attained *samadhi* can fall if they stop practising.

Iyengar gives great importance to simplicity and purity in life. His definition of meditation is: "To bring the complex mind to a state of simplicity, so that we are pure inside and out." It is this sadhana which gives Iyengar a clear vision and helps him to diagnose the cause of trouble and succeed with problem cases where conventional modes of treatment do not give effective response. It is said: "He that studies only men, will get the body of knowledge without the soul; and he that studies only books, the soul without the body. He, that to what he sees, adds observation, and to what he reads, reflection, is on the right road to knowledge, provided that, scrutinizing the hearts of others, he neglects not his own."

Intellect lies behind genius. Iyengar has used his intellect, not as a lamp in his study for his own seeing, but as a lighthouse uses its lamps so that those far off on the sea may see the shining and learn their way.

Iyengar considers himself an old-fashioned teacher. He will carefully watch and assess the performance of his pupils and the progress made by them. Even if they are good, he will not tell them that they are good. He tells them: "For me, if I see there is good I have to be satisfied within myself, but I will never say it outside. The moment I say it, I close the door to your progress. To be a teacher you must roar like a lion outside and be meek as a lamb inside."

To Iyengar, the skin which envelopes the body is a very important part of the anatomy. It is a highly sensitive organ; it is also the weightiest. An average human brain weighs about four pounds, while the skin weighs about six pounds. He observes the colour of the skin, its texture and dryness, and also the subtle movements which are not perceptible to the untrained eye. The colour and texture indicate points of pressure or swelling. Dryness indicates that the energy within the body has not been distributed evenly within. The movement and tension of the skin at certain spots while performing asanas create new dimensions for the pupils. The tension of strings of a musical instrument or lack of it can create music or cacophony. The same is true about the tension of the skin for the health of the body. According to Iyengar, the skin is the outer layer of intelligence, while the Self is the inner layer, and there ought to be tremendous communication between the two layers. To get the maximum stretch, to get correct alignment of the body and the consequent even distribution of energy within it, Iyengar often makes use of props like the wall, doors, window-ledges, chairs, tables, stools, ropes or towels. He has some specially designed equipment at his Institute for providing relief to patients with heart complaints or with breathing difficulties.

Adjusting the mind (the seat of emotions) and the brain (the seat of intelligence) during the performance of the asana is regarded as essential by Iyengar. Every asana has three stages. The first stage in the performance of an asana is designated as *motion,* which prepares the pupil to get into *action* to achieve the pose which is the second stage. Then comes the third stage of maintaining the pose till the pupil developes *stability* in it. An asana is performed when it is maintained with stability and comfort, says Patanjali in his *Yoga Sutras.* The brain must be taught to relax during each stage, as otherwise there is great wastage of energy. The muscles are stretched, the breathing is relaxed and the nerves are under correct tension. The body is well-balanced. The mind is silent, for there is no hatred nor passion, there is no delusion nor greed; there is no touch of pride or envy. The brain is at rest as there is no movement in time, either the past or the future. The pupil is held in the eternal now. The pupil has achieved mastery over aching limbs and panting breath. No barren thoughts assail his mind. He has gone a long way in the conquest of fear. This stage becomes meditative, where motion, action and stability get integrated. With total awareness and attention to minute details, the pupil learns to bring out the classic sculptured beauty of the asana. He realises that little things make perfection, but perfection is no little thing. He also realises what Iyengar often repeats, that precision leads to divinity.

It has been said that knowledge without common sense is folly; without method, it is waste; without kindness, it is fanatacism; without religion, it is death. Iyengar used his knowledge with common sense and it became wisdom. He evolved methods whereby it became a power that spread around the world. He used his power with charity, and it became beneficient. He yoked his knowledge to Yoga, the root of all religions, and it led to virtue, life and peace.

ISSUE OF CERTIFICATES BY YOGACHARYA B.K.S. IYENGAR

Swaziland, October 1975

How SHOULD I ADDRESS YOU? **Fellow Sufferers?**

You are my children in a way which I term "spiritual children," because you are all born in Yoga through my intellectual and spiritual approach. My biological children are only born by my physical behaviour, but you have all become children of mine from my spiritual behaviour. You are all my spiritual children, so I, being a parent who is a sufferer, you also have to suffer with me. Responsibility has to be taken by the children to live and bear with the sufferings of the parent, so I am One with you.

You all started Yoga in 1968; at that time eleven people came to me. As a spiritual father I never dreamed that within a few years this subject would have produced so many children in your country. As you are my direct spiritual children, your responsibility is to my grandchildren. We all know that grandparents love grandchildren more than children, and probably the same thing may apply to me; that I may love my spiritual grandchildren

471

more than you people, provided you all work with zeal and make them true human beings to serve not only themselves, but to serve their brothers and sisters in their own countries.

Yoga is a very intricate subject. It is a fascinating subject. It develops tremendous will-power, tremendous tenacity. This is the good side of the subject. The bad side of the subject is that in seeking the Truth or seeking Oneness within ourselves, we may develop a sort of pride—thinking that we are better than others. If we do not become victims of that behaviour, we will become the true children of Yoga.

I am giving the certification. It is the first time that I am giving it, so the honour is for you people. Still in my Mother Institute I have not yet started issuing certificates.

A teacher should have two qualities : —

1.   Quality to be strong in the beginning, though you do not know the subject correctly. You should be strong to give with an affirmative approach, but inside you should have a doubtful approach—"Am I going in the right path?" The moment you show doubt in your teachings, that means you have given the seed of doubt to your pupils. Teaching is very difficult, but it is one of the best human services one can do. You have to work, not as a teacher, but as a learner in the art of teaching. You are learning from the pupils, because the human mind and the human body are not the same in each individual. It all varies, so it is the duty of the teacher to bring that Oneness both in body and mind. A teacher is gifted by providence to learn, so that you can impart your knowledge; not to say, "I am a teacher, so I can give." That is where pride comes in. You have to teach affirmatively and yet be doubtful in your approach. Affirmative at the

472

moment to create confidence in your pupils, and negative within yourself so that you can come back and rethink whatever you did—whether you did right or wrong. Then work on your own self to find out where you committed mistakes in your explanations or in your corrections, because you protect your body quicker than you protect your pupils. This is the nature of each individual.

It is very rare where a teacher is tremendously strong outside, but tremendously humble inside. I am a teacher and you are my pupils only in the outside appearance, but inside you have a soul and I have a soul. There is no difference between your soul and my soul. I consider that it is my privilege that you have come to me, so I treat you as gods inside. As we serve God by going to church or temples, so in your heart each pupil is a god for you. Outside you should not show that you consider your pupil to be God. Outside you are strong, but inside you have to feel that you are serving a person who has come to you in the form of God and this brings you definitely to the level of true teaching. The moment you consider yourself a teacher and just say, "Come on, do this," your downfall is written.

Consider this with humility inside. The Self is one, so feel your pupils as gods inside. If you have faith in God, serve your pupils as you serve your God; if you have no faith, serve them as you serve your parents or your best friends. This is the attitude you must have towards your pupils. Outside you have to show the differentiation that a pupil is a pupil and you are a teacher, but inside you should not. This is one point for the development of a good teacher.

2. The second characteristic of a teacher is that the teacher should not expect too much from the pupil, but

at the same time you have to create, ignite interest and convey that, "I expect more from you." This is a very difficult quality of a teacher. No one can know exactly another person's limits. The moment you say, "That is all this person can reach," your knowledge gets stagnated and the pupil's approach gets stagnated. Both should have new avenues—that this is the minimum or this is the maximum of my pupil, but let me go ahead. Let me see. You should go on building your pupil—physically, mentally and spiritually.

Outside you have to show duality. There is a difference between father and child. Inside the father does not separate the child, but outside, yes, the child is dependent, is it not? Initially children are dependent on their parents and as head of the family you try to show them the Path; but after a certain age they become equals. So also in the teaching you have to take that approach.

Admonishments are needed, but never tell a student, "You are very good," because the moment you praise, it is praising your own self and that is the downfall of the teacher. You have to create a sort of newness to show that even though the pupil has advanced, lots of things are missing. You have to see not the good points of your pupils, but the points which are not there at all. Then only the teacher will become a humble teacher, a respected teacher, a lovable teacher.

These certificates are not needed from the truest point of view, but unfortunately the world demands them. Adulteration is everywhere, in everything—physical or spiritual. The moment we become loose in giving the certificates to one and all that means we are also getting adulterated. If you want to teach, the world will demand—"Where have you learned? Have you got a certificate to

474

teach?" If you have a certificate, they get confidence, but in the truest sense it is not needed at all.

The certificates are not given for misusing, saying—"I am a teacher." The pupils are paying you fees not as a teacher, but actually they are paying you a stipend for you to learn to become a good teacher. So the certificates are stipends for you to become a good teacher. You have to use the certificates like that. Even though you may charge fees to your pupils, in your heart of hearts you should have the quality that they are paying you to learn to impart the art.

Yoga gives tremendous inspiration, tremendous will-power and confidence, but against this positive side, the negative side is that we become self-praising. If you are careful not to inflate your self, but to be in the real Self, I say that I have done a good service for you and you are also doing a good service. I cannot expect that all my pupils will be honest to the core throughout their lives. This also you should know—that all students who come to you do not come for spiritual knowledge. Some come because their health is broken and they want to get it back. Others may come to you (although they may not tell you) to maintain good health, so that they can abuse more—indulge more and abuse their strength. Some people come for amusing; some people come for abusing! You have to know the natures of these people when they come, and you have to wait to tell when they are crossing the border of indulgence; then only your help is needed, not in the beginning. That is known as psychological study by the teacher—knowing when it's time to have a word with the pupil.

You may have a student with heart trouble. His doctor has told him not to smoke. You also say, "Don't smoke, don't eat meat," and the pupil says, "Why should I come to you?" Do you mean to say that by telling him not to do it, he will not do it? You have to see the other point of view also. A man who is intelligent will never stop immediately. Without giving the clue, you find out how to stop those inner urges which make him indulge. That is also the art of teaching. You have to study both his intellectual calibre and the physical calibre. Yoga plays all these roles.

Although they may come just to enjoy more in life, Yoga is a key which gives sensual satisfaction and also takes you to spiritual satisfaction. A man who is indulging in sensual satisfaction, I will not say anything to him, but my job is to see whether I can convert him into the subject of Yoga. You also have to do the same thing; not say, "He is no good, I do not want to teach him."

If you do not like a person and you teach that person, your brain is washed. Sometimes you get pupils who give you nausea. Remember they are the real Gurus for you, because they train you to build yourself. God has sent that person to you, so you cannot just say, "Get out, I am not prepared to teach you." It is a test of God whether you can improve or not. That is the crossroad in our approach to Yoga. In these crossroads we have to be very careful. We have to accept. We have to find out whether we can take this ugliness—whether in character or in personality— and blossom something out of it. This is a challenge for the teacher. Do not gauge a student from your standard. Gauge a student from his or her standard. Her way of talking and behaviour will tell you whether that person is in a primitive, medieval or advanced spiritual state. We have to come to the level of the pupil. You have to go down to show the way. As you know the Path and the pupil does not, you have to build the pupil slowly from their standard to your standard.

In my heart of hearts I am happy that from 1968 Yoga has grown into a gigantic tree in your country. Your responsibilities have increased and you have to carry a heavy weight on your backs and because of this, you cannot neglect your practices. If you cannot practise, you cannot teach at all.

If a pupil comes to you with some disease, imagine that disease is with you. What do you do? How can you work? Which organs are defective? etc. If you take these avenues on your own self, your subjective experience will go a long way in helping those pupils who are sent to you by God as his servants. He tests us through our pupils.

Carry on your work. It is God-sent. Through His will we have come together.

Do not inflate any misunderstandings between yourselves. There are three ways—you can forget, forgive or be indifferent. If ill-feeling grows between you, you are not practising Yoga at all, except to inflate your own self. Give and take is the only way to be friendly in Yoga. If you look at a tree—some branches are straight, some branches are crooked; some leaves are beautiful, some leaves are not; some are dry, some are fresh. As this is one family— all these zigzags will be there. Allow certain margins. Each person will have a different understanding according to the growth of their intellect. One may be mature, one may be premature, one may be in the state of maturing. We have to consider all these things and show the way. To show the way we cannot criticise. We can only criticise or admonish when the same mistakes are

477

repeated several times. In the beginning when a rupture takes place it grows into such a gigantic growth later, so that it becomes a cancer of the mind.

If something goes wrong, I feel it. I have given freedom to one and all. I have not asked how many pupils you have or what your earnings are. When there is freedom, there should be no misunderstandings. If you had no freedom, it would be different.

My practises are completely pure. We have to be honest with ourselves. We have to be honest in our work. We have to be honest to our pupils. Then you can do wonderful work. Carry on the work with humility inside, but when you teach show vanity. When I practice I am sattvic. When I teach, I cannot be sattvic. If I am sattvic, my pupils are tamasic. Sattvic nature is silence. Tamasic nature is dullness and inertia. I am rajasic in my teaching, so that the pupil will not become dull. Rajasic teaching makes the pupil do sattvic Yoga. If you are sattvic in your teaching, you are leading your pupils to darkness and not to light. While you are teaching you have to be rajasic; when you are practising alone or with your colleagues, you should have humility. To improve your pupils, you have to show a little bit of self—the inflated self. If you are soft, the pupil's brain becomes inflated. To humble the pupil, you have to be rajasic. The teacher has to play a dual role. This double role is not dishonest. When you practise, you are inwards; you have to be within your inner body. When you are teaching, you have to forget yourself and your pupil is your entire Self. You become a non-self, but your Self has entered into that body. You have to feel you are in that second body—the pupil's. To enter that body you have to make a noise

Teaching is external. Practice is internal. If you know all these things, you can avoid the pitfalls and God will bless you. The tree can give fruit only when it is ripe. There are several trees which never give fruit. In order to get the fruit, we have to get the whole inner organism ripe so that the Self becomes ripe. I wish you all the best in your life.

(A speech by B.K.S. Iyengar when he issued the first certificates, in any part of the world, to teachers from Southern Africa. Published with the permission of the B.K.S. Iyengar Yoga Institute of Southern Africa.)

Sri B.K.S. Iyengar

ESSENTIAL QUALITIES OF A YOGA TEACHER

by B.K.S. Iyengar

1. Teaching is a difficult art, but it is the best service you can do to humanity.

2. Be strong and positive in your approach. The moment you show doubt in your teaching, you plant seeds of doubt in your pupil.

3. Be affirmative when teaching so as to create confidence in the pupil. Be negative within yourself so that you can reflect upon your work.

4. In the art of teaching you have always to work as a learner. Teachers learn from their pupils, as every pupil is different in body and mind. It is the duty of the teacher to bring about unity in the body and mind of each individual pupil with varying traits.

5. You should have the humility to say that you are still learning the art. Never say, "I am a teacher so I can teach." That is pride.

6. It is the nature of us all to protect our own bodies. When taking care of the bodies of your pupils, you have to be much more vigilant than of your own body.

7. Outwardly the teacher should be tremendously strong but deeply receptive to the needs of the pupil. Serve the pupil who has come to you, as if serving divinity.

8. Whilst teaching, show the differentiation that your pupil is a pupil and you are his teacher.

9. Do not expect too much from your pupils, still generate the interest of the pupil so that you can extract more effort from him.

10. Never fail to admonish your pupil for mistakes or for not putting forward his best effort. Never praise a pupil, telling him that he is very good. The moment you lavish praise, you are praising your own self. This self-laudatory praise leads to the downfall of both teacher and pupil as it creates an attitude in the mind of the pupil that he is a very superior person.

11. Strive to forge ahead with your pupil. Build him up physically, mentally and spiritually by your own actions and example, and not mere words.

12. In the beginning, children are dependent upon their parents. When the children mature, wise parents treat them as equals. Your approach towards your pupils should be similar, for you are the parent and your pupils are your children. When your pupils become mature, tread the path of learning together with them, for further refinement.

13. When you notice a pupil using the energy created by your Yoga teaching only for gratification of the senses, never tell him that he is indulging in sensual pleasures. Attempt to turn his mind towards the spiritual aspect of life. This is a challenge to you as a teacher.

14. Do not judge a pupil by your own standards. The way your pupil talks and behaves will tell you his state of development. Descend to the level of your pupil and then guide him onwards slowly, with love and affection, till he reaches your standard.

15. Try to have a fresh approach for every lesson. Though you may be greatly advanced in your studies, you have always room for improvement. The deeper you probe, more fresh points will come to light. Then you will become a humble, respected and a lovable teacher.

WISDOM
of The
MASTER

WISDOM OF THE MASTER

Maxims by Shri. B.K.S. Iyengar
compiled by B.I. Taraporewala and
Shirley Daventry French

YOGA

Yoga is a Darsana,
a mirror to look at ourselves from within.
Control of the mind is Yoga.
When the mind is controlled, stilled and silenced,
what remains is the soul. It is the quest of the soul,
the spark of divinity within us,
which is the very purpose of Yoga.

Yoga is like music.
The rhythm of the body, the melody of the mind
and the harmony of the soul,
create the symphony of life.

Yoga is nothing
if it is not perfect harmony of the body, senses,
mind and intellect, reason, consciousness and self.
When all these are integrated that is true Yoga.

Why should you practise Yoga?
To kindle the divine fire within yourself.
Everyone has a dormant spark of divinity in him
which has to be fanned into flame.

According to ancient texts,
Yoga is a sacred subject, to be kept secret.
Hence it became mystical. I try my best to show
that it is practical and I give the secrets to you. The secrets,
when experienced, will make you sacred in practice.

Yoga is the most abused
as well as the most respected subject in the world.
Question: Is Yoga exclusively Indian?
Answer: Yoga is for all. To limit Yoga
to the boundaries of one nation is the denial
of universal consciousness. Human feelings, emotions,
joys and sorrows are the same the world over.

****

The great Patanjali said
be careful when you accept anything from anyone.
If the thing is given with a cause or a thought
it will add to your karma.
Without thought or cause it is well given.
In the same way do your Yoga
without any special thought or cause.

Words fail to convey the total value of Yoga.
It has to be experienced.

The body is the temple of the spirit.
Let the temple be clean through Yoga.

Yoga is the music of the soul.
So do continue and the gates of the soul will open.

As a farmer plows a field and makes the ground soft,
a yogi plows his nerves so they can germinate
and make a better life.

This practice of Yoga is to remove weeds from the body
so that the garden can grow.

Work is Karma Yoga,
Word is Jnana Yoga.
No conflict in work and word is Yoga.

Yoga works not with a physical body,
but with a physiological body.

The body is made up of five layers :
the anatomical layer,
the physiological layer,
the psychological layer,
the intellectual layer,
Bliss.

Yoga develops all five layers,
not merely just the physiological layer
as in Western disciplines.

Yoga has to be done using the intellect of the head
as well as the intellect of the heart.
This is spiritual Yoga.

Yoga aims for complete awareness in everything you do.

HEALTH

The capital we are born with,
the human body,
remains unutilised for most of us.

Health is a state of complete harmony
of the body, mind and spirit.
When one is free from physical disabilities
and mental distractions, the gates of the soul open.

Health is that state
when one becomes carefree of the body.

A healthy person is one who detaches himself
from the body, by making it pure and perfect.

You have not understood the working of your body,
yet you want God-realisation?

Unless freedom is gained in the body,
freedom of the mind is a far cry.

To a yogi his body is a laboratory,
a field for perpetual experiment and research.

490

It is through the body that you reach
the realisation of your being a spark of divinity.
How can you neglect the body
which is the temple of the spirit?

Health is the state when the soul is given
the key of the body to roam at will.

****

Without health one cannot have a strong root
in the mind.
The movements of the mind
(laziness, carelessness, believing illusion to be the truth)
have to be stilled in order to know what the soul is.

Health is not a commodity to be bargained for.
It has to be earned with sweat and toil.
All of us know that life, like a river, is a perennial flow.
As such, it needs careful attention
to keep the flow under control.

It is a fact that healthy plants and trees alone
yield fragrant flowers and tasty fruits.
Similarly, from a healthy man,
smiles and happiness blossom out like the rays of the sun.

Though man demarcates body, mind and soul,
it is impossible to pinpoint where the body ends
and the mind begins,
or where the mind ends and the Self begins.
They are interrelated
and interwoven together by the string of intelligence.

491

The eyes are the windows of the soul, the ears are the windows of the mind.

Health is firmness in body,
stability in mind
and clarity in thinking.
If a mirror is clean, it reflects objects clearly.
Health is the mirror of man.

Nature provides the means to adjust to the rhythm of life
with all the turmoils of day-to-day
pressures and environments.
The body astonishingly adjusts to the imbalances
created by the possessor of the body.
When these are overstepped,
the physical, physiological and psychological diseases
set in, creating psychosomatic diseases.
It is similar to the ecological imbalances of mother earth
when man taps and exploits nature.

The positive way of earning health
is by exercising the body and mind
so that a perfect state of concord is developed
with joints, tissues, muscles, cells, nerve, glands,
respiration, circulation, digestion,
distribution and elimination,
and a happy disposition of mind is maintained towards
sorrow and joy, pain and pleasure, evil and good,
inspiration and expiration,
and aspiration and resplendence.

Yoga has a threefold impact on health.
It keeps healthy people healthy.
It aids recovery from ill health.
It inhibits the development of diseases.
Anything that disturbs your spiritual life
and practices is a disease.

493

In each asana, if the part of the body in contact with the
floor—the foundation—is good,
the asana is performed well.

Yoga does not require costly gadgets.
It can be done according to one's convenience
and irrespective of place, age, sex or condition.
it covers the total involvement of man as a whole,
and hence I consider Yoga
a gateway to the heaven of health.

ASANAS

The body is my temple
and asanas are my prayers.

While practising asanas,
learn the art of adjustment.

When your posture is imbalanced,
the practice is physical;
balanced asanas lead to spiritual practice.

As a goldsmith weighs gold,
you have to adjust your body so that it is
perfectly balanced in the median plane.

As pearls are held on a thread,
all the limbs should be held
on the thread of intelligence.

If your body *can* do more and you do not do it,
that is unethical practice.

Leave no outlets for the energy to flow out.

Ethical discipline of the asana is
when you extend correctly, evenly
and to the maximum.

The goal is far for those who do asanas casually,
it is near for those who are intensely intense.

Never perform asanas mechanically,
for then the body stagnates.

The brain is the hardest part of the body
to adjust in asanas.

While performing asanas the brain should be watchful
and alert to direct the movements of the body.
Activate the body, relaxing the brain.

If the brain is silent but attentive
while performing asanas,
your practice is non-violent.

Use your intelligence to control the body
before starting the movements of the body.
In the beginning,
the brain moves faster than the body;
later, the body moves faster than the brain.
The movement of the body
and the intelligence of the brain
should synchronise and keep pace with each other.

To bring a part of the body in correct alignment,
you have to work with the whole body.
To bring the whole body in correct alignment,
you have to work each and every part of the body.
When performing asanas,
no part of the body should be kept idle.

Repeated mistakes become habits.

In each asana, if the part of the body
in contact with the floor—the foundation—is good,
the asana is performed well.

When an asana is done correctly
the body movements are smooth,
there is lightness in the body
and freedom in the mind.

When you feel that you have attained
the maximum stretch,
go beyond it. Break the barrier to go further.

In asanas there are two stages—
motion and action. Motion needs mobility.
We waste our energy in motion, leaving none for action.
Action is not motion but a stage beyond it.
Only action can release us.

When stability becomes a habit,
maturity comes and clarity follows.

If the body is constricted and heavy,
the pose is immature and done wrongly.

Long uninterrupted practice of asanas,
done with awareness, will bring success.

Allow your intelligence
to penetrate evenly throughout the body to its extremities,
like the rays of the sun.

Everything cannot be observed by our two eyes.
Each pore of the skin should act like an eye.
Your skin is a most sensitive guide.

Fear and fatigue block the mind.
Face both,
then courage and confidence flow into you.
Do you know when you get exhaustion?
It is when you change the balance of energy.

When practising asanas,
go beyond thoughts of pleasure and pain.

Do not allow past experiences to be imprinted
on your mind. Perform asanas each time
with a fresh mind
and with a fresh approach.

Balance is a gift of the Creator.

You have to work to obtain a perfect balance
between both sides of the body.

Your whole being should be symmetrical.
Yoga is symmetry.
That is why Yoga is a basic art.

Extension means creation of space.
Space leads to freedom. Freedom brings precision.
Precision leads to perfection. Perfection is truth.
Truth is God.

****

God is the pose. Meditate on God.

Each movement is my mantra.

Self-realisation must exist in every pore of the skin.

In postures intelligence should be uniform.

When movement becomes mature, effort ceases.

A sense of direction is right intelligence.
To move the part you have to move the whole.
Motion means freedom. Action is rigidity.

All skin will be soft when space is created.

Horizontal and vertical action
brings circumferential action.

As there is a space between thoughts,
there is a space between action and thought.

Your body is your child—look after it.

You have a problem part?
That is your problem child.
Learn how to deal with it.

500

Self knowledge
starts from the skin on the soles of the feet
when standing.

The inner body must be an extrovert.
The inner brain must be an introvert.

The brain must be quiet,
the body active.

Physical, mental and spiritual in harmony.
That is the Self.

Involuntary, unconscious movement
in any posture is sensual.
We have to learn to distinguish between
that which is spiritual
and that which is sensual.

In Savasana, when you are intent on stillness,
any movement of any sort is a sensual movement.
In Savasana the intelligence of the head
is brought to rest on the seat of the heart,
and that is relaxation of the soul.
The body
which is the child of the soul
embraces the soul.

Because you cannot see the back, it is forgotten.
The back must be activated in all the poses.

The frame has to hold the inner energy properly.
Work from the energy body.
The energy body, not the physical body, holds poses.

5 0 1

Do not contract your brain when you stretch your body.

Any dull posture must be made active.

We waste our energy in motion,
it should be used in action.
Motion requires softness.

The brain is the heaviest limb in the body.
Inspire the brain to stretch the body.

Sunken eyes, sunken brain—exhaustion.

Go to the source of the pose.

Balance is the state of the present—
the here and now.
If you balance in the present
you are living in Eternity.

Move the body with the Self—no separation.

When the pose is correct,
there is a lightness, a freedom.
When the pose is wrong, it is heavy.

Look at the Self, not the Ego. If your throat is tense
while doing an asana or pranayama,
you are doing it with your brain instead of your body.

The whole body must work—not partial.
When there is hardness, there is no intelligence.
Eliminate dullness anywhere.
Tension is aggression.
Without disturbing the external body,
stretch the internal body.

Yoga is working your body equally on both sides.

Your body must break into pieces
to know the peace within.

It is when the inside of you becomes subtle and fine
that the Yoga postures improve.

Doing asanas is a grace from God.
Take it or He will walk away.

Marriage between the body and the mind is essential.
When the two parties do not cooperate
there is unhappiness on both sides.

When the consciousness dissolves within the self
it is true Savasana.

You must savour the fragrance of a posture.

We are always beginners
from the point where we get a new point.

In asanas we are chanting with our bodies.

When you clasp the hands in Marichyasana,
you are holding your own dual personality—
the mind and the self are linked.

Each posture must show growth;
if not precisely, meaningfully.
It must produce fruit—
some are not even finding roots.

Stand erect or you cave in the very Self.

The flame of the body should be kept burning.

Rotate and stretch the torso.
Your self writes on the spine.
Flow the ink to write with your soul
imprinting the messages where needed.

Is your intelligence controlling the body
before you do the movement?

Your energy has to flow in the body
as between the banks of a river—
no disturbance to the banks, or they collapse.

Activity and passivity must go together in asanas.

Perform each asana as a mantra
and each pose as a meditation,
then the light will dawn
from the centre of your being.

Treat each part of your body as if it were a jewel.

I am standing on my own altar;
the poses are my prayers.

Skin of back body should roll towards the Self—
that is Tadasana.

When you stretch,
if the stretch is even there is no strain at all.

What is the difference between perfection and divinity?
Harmony and balance.
So is not asana working for perfection?

Life is dynamic, so the poses should be dynamic.

Today's maximum should become tomorrow's minimum.

Question: How do you know correct postures?
Answer: By doing it—trial and error.

When the movement is finished—to the maximum—
then the action begins.

The skin is the intellect—a sense organ;
flesh is physical.

My ending should be your beginning.

In each pose there should be repose.

If you look you can see that his eyes are always soft.

You have to work through the gross body
to the subtle body (the spine)
and then through the spine to the mind.

The body has to be transformed.
It must be brought to stability.

The spine brings physical stability.
The mind brings emotional stability.
The brain brings intellectual stability.

It is the job of the spine
to keep the brain alert and in position.

Your skin is a most sensitive guide.

Freedom in a posture is when every joint is active.
Let us be full in whatever posture it is we are doing.
Let us be full in whatever we do.

The body must be trained to be the servant,
not the master.

What is the use of merely developing the muscles
if the brain is not working?

The body is still in one piece,
that is why we are in pieces.
The body must be broken down into pieces
for there to be peace.

How can you have peace of mind,
when there is no peace in the body?

You must develop the same character as the Kurma,
the tortoise.
When once it is in its shell,
nothing at all can disturb it.
In Kurmasana you are unable to see anyone or anything,
obliging you to turn the attention inwards.

Do not ridicule even the poses you can do well,
there is always further awareness in each pose.

In all poses—ascend to descend.

If you open the armpits the brain becomes light.
You cannot brood or become depressed.

If the lungs collapse, the brain becomes dull and morose.

If the joints are hard,
there is a traffic jam in your body.
There should be freedom to act.

If you keep your aim to the maximum,
Self-knowledge will come.
With the minimum, it is sensual Yoga.
The moment you go a little more than the body can take,
you are nearer the Self.
The minute you say, "I am satisfied,"
the light is fading.

The mind is the outer layer of the Self
and the Self extends everywhere.
When you do the pose
you should have that vastness of the mind.

The nervous system should be completely clear.

Sutra means a thread.
As the pearls are held on a thread,
all the limbs of your body should be held on that thread
which is called the intelligence.
Work from your heart, not your brain,
to create harmony.

Presence of mind
means synchronising your body and mind.

Do not contract your brain when you stretch your body.
An active brain is an aggressive brain.
Do not clench your brain as you clench your teeth.

Opening the eyes wide releases pain
and stops dullness of the brain.

There should be harmony in action.
See and act!

Body is first treated as physical,
then body is used for discipline of the intellect.
By creating intelligence in the body,
you refine the intellect.

There should be constant analysis throughout the action,
not afterwards.
This is understanding.
The real meaning of knowledge is
that action and your analysis synchronise.

We all work for the supreme goal—to be perfect.

It is never a question of what I am doing,
   but what am I not doing?

Know the morality of each posture.

Attach the flesh to the bone when doing the poses.

When you have conquered the microcosm
      (the physical body—minature universe),
you have conquered the macrocosm (Universe).

If the mind does not see, it is a small mind.
   If you cannot see your little toe,
      how can you see the Self?

Without art there is no science.
A philosopher is always an artist and vice versa.
   Our body is the instrument for our art.

You have to get freedom in your body
   before you can see the spiritual light.

Body is the bow, asana the arrow
   and soul is the target.

The median line is God!

SADHANA (Practice)

A battle ensues when the mind says,
"I want to," but the body says, "I cannot,"
It lies in your hands to see who wins.

Convert talent into genius by hard work
and uninterrupted sadhana.

Just like a river, the Self has two banks—
a material and a spiritual bank.
Spiritual practice is the boat
that takes you from the material to the spiritual bank.

Over-enthusiasm is short-lived.

Spiritual sadhana begins when you go beyond
what you consider to be your maximum effort.

Hard work and humility are essential
for spiritual sadhana.

Earnestness in effort is *tapas*.

To be dull is easy. To be totally dull
is as difficult as to be totally alert.

Slouching acts like dope to the body.

Intensified action brings intensified intelligence.

Each part of the body has to be impregnated
with intelligence.

512

Have total attention. Pause between each movement.
Then in the stillness be filled with awareness.
Ask yourself,
"Has every part of me done its job?"

Total extension brings total relaxation.

If you know the extension of the body,
you know the extention of the mind.

Precision in action comes
when the challenge by one side of the body
is met by an equal counter-challenge of the other.
This ignites the light of knowledge.

Knowledge grows when action and analysis synchronise.

Sincerity and stupidity cannot go together;
only sincerity and intelligence can.

Do not mar the beauty of the asana
by the ugliness of your motions.
Rather, transform the ugliness of your motions
into the beauty of the asanas by right presentation.

Prajna (illuminating knowledge) is the child of
intelligence and maturity.

As asana performed with total awareness
is as good as a mantra or as meditation.

Position God for every asana,
then reach towards Him.

513

We are always seeking contact with heaven,
but how many of us
have made any reasonable contact
with mother earth.

Inflated egoism and intoxicated intelligence
is failure in spiritual life.

Conquer fear,
then Self-knowledge will come.

Until you have the inner light,
you must use the outer light.

The eyes are the windows of the soul,
the ears the windows of the mind.

Mind must remain in the state of the present.

Energy must flow everywhere like a river.

When I practise, I'm a philosopher.
When I teach, I'm a scientist.
When I demonstrate, I'm an artist.

Leave no outlets for energy to flow out.

Differentiate between self-culture and physical culture.

Use each experience as a stepping stone.

We should be humble within.

We are all intoxicated with our own confusion.

If the mind is to be made still,
the eyes must be still.
If the nerves are still,
then the Self is still.

The mind must not stop at one point and say,
this is enough.
It must go further;
the Self must be everywhere.

To live in the moment is spirituality.
To live in the movement is divinity.

Be a fanatic with yourself while practising Yoga.

When you are fully in the body,
you meet the soul.

Freedom starts inside,
freeing man from dualities like mind and body,
spirit and material.

Training of mind and body
leads to awareness of the soul.

You say, "Mind over matter."
I say, "Matter over mind."

515

To achieve the end in Yoga,
uninterrupted practice is demanded.

Freedom is precision and Yoga takes me to that.

Persistent practice alone is the key to Yoga.

Motive is essential to ignite the fire within yourself.

Perfection is not at all easy.
This body is only an instrument of the soul
to reach what is within.

We all work for one supreme goal—
to be perfect.

When there is perfection, there is no thinking;
when there is no thinking, you are one with the truth.

Man can be carried away by words
but not by actions.
Action brings that light which is hidden.

Unless freedom is gained in the body,
freedom of the mind is a far fetched idea.

Ultimate truth should be completely naked.

Death is a certainty.
You have to die gracefully, nobly—
not like a worm suffering from diseases.
Let death come naturally,
not unnaturally.

If you feel death approaching,
finish the exercise first and then die!

Life is immortal, death is mortal.

Use caution and be bold.

You have to take a chance, then balance comes.

Use the body as an instrument of recognition—
an instrument to purge the egoistic intelligence.

All knowledge comes only from the skin.

If my physical body joins with my spiritual body,
that is a divine marriage.

Just as a goldsmith purifies gold,
so must the body be constantly purified and purged,
so that the inner gold may shine.

In our spiritual quest,
it is required of us
that we develop our body in such a way
that it is no longer a hindrance, but becomes our friend.
Similarly our emotions and intellect
must be developed for divine purposes.

Let the breath and the intelligence move simultaneously.
If the intelligence moves first, it is force.

The intellect needs to be humbled for the body to become the temple of God.

Through the emotional centre
one cultivates the intellect of the heart.
Through the intellectual centre
one cultivates the intellect of the head.
Most Westerners try to solve their emotional problems
through the intellect of the head.
Emotions can, however, only be solved
through the emotions.

Analytical intelligence is easy to come by,
but not practical intelligence.

You cannot say you are intelligent,
if you do not also have body intelligence.

To live totally in the body
is to live totally in the Self.

Where does need end and greed begin?
One who knows this has a religious mind.

Anything that sustains and supports is religion.
If you are well and allow yourself to become unwell,
that is being irreligious.
To help someone who is down is religion.
The upliftment of one who is about to fall,
or who has fallen,
is religion.

Purity is when there is no anxiety, no worry, no thinking.

Memory is useless if it brings about
a repetition of the past.
Memory is useful if it helps to prepare you for the future,
to know whether or not you are proceeding forward.

When the means are good,
the end cannot but likewise be good.
The means must be good or the end will be meaningless.

The presence or absence of intelligence
is shown when you face insecurity.
Security lies in insecurity.

The intellect needs to be humbled
for the body to become the temple of God.

In your discipline,
if doubt comes let it come.
Do your work,
let doubt carry on with its work,
and see which gives up first.

Why think of liberation at some future time?
Liberation is in the little things, here and now.

The mind, the thinker, must be made
utterly and completely still
to know what the Self is.

All discipline must come from within.
All fire and purity must come from within.

Love, labour, laugh.

Singularity of purpose should be your aim.
Any holy person is a yogi.
Any yogi is a holy person.

Limited knowledge will give you a limited approach.
Unlimited knowledge has an unlimited source.

To love is to be merciless.

Some turn ugliness into beauty,
and some turn beauty into ugliness.

What we were is unimportant.
What we are doing now is important.

The end of discipline is the beginning of freedom
Only a disciplined person is a free person.
So-called "freedom" is only a licence
to act and do as we like.

Love, labour and laugh.

LEARNING AND TEACHING

Know your capacity. It is an index
of your own internal strength.

Test your pupils. Know their capacity.

Treat casual pupils casually,
and dedicated pupils with dedication.

It is better to train one pupil honestly,
than to train many pupils casually.

Do not teach what you do not know.

Over-enthusiasm in teaching is nothing
but the expression of ego.

Create awareness in your pupils.
Teach them to be self-aware, not self-conscious.

Teaching is not merely teaching to earn your livelihood.
Teaching is learning also—learning to refine
your body, nerves, intelligence and self,
so that you can refine those who come to you.

Never forget that the pupil
also teaches the Master.

Learning is as much an art as teaching.

To be a teacher requires vigorous discipline
over one's own self.

523

If a teacher makes a mistake,
all his pupils imitate him.
So the teacher has to be doubly careful.

You must purge yourself
before finding faults in others.

Only a pupil may commit mistakes,
a teacher must not commit mistakes.
I purge my pupil-teachers
so that they will teach better.

When you see somebody making a mistake,
try to find out if you are not making
the same mistake.

Self-correction comes with perception.

On the outside, treat your pupils as your pupils,
but within you treat them as having
the same spark of divinity within them as you have.
Be humble inside and strong outside.

To make the pupil *sattvic*
the teacher has to be *rajasic*.

Pay twice as much attention
to the duller and inactive side of the body
as to the active side.

The work of the pupil is to adjust his body
according to the words of the teacher.

Give a hint, nothing happens,
Give a hit and see what happens!

The teacher helps the pupil to master fear.

The teacher plants the seed of knowledge.
The pupil must work hard to nurture it.

The teacher lives to give life to the pupils.
He should have courage, vitality, memory, awareness
and absorption which he should instil in his pupils.

It is hard to teach a pupil
who thinks he is superior to the teacher.

Memory is necessary to see
whether we are regressing or progressing.
If you use memory to live in past experiences alone,
it becomes your foe and hinders progress.
Memory is a friend when used for progress.

Cleverness and clarity are not the same.
Cleverness is dexterity, clarity is wisdom.

The reasons for failure in self-culture are
intoxicated intelligence and inflated ego.

Subjugation of the ego leads to harmony and happiness.

If the body is to become the temple of God,
the intellect must be humbled.

First learn to keep healthy people healthy,
before trying to cure unhealthy ones.

Injuries come by doing aggressive movements,
not by doing Yoga.

Limited knowledge can only give limited experience.

Learning can be acquired,
but wisdom has to be earned.

Intelligence alone will not solve problems,
unless it is linked with observation.
First observe, and then use the intelligence.

Concentration is focussing your attention on an object.
Awareness is the faculty of concentration
without any bondage.

Awareness must be like the rays of the sun:
extending everywhere, illuminating all.

Beyond the intellect there is will-power.

Will-power develops by regular discipline.

The Guru, the sisya and the vidya
—the teacher, the pupil and the knowledge—
all should become integrated.

Yoga turns an extrovert into an introvert,
and an introvert into an extovert.
The sadhaka has to find the balance of the two.
This is harmony.

Discipline and purity must come from within.

You have to build and create within yourself
the feelings of beauty, liberation and infinity.

Nothing is achieved by a mind that doubts.

When doubt ends by discrimination, wisdom dawns.

Nothing is perfect; you can
always improve. That is creation
of life, and interest.

What I was is unimportant; what I am now is important.

****

The parts of your body are your pupils.
Teach them well.

Digest the poses yourself
before you teach them to others.

Correct from the source.
Find the source.
Go to the source of the problem.

In a total stretch, there is a chemical change in the brain.
Brain and body become completely light, cool and still.
There is no thought.
The consciousness moves only in
the body, not outside.
So you do not have to tell the pupil to go into the Self;
it happens by itself.

527

Can your intellect penetrate
to stretch the hidden areas of your body.
One can criticize only when one knows
the depth of the subject.

You see the external world with the eyes;
the internal world with the ears.

If you cannot do,
you cannot find fault in others.

A teacher must first have experienced in his own life
what he is teaching.

There is no end to knowledge.

Pleasure belongs to the emotional centre.
Desire belongs to the emotional centre.
Only ignorance belongs to the intellectual centre.

A teacher should be like a tiger to the pupils
when they are doing wrong.

Like sprinkling a drop of water in hot oil to see if it sizzles,
make sure as a teacher
that you also see and keep that kind of heat in students.

Teachers should roar like a lion outside
but be like a lamb inside.
The grace of God has come to you if students come to you;
treat them as God, but outside be strong.

Positive silence is spiritual,
negative silence is sensual.

A good book is better than a bad teacher.
A good teacher helps you explore to the maximum.

God requires only this of us:
that we learn to distinguish
between that which is spiritual
and that which is sensual.

Why develop like a race horse,
as is the case with so many
wrestlers, athletes and gymnasts?
In time the race horse becomes a cart horse.

Nobody should become a graduate
if he is unfit in his body.
Of what use is a degree
if the body is not going to last;
if the body is one day going to corrupt that knowledge?

A crooked body means a crooked mind.
It's a crooked mind that says, "I think I can."
Be positive!
Never say, "I'm trying."
If you are trying,
you wouldn't be able to open your mouth to say anything.

The body is the institution.
The teacher is within.

Irritability is a measure of insanity.
If the pupil becomes irritable,
the teacher must treat him likewise with irritability.

The highest form of sensitivity
is the highest form of intellect.

Create the pupil's mistakes in your own body
and then do the pose
to get the feeling of the wrong movement.

A confused mind finds a confused teacher!

Use fully whatever limited intelligence you have,
then automatically it opens a little more
—it can accumulate more.

The eyes are the windows of the brain
and the nerves are the windows of the soul.

Discrimination means that doubt is still here.
When doubt has completely gone,
there will be no need for discrimination.

You all want to learn Yoga,
but you are not willing to accept
the challenge that comes.

I prune human beings.

I am creating in you
and you cannot face that creation.

Come with me!

Clarity, faith, devotion and passion makes a good pupil.

PAIN

Pain comes to guide you.
When you have known pain,
you will make friends with those who suffer,
you will be compassionate.

In the struggle alone, there is knowledge.
Only when there is pain you will see the light.
Pain is your Guru.

****

Pain is a toxin which must be eradicated.

Unbearable pain must become bearable
before it can be eradicated.
Then we can learn to remove it.

No pain—no gain.

Where there is a pain, there must be a cause.

Westerners are certainly more developed
than the average Easterner,
but emotionally more immature.
Westerners tend to rationalize or brood over things,
over what they can do to get over or change their pain,
which is an escape from actually facing it.
They are seldom prepared to face that pain
and work through it.
Take, for example, the terrible shouts, cries and groans,
when you are taken intensely into a posture,
thus bringing you face to face
with the reality of your body's nature.

WEALTH

Where does need end and greed begin?
One who knows this has a religious mind.

Giving does not impoverish,
nor does withholding enrich us.

What has a yogi to do with wealth?
That wealth is within him.
His body and mind are his wealth.

PRANAYAMA—DHYANA—MEDITATION

Peace in the body brings poise to the mind.

Pranayama is a prayer,
not mere physical breathing exercise.

If breathing is defective,
the energy does not circulate freely to ignite intelligence.

As leaves move in the wind,
your mind moves with your breath.

The mind (manas) is shaped,
formed and coloured by your emotions and thoughts;
breath (prana) is not. Hence, prana is superior to manas.

If you understand how to distribute prana,
you can bring about the union of the energies
of the individual and of the universe.

Eyes teach you the art of action.
Ears the art of silence
When you become aware of this,
you begin to learn the art of meditation.

To understand the outer world, open your eyes.
To understand your own inner world, close your eyes,
and open your ears.

Resting the conscious brain
on the floor of the unconscious one,
is meditation.

Physical firmness, emotional stability
and intellectual clarity
are the keys to meditation.

As long as the body is not held firm,
meditation is impossible.

It is the job of the spine to keep the brain alert.
The moment the spine collapses, the brain collapses.

In meditation, the mind is still, but razor sharp,
silent, but vibrant with energy.

Introspection is meditation.

Meditation is the hardest and finest adjustment
of the intellect.

To bring the mind to a state
of innocence without ignorance is meditation.

The secret of meditation is the adjustment
of all the finer things,
the joy of tranquillity in body and mind.
Till you experience this,
you have not mastered Yoga at all.

First learn about concrete meditaton before jumping to
abstract meditation.

In meditation the character of the person glows from
within and illumines him.

534

Samadhi comes like lightning. It is a moment of eternity.

Samadhi is an electrifying experience. The body of the sadhaka has to be strengthened by the discipline of Yoga, otherwise the experience of samadhi will consume him instead of illuminating him.

Total living is samadhi.

The marriage of nature (prakrti) and consciousness (purusa) is the divine union.

Samadhi is the state where there is only pure awareness.

Your body lives in the past, your mind in the future.
They come together in the present
when you practise Yoga.

Do not live in the future; only the present is real.
Self-culture begins when you get completely engrossed in
whatever you are doing.
Selfishness means rigidity;
selflessness, pliability.

To know oneself is to know one's body, mind and soul.

If a man has courage, but his sword is rusty,
of what use is his courage?
If the sword is sharp, but it's owner lacks valour,
of what use is the sword?
If a man has divine aspirations, but his body is diseased,
of what use are his aspirations?

Look after the root of the tree
and the fragrant flowers and luscious fruits
will grow by themselves.
Look after the health of the body,
and the fragrance of the mind
and richness of the spirit will flow.

If the foundation is firm,
the building can withstand calamities.
The practice of Yoga is the foundation,
so that the Self is not shaken
under any circumstances.

Freedom is to be free from the chains of fears and desires.

The known is limited, but the unknown is vast.
Go to the unknown more and more.

Spiritual knowledge grows from the union
of the head and the heart.

Perfection eludes us,
but this should not lead us to reduce our efforts.

The more I work,
the more insignificant my efforts appear to be.
I have to be content with this divine discontent
which drives me on.

The body is gross, the mind subtle
and the spirit infinite.

A sculptor gives expression
to perfection and beauty through mediums
like stone, wood or metal.
We should give expression
to the latent divinity within us through our whole being,
thoughts, body and love.

Question: "How many languages can you speak?"
Answer: "Only one, the language of love."

What is required
is culture of the heart, and of the hand,
not merely of the head.

In the midst of death, life persists:
in the midst of darkness, light;
in the midst of falsehood, truth.

Surrender to God all your experiences.
Start your work and end it with the name of God.
Then your life will be full of harmony.

****

Inhalation is taking in the spirit of the Lord.
Exhalation is resigning yourself to the Lord.
Surrender to him.

The ears control the mind.
The eyes control the brain.
Tenseness of the eyes affects the brain.
If the eyes are still, the brain is still.

The eye of the soul is between your brows
but a little higher.
If that is still, your soul is still.

Imagine the Lord is standing above your chest.
Turn your eyes to the feet of the Lord.

If the eyes waver away from the mind,
then you know that the Lord wavers away from you.
You know that you are only in the material world.

Your God is the sound of your breathing.

When you hold the breath,
you are retaining the Lord within yourself.
When you exhale
you give out your individual self to the material world.

Pranayama requires intelligence.
You become intellectual through books.
As long as you do not live instant to instant
in the breathing
you are an intellectual.
The brain supercedes you when sound is rough.
To tame the brain—tame the breath.

In pranayama
your intellect should be as firm as a burning candle
in a windless place.

Inhalation and exhalation should flow without ruffle,
soft and smooth.
Live from moment with these two breaths;
like a very full river that is moving,
but its movements cannot be seen.

When a host receives an honoured guest,
he receives him with his total self,
not with his mind merely.
All his worries and anxieties are forgotten
for that moment.
So should the inhaled breath be received into one's being.

Tolerance is developed in pranayama.

Breathe! Don't blow like a windmill.

When you hold the breath, you hold the soul.

The thoracic diaphragm is the cradle
in which the Lord, the honoured guest, is resting.
He is not to be disturbed there,
especially during retention.
The intellectual centre must surrender
to the emotional centre,
to the Lord in this cradle.

If the intellectual centre ascends during inhalation,
you are doing egoistic pranayama.
If the intellectual centre descends
and the emotional centre ascends,
you are doing true, humble pranayama.

Learn the art of descending the mind
so that the self ascends.

During exhalation the intellectual centre
is completely purged—
this is renunciation.

Just as a goldsmith removes impurities from the metal,
in pranayama the body will gradually remove the impurities.

One who knows the art of relaxation,
also knows the art of meditation.

To rest the brain,
sit in such a way that the unconscious and conscious brain
must meet in the centre.
Patanjali says, when sitting
the body must be firm as a mountain.
Iyengar says, it is better to suffer
and learn the right method.

Your body is in one piece like a block of wood,
intellect split.
My body is in several pieces,
intellect is one—
and that is meditation.

The brain deals only with the external world.
To keep the brain quiet
is to retire from the external to the internal world.
The front brain
(the external, material centre of the brain)
must be kept quiet.
The back brain
(the internal, spiritual centre)
must be kept active.

Yoga is nothing but a sense of direction,
and meditation is nothing but a sense of direction.
Yoga means meditation.
Dhyana is a definition of Yoga.

Meditation is a fine, supreme consciousness
in which there is no duality.

Mind is the outer layer of the soul.
Mind must merge with the self in meditation.

Body, mind and self,
all three have to be kept in a state of suspension.

Surrender to the Lord who is within you.

542